THE PRACTICE OF TRANSPORT INVESTMENT APPRAISAL

The Practice of Transport Investment Appraisal

Edited by
K. J. BUTTON
Loughborough University
and University of British Columbia

and

A. D. PEARMAN
University of Leeds
and University of North Carolina

Avebury

380.5
P895

Published by
Avebury
Gower Publishing Company Limited
Gower House
Croft Road
Aldershot
Hants   GU11 3HR
England

Reprinted 1987

British Library Cataloguing in Publication Data
The Practice of transport investment appraisal.
    1. Transportation - Cost of operation
    I. Button, K.J.   II. Pearman, A.D.
    380.5'2   HE5618

ISBN 0 566 00464 X

Printed and bound in Great Britain by
Antony Rowe Limited, Chippenham, Wiltshire.

Contents

Contributors

N.J. Ashford	Department of Transport Technology, Loughborough University
M.E. Beesley	London Business School
K.J. Button	Department of Economics, Loughborough University and Faculty of Commerce and Business Administration, University of British Columbia
J.M. Clark	Centre for Transport Studies, Cranfield Institute of Technology
D. Gillingwater	Department of Town Planning, Trent Polytechnic
K.M. Gwilliam	Institute for Transport Studies, University of Leeds
D.A. Hensher	School of Economic and Financial Studies, Macquarie University
J.A. Holt	Department of Maritime Studies, Liverpool Polytechnic

D.S. Kirby

Barrister-at-Law,
Inquiry into the Kyeemagh-Chullora Road,
Sydney

P.J. Mackie

Institute for Transport Studies,
University of Leeds

A.D. Pearman

School of Economic Studies,
University of Leeds, and
Department of Economics,
University of North Carolina

C.H. Sharp

Department of Economics,
University of Leicester

Preface and acknowledgements

This book is concerned with the application of cost–benefit analysis to the appraisal of transport investment projects. It is, however, far removed from being a textbook of economic theory. Several excellent books have been written about the theory of cost–benefit analysis, both generally and specifically in the transport field. Little would be achieved by adding to the list. Much less available are insights into how theory translates into practice in this very important area of applied economics. When data is scarce, understanding of behaviour limited, and appraisal constrained by institutional and political reality, what emerges as transport investment appraisal is frequently quite distinct from the elegance of textbook exposition.

We believe that an understanding of the compromises and adjustments which have to be made in undertaking the social appraisal of projects in the transport sector is every bit as important as a familiarity with the underlying theory. To try to broaden such understanding, we have asked a number of professional transport planners and economists, each with considerable practical experience, to contribute a chapter specifically concentrating on the application rather than the theory of appraisal. Some of the contributions are in the form of case studies which emphasise the importance of institutional framework in determining the way appraisal takes place in practice. The remainder take specific topics in transport appraisal and survey their present standing, again with the focus on problems and recent developments in application.

All the authors have refrained from the use of excessive mathematics with the result that the book should be accessible to a wide audience — not only professional economists and economics students, but also transport engineers, transport planners and geographers. The range of applications and issues considered will, it is hoped, stimulate fresh thoughts about the problems of appraisal from a number of viewpoints.

We should like to express our thanks here to all the contributors to this volume. Their careful attention to detail, not to mention deadlines, has made the process of amalgamating the contributions into a coherent unit far simpler than it might otherwise have been. Thanks, too, to all those involved in preparing the individual typescripts, and especially to Jill Dunham, who took on the handwriting of both of us, and lived to tell the tale!

KJB
ADP
July 1982

1 Introduction

General introduction

The literature on transport economics and, in particular, the appraisal of transport investments is extensive and evergrowing, so why has it been felt necessary to add this collection of papers to the list? First, much of the published material on transport investment appraisal, and especially that in readily accessible sources, tends to focus on the more theoretical issues. There is considerable emphasis on the analytically 'correct' application, in principle at least, of the so-called New Welfare Economics to the problems of transport infrastructure expansion, and on the appropriate theoretical foundations of social cost–benefit analysis. The actual conduct of investment appraisals and the practical problems of applying economic principles has received much less attention. The links between theory and application have, in effect, often been neglected in the literature.

Further, even when there is discussion of practical appraisal problems the range of applications and examples considered tends to be limited, often concentrating exclusively on one sphere of transport activity, e.g. the appraisal of road schemes or airports. In contrast, the papers offered in this volume cover a diverse range of both transport modes and appraisal situations. The contributions place particular emphasis on the actual conduct of transport investment appraisal and on the types of compromise which are often necessary if decisions are to be taken. They also highlight some of the limitations of current transport investment appraisal procedures.

It is hoped that this book will be of interest to a wide audience. The form of exposition chosen by the authors, combined with only minimal recourse to mathematics in the writing, should make the various contributions easily accessible. The material itself will, hopefully, prove useful to those engaged in the teaching of transport studies and planning and provide them with useful case-study material, in addition to practical insights into the appraisal process. It is also anticipated that it will be of interest to many practising transport analysts — including planners, engineers and economists — who wish to look at some of the wider problems of transport appraisal. The extensive range of applications and issues considered may stimulate fresh thoughts about the problems of appraisal in a specific sphere.

This Introduction is intended to serve three main purposes. Firstly, it offers a general review of the development and methodology of transport investment appraisal. Transport economics is one of the oldest branches of the discipline and interest in techniques for improving the overall efficiency of investment decision making has a long history. Much of the earlier work, interestingly, shows rather more recognition of the real world problems of investment analysis than does some of the highly abstract literature of today. Secondly, the Introduction provides a general critique of some of the current methods of transport investment appraisal, to complement the practical papers contained in the body of the book. Finally, this chapter attempts to place the various contributions in their wider context.

The problems of transport investment appraisal

Before proceeding to review the development of transport investment appraisal techniques it is useful to spend a little time examining in more detail the specific difficulties of such analysis and to consider carefully why standard micro-economic, commercial criteria will not suffice.

Transport may broadly be divided into those activities which are viewed in commercial terms and those which are not. In general, but not exclusively, the former embraces mobile plant (lorries, ships, cars, aircraft etc.) and infrastructure which is provided on purely financial criteria. While decisions regarding investment and pricing policies for those sectors pose interesting and often complex problems for management they are, in general, outside the main focus of this book. The papers here are concerned primarily with investment in transport infrastructure, especially publicly provided infrastructure. In some instances, where public undertakings have a remit to operate 'commercially', financial decision criteria may be applicable, but such cases are

2

exceptional and circumstances where financial appraisal is strictly legitimate are more limited than might sometimes be thought.

In the majority of cases, certainly in Europe, transport infrastructure is neither provided nor operated so as to maximise either long- or short-term profits. Indeed, in the case of most roads there is no direct charging for their use at all. Financial criteria are replaced in these circumstances by appraisal techniques concerned with the much wider implications and importance of the transport system.

The lack (or inadequacy) of a charging mechanism may be accounted for by two main features of transport infrastructure. Firstly, it exhibits some of the properties of a public good — it is difficult to exclude those who wish to use it, and any single person's use has minimal effect on other users. The degree of 'publicness' clearly varies with the type of infrastructure under consideration, with ports and airports exhibiting few characteristics of excludability or non-rivalry, but roads being nearer the theoretical notion of a public good. Even when excludability is possible and the so-called free-rider problem of non-paying inter-lopers is minimised, the costs of exclusion may prove excessive.

Secondly, even when the public good characteristics of transport infrastructure are minimal and commercial pricing policies (and invest-ment criteria) could be applied they are often ignored for distributional reasons. The standard commercial pricing approach implicitly assumes that transport services should be allocated by the strength of effective demand and, thus, those with the highest income are potentially the largest consumers. Since transport is important both in the final costs of production and in the access individuals enjoy to work and leisure opportunities, successive governments have in many instances replaced effective demand for transport services as the allocative tool by the notion of 'need'. Over the years the exact definition of need has varied and a series of alternative quantitative measures have been advanced, but this does not concern us here — the simple point is that price is not used as the main method of resource allocation in many spheres of transport activity.

Even if transport infrastructure were allocated on commercial grounds it is not altogether certain that financial investment appraisal techniques would be appropriate. Transport infrastructure imposes many external effects on those not necessarily concerned with its use. Airports, roads and railways generate considerable noise nuisance, are frequently visually offensive, and intrude into the life of local com-munities. The existing methods of costing employed by commercial firms take little account of these wider social implications, quite simply because they are not traded in conventional economic markets. Additionally, the full implications of large transport constructions are difficult to trace, and without considerably more wide-ranging techniques than those employed in financial appraisal there is the possibility of 'double-counting' even of monetary items in the investment account.

The longevity and high costs of most major pieces of transport infrastructure also mean that elementary commercial criteria such as the payback method or simple rate of return cease to be of any real use. In particular, many of the costs of transport investments are incurred early in the life of a project while the benefits only accrue over many years. This means not only that one must take account of the temporal weightings people attach to current outlays *vis-à-vis* future social returns, but also that there are considerable risks and uncertainties associated with the magnitude and profile of the eventual benefit stream. Rather more detailed forecasts of the long-term effects of the project are, therefore, normally sought by those concerned with transport schemes than in other areas of investment policy.

The pioneering work

The inappropriateness of the conventional commercial criteria in the transport context became increasingly apparent during the upsurge of activity which accompanied the Industrial Revolution. Technical advances in transport, mainly in terms of improved roads and inland navigation, removed many of the former constraints on the bulk movement of industrial goods. The problem became one of devising appropriate allocative techniques to ensure that resources were directed optimally within the transport sector. In particular, the wider importance of transport to the wellbeing of the economy needed to be embraced within the appraisal methodology. This was certainly the approach of the French Engineering school of economists in the first half of the nineteenth century, when it worked to establish the first set of formalised public investment criteria. (There are references to the general idea of wider appraisal criteria in earlier literature. Benjamin Franklin, for example, talks of attempting to establish the pros and cons of alternative actions and to estimate their respective weights, but they do not really lay out a formalised procedure.) Prior to this the majority of transport infrastructure had been provided for *ad hoc*, often military or political reasons, or, in a limited number of cases, was operated on quasi-commercial grounds, e.g. the turnpikes. The French Engineers were pragmatists who, while implicitly accepting the need for public expenditure on transport infrastructure, were concerned to devise systematic and sensible methods of analysis which would ensure acceptable provision and use.

Of these, Navier (1832), established one of the first cost—benefit

4

criteria, arguing that public works in transport should be provided only if the total benefit (in the form of total *transport* cost savings) exceeds total (recurring) costs. Projects meeting this criterion, it was argued, may then be ranked from highest to lowest according to their benefit—cost ratios irrespective of whether they are financed directly by public funds or by *regulated* private monopoly, although in the latter case some allowance may be necessary to reflect additional risk and uncertainty. He felt these costs and benefits to be measurable in a financial sense and, indeed, tested his rules on several specific cases taken from the researches of his fellow engineers at the École des Ponts et Chaussées. In much of his later work, Navier paid particular attention to the direct economic costing of railway operations since these, he felt, constituted the major part of total costs. This information appeared central to the application of his rule to the ranking of projects because, given the demand for transport, the different net benefits realised by the railroads become dependent almost exclusively upon costs. His approach to the costing problem was, again, however, pragmatic and, unlike many modern practitioners of cost—benefit analysis (CBA), he clearly recognised the weaknesses and imperfections of the cost estimates he produced.

Navier's work had its limitations and, in particular, his view of costs and benefits, concentrating on items directly measurable in financial terms, would now appear inadequate and rather narrow. Minard (1850), one of his colleagues, made a major contribution to the debate by broadening out the notion of opportunity cost in this context. In addition to the financial savings to transport undertakings associated with an investment, he also highlighted the importance of time savings, arguing that these should be credited with a monetary value

> because a service rendered more promptly is almost always a better buy; 'time is money', as the English proverb says.

In the absence of an established methodology he resorted to subjective monetary evaluations of time savings in his applied work. He was also the first to appreciate the problems which arise from what is now known as 'double-counting', citing the example of increased property values which generally followed the construction of a new river bridge being offset by a fall in property values at sites near older crossings. Minard also made two further significant contributions to the development of modern transport investment appraisal. Firstly, he implicitly recognised the importance of timing, especially in relation to the effects of compound interest on the present value of capital. He additionally cautioned that the benefits from most public works should not be assumed perpetual when undertaking project evaluation, because 'the truth is that the utility and value of public constructions change with time'. Secondly, Minard was concerned with the distributional aspects of investment appraisal, especially in relation to the method of financing to be employed. While opposed to excessively high tolls which would reduce the aggregate benefits of an investment, he equally rejected Navier's case for zero tolls (which would maximise gross transport-benefits), since this would spread the cost evenly over all taxpayers irrespective of whether or not they benefited from the availability of the facility.

Dupuit (1844) is considered to provide the true basis of modern transport investment appraisal methodology, offering both a critique of Navier's position and several major advances in micro-economic theory on the work of J.B. Say. (Historically, it is worth noting that Dupuit's work followed that of Minard – the latter's findings suffering from delayed publication.) Specifically, he developed the idea of consumer surplus whereby increases in quantity taken at a reduced price do not all take the same value, but are valued discretely according to the law of diminishing marginal utility. He recognised that price merely represents consumers' evaluations of the marginal unit of a commodity purchased and that intramarginal units will have associated with them a higher level of utility ('the utility of . . . articles is at least Op [the price] and . . . for almost all of them the utility is greater than Op'). It is not, therefore, the market price which reflects the utility of a good but rather the price the consumer is willing to pay:

> in general the relative or definitive utility of a product is expressed by the difference between the sacrifice which the purchaser would be willing to make in order to get it and the purchase price he has to pay in exchange.

Further, Dupuit argues that Navier placed excessive emphasis on savings in transport costs. By recognising the importance of the derived nature of the demand for transport, Dupuit redirected the attention of the analysis to the ultimate aim of an investment, namely to 'reduce not the cost of transport but the costs of production'. The measurement of net benefit derived by Dupuit tends, therefore, to differ somewhat from Navier.

The modern development of CBA

Despite the pioneering work of the French Engineering School it is only comparatively recently that systematic applications of what is now generally called cost—benefit analysis became standard practice in the transport sector. The emergence of a larger public sector combined with the greater complexity and wider implications of modern transport (not to mention its extremely high cost) largely account for this. As we see below, however, the application of economic appraisal has met with some opposition and, in addition, the emphasis of the appraisal methodology has not been uniform but has tended to vary, even within the broad CBA framework, as concern has switched, for example, from the environmental implications to distributional questions and from comprehensive transport planning to piecemeal project assessment.

Cost–benefit analysis as a standard tool of analysis first came into use in the United States at the turn of the century, although its adoption in this context owes more to the need for an administrative device allocating resources to the improvement of navigation than to any theoretical consideration. Prest and Turvey (1965) point to the River and Harbor Act of 1902, and the role of the Army Corps of Engineers in working out the costs and benefits, albeit only tangible ones, of river and harbour projects, as a major early application. In a wider context, the Flood Control Act of 1936, founded in the social ideals of the New Deal, led to the widespread use of CBA ideas in the United States for the assessment of water-development projects. At about the same time, i.e. 1937, a pioneering CBA traffic study was conducted in Oregon. While these examples illustrate the prewar growth of interest in the application of CBA, the majority of public-sector projects at the time were still being assessed according to older, political, random and *ad hoc* criteria. It was not until the 1950s, and the publication of *Proposed Practices for Economic Analysis of River Basin Projects* by the US Federal Inter-Agency River Basin Committee, that a systematic set of clear guidelines were established to conduct a CBA study.

While enthusiasm for CBA grew in the United States — indeed many felt it offered the opportunity for the establishment of a set of universal, 'scientific' rules for the conduct of public sector decision making — its application to transport investment in the United Kingdom did not come until a little later. The use of economic appraisal on a large scale in the transport sector began with its employment in the analysis of a series of major investment schemes. Most notable of the early appraisals were the CBA studies of the Victoria Underground Railway Line and the M1 Motorway.

These appraisals, though, tended to be one-off studies, each having its own specific methodology and emphasis. A survey of some 21 transport cost–benefit studies conducted by Barrell and Hills (1972) covering the years from 1960 to 1970 provided an ordinal comparison of the various approaches which had been adopted over that period. They used some thirty criteria for their comparison covering differences in problem definition, enumeration of costs and benefits, valuation of costs and benefits, discounting of future values, allowance for risk and uncertainty and presentation of results. The overall findings of Barrell and Hills at that time are of interest, namely:

> The main conclusions to emerge from the survey, which have been reinforced by discussions with consultants and government officials, are that economic evaluation in transportation is usually very narrowly conceived and, in many cases, takes such a restricted view of the term 'community' that it is doubtful whether the methods applied deserve the description of cost—benefit analysis, or even whether the objective really is to measure net community benefit.

The belief that CBA could provide the panacea to many of the problems associated with public transport investment appraisal was, however, strongly ingrained in official thinking by the late 1960s and more standardised CBA formulae were beginning to be developed in several areas. The White Paper on *Transport in London*, published in 1968, provided, in an appendix, a short-cut method of evaluating public transport proposals where there may be substantial potential benefits to non-users, especially in the form of reduced traffic congestion. This method formed the basis of evaluation for a number of schemes between 1968 and 1974, when public transport operators were applying for infrastructure grants under the 1968 Transport Act. Standard methods of appraisal were also developed for inter-urban road investment analysis (the COBA computerised methodology) and for the allocation of social passenger service subsidies to the railways. The introduction of strategic, rather than physical planning, into local level land-use planning under the 1968 Town and Country Planning Act, together with the introduction of a common test discount rate for nationalised industries in 1967, provided further encouragement for those supporting the wider use of cost—benefit type techniques. The later years of the 1960s had witnessed a steady spread in the use of economic appraisal methods and a gradual refinement and acceptance of the techniques of CBA, although possibly rather more so amongst the theorists than the practitioners.

The standard methodologies of the day attempted to follow the comprehensive definition of CBA laid down by Prest and Turvey (1965):

> CBA is a practical way of assessing the desirability of projects where it is important to take a long view (in the sense of looking at repercussions in the further as well as the nearer future) and a wide view (in the sense of allowing for side effects of many kinds on many persons, industries, regions etc.) — i.e. it implies the enumeration and evaluation of all relevant costs and benefits.

8

In essence the approach involved attempting to estimate the net present social value of a transport investment by employing the following formula,

$$\sum_n \sum_i \left[\frac{P(a_i B_{ni}) - P(b_i C_{ni})}{(1 + r)^n} \right]$$

(1.1)

where:

$P(a_i B_{ni})$ = the probable social and financial benefit of the transport investment expressed in money terms to be gained by individual (or group of individuals) i in year n as a result of the project's completion. The benefit, B_{ni}, is given a weight of a_i to reflect the importance attached to i's welfare.

$P(b_i C_{ni})$ = the probable social and financial cost in monetary terms to individual i in year n associated with the investment. C_{ni} is given a weighting of b_i to reflect the importance attached to the costs borne by i.

$(1 + r)^{-n}$ = the relative weight attached to a cost or benefit occurring in year n. The form of the weight reflects the decreasing importance attached to the more distant attributes of the project.

A change of emphasis

The 1970s witnessed a marked reaction. CBA appeared to fall from favour. To some extent this is an exaggeration, in the sense that CBA continued to evolve during the decade, but public and professional confidence in the strength of the technique certainly declined. One reason for the increasing doubts about the power of conventional CBA stemmed from a shift in public attitudes and priorities. The early studies were concerned primarily with questions of economic efficiency and placed minimal emphasis on either distributional questions or matters concerning the environment and less 'material' items. However, in the 1970s changing social concerns highlighted questions of energy and ecology. These issues also began to assume greater importance in the types of transport application to which CBA was now beginning to be applied (e.g. to airports and urban motorways) and, as Wildavsky (1966) says:

Although cost—benefit analysis presumably results in efficiency by adding the most to national income, it is shot through with political and social value choices and surrounded by uncertainties and difficulties of computation.

9

A further reason for the change in attitude is that a general mistrust developed of any procedure which appears to offer a simple, numerical answer to difficult and delicate decisions which, by their nature, involve a variety of subjective considerations. This view grew along with a suspicion that CBA can be manipulated to provide justifications for specific lines of action corresponding to the view of the practitioner or of pressure groups. It also became apparent that there is no single 'proper' way to perform a CBA, but rather that a number of alternative approaches exist, each corresponding to a particular set of moral notions. These were, in fact, problems which had been explicitly recognised by early theoreticians in the field but their suggested qualifications and reservations were not always carried into practice. The need for decision makers using a CBA framework to make their assumptions explicit, however, became more widely accepted and the rather mechanised appraisal procedure, which had become best practice methodology, was now seen as a starting point for a much wider evaluation of different courses of action rather than an end in itself. This introduced more scope for disagreement over the appropriate method of appraisal.

More specific problems with the 'pure' CBA model stem from putting the underlying welfare economic theory (based upon the Kaldor-Hicks compensation criterion) into practice. There are often considerable difficulties in physically tracing out and measuring all the consequences of a transport investment and, even when measurement is feasible, it is frequently almost impossible to place anything more sophisticated than arbitrary monetary values on such effects. In fields where research work on evaluation has been long standing, e.g. in the evaluation of travel time savings, the techniques developed rely upon estimating the hypothetical market prices for intangibles which would prevail if they were traded in competitive conditions. Evaluations depend, therefore, on the willingness of the affected parties to pay and government dictates and priorities are considered inappropriate. The partial nature of CBA also makes it particularly unsuitable for appraising large-scale schemes or investments where wide-ranging multiplier repercussions on the economy, even at the local level, can affect the constellation of relative prices and production which form the basis against which intangibles are evaluated.

The weighting schemes required in the standard CBA procedure are particularly difficult to devise. The distributional weights reflecting the impact of a decision on different sectors of the community pose specific problems of interpersonal comparisons which must, by their nature, be subjective. In addition, although the test discount rate, and more recently the recommended rate of return, represents an attempt to introduce standard temporal weights across areas of public sector activity, the rates used are somewhat arbitrary and only partially reflect the social opportunity cost of resources. The actual estimation of the time stream of costs and benefits is itself difficult and the introduction of sensitivity and other, usually cruder, techniques to reflect the stochastic nature of the forecasts introduces further elements of subjectivity.

More recent developments

The major change in attitude towards the conventional CBA framework came in 1971 with the publication of the Roskill Report on the siting of a third London airport. This represented the largest single CBA study (strictly a cost-effectiveness analysis since it was only concerned with where to build and not with the basic question of whether to build) conducted in the transport sphere, costing over a million pounds at 1970 prices. Debate about the final conclusions and the appropriateness of the methodology began almost immediately and subsequently the government overturned the recommendations reached by the Commission of Inquiry. In itself the official rejection of the Commission's views need not seem damning – after all it may simply reflect the different value judgements of government – but the attacks on the basic methodology were of more serious consequence.

A second challenge arose more gradually as objectors at public inquiries into new trunk road proposals became both more vocal and sophisticated in putting their case. The main lines of criticism included doubt about the reliability of the traffic forecasts then employed, the inability of objectors to question the 'need' for a new route (the inquiries were only concerned with specific alignment) and the apparently excessive emphasis which was placed on the quantifiable effects of a new road (notably the COBA package looked mainly at time savings and operational economies) to the neglect of important, but less tangible, items. The problems were possibly compounded by the initial, official reactions to the situation which, rather than attempting to improve the procedure, exhibited a remarkable degree of intransigence to the extent that certain lines of objection (e.g. to the 'official' traffic forecasts) were not permitted at inquiries.

The study of the transport component of the Greater London Development Plan highlighted a further problem which was confronting CBA practitioners namely the impossibility of assessing the longer term effects of a particular decision. In the case of the London urban motorway proposals, for example, the sheer complexity of tracing out the temporal pattern of interacting transport demands over a complicated road system resulted in the calculation of only a first year rate of return.

Those concerned with transport investment appraisal have subsequently attempted to meet these problems and criticisms by developing techniques in two different directions. Firstly, the conventional CBA approach, with its emphasis on utility maximisation, has been subjected to further modification and improvement. In particular, more attention has been focused on the less tangible costs and benefits and on incorporating distributional considerations more fully. Secondly, the emphasis within the criteria underlying investment appraisal has shifted and important variations on the conventional CBA methodology have emerged offering a range of alternative economic appraisal techniques. In general, official practice has tended to follow the first line while academic studies have been concerned with the second. In essence the contributions in this book look at both of these approaches.

The official attempts to improve what we have called the conventional framework of CBA have involved considerable expenditures on research programmes into traffic forecasting (e.g. the development of the Regional Highway Traffic Model) and a series of research projects and inquiries looking at the wider impact of transport on the community (e.g. the Armitage inquiry into the social and environmental impact of heavy goods vehicles and the monies invested by the Department of Transport in the valuation of time project conducted at the Universities of Oxford and Leeds in conjunction with the consultants Martin and Voorhees Associates). Also rather more attention is now paid to the problem of giving greater emphasis to the less material elements of the CBA account.

The alternative approach, a substantial change in methodology, represents a response to the difficulties of those who actually have to make the investment decisions. In particular the chairman of British Rail points to the need for an approach which

> can be understood by ordinary intelligent people . . . incorporates the methods of analysis developed by welfare economists over the last decade or so . . . gets away from the naive position adopted by the early cost—benefit man which seemed to imply that every consideration could be perfectly weighted and that therefore there was a single best solution. (Parker, 1978)

Multi-criteria decision-making techniques move away from the idea of utility maximising which underlies CBA, and are more akin to the management theories of satisficing. Rather than attempt to seek optimum solutions which, for practical reasons, are likely to be unobtainable, the decision maker selects actions complying with a range of criteria which describe minimally satisfactory alternatives. In the case of a road scheme, for example, one seeks an option which provides certain set levels of access (somehow defined), safety, noise abatement, cost economy etc., rather than alternatives which maximise some goals, say access, at the almost total expense of others.

The planning balance sheet (PBS) initially developed by Lichfield (1956) for town planning purposes is similar to CBA in that all costs and benefits are included and that distributional considerations are not neglected, but it represents a movement in the direction of multi-criteria analysis in that not all the effects of the various schemes are translated into monetary terms. It has subsequently been developed and employed in the evaluation of urban transport and airport invest-ment proposals. Where evaluation is difficult, the PBS approach employs physical values and when quantification is impossible, ordinal indices or scales may be used. A socio-economic account is drawn up setting out the full effects of each course of action and indicating the extent to which various groups in the community will be affected. A modified version of this type of approach, the project impact matrix, has recently gained the favour of the Leitch Committee (Department of Transport, 1978).

Critics of the PBS methodology point to the need to develop ordinal ranking criteria to permit the various items of the PBS account to be set against various planning goals intended to reflect community preferences. The ranking process has to reflect social preferences which are themselves difficult to ascertain and, even if a concensus is possible, the ordinal nature of the ranking suggests a loss of efficiency in the techniques. Peters (1968), for instance, argues that PBS only offers

> a bombardment of monetary measures, quantitative measures and qualitative judgements in confusing array, without a single indicator, with a danger of double counting and an embarrassing degree of circularity.

These criticisms, although partially valid, tend to contrast PBS with an idealised conventional CBA framework rather than the pragmatic CBA approach adopted in practice.

The PBS attempt to extend CBA into a multidimensional framework, however, requires substantial data inputs and only offers a partial solution to the problem of making interpersonal comparisons. Despite this and although PBS does not avoid the problem of making value judgements, the technique has the merit that, unlike the pure CBA model, these normative judgements are made explicit rather than hidden in a final, single net present social value calculation. The con-struction of the initial socio-economic account can often, in itself, be educational and shed considerable light on salient questions the decision maker should be asking.

The PBS method falls somewhere between the traditional CBA approach and true multi-criteria decision-making techniques. It contains elements of the maximisation principles which underlie CBA, but without the exclusive reliance on monetary evaluation of all an investment's impacts. Multi-criteria decision-making techniques, which have been extensively developed at the theoretical level in the context of regional impact analysis generally involve introducing weights to reflect the relative priorities attached to the various outcomes associated with different courses of action (Pearman, 1978). They have not yet been applied in the transport field but are attracting the attention of many concerned with the inherent limitations of the CBA approach. A number of multi-criteria approaches have been devised, each attempting to achieve a multidimensional compromise between the wide diversity of goals and costs which are embodied in public sector choice. The approaches differ in their method of presentation, the level of mathematical sophistication involved and the amount of data input required. Several of the techniques rely upon geometrical representation to produce multidimensional scalings, while others involve a considerable degree of intuition. In general, however, these particular techniques tend to be rather specialised in their nature and are only of practical use in certain specific circumstances. Of more practical value in the transport field are some of the simpler weighting techniques which already enjoy a degree of acceptance and for which the theory is comparatively well advanced.

The introduction of weightings permits the effects of a projected action to be reduced to a single, summary figure. The goals achievement matrix approach, which has been used in urban transport planning (Hill, 1968), for example, offers an explicit treatment of various goals and applies a set of predetermined weights to them so that each option can be assessed in terms of goal achievement. To facilitate this, the goals are related to physical measures to reflect the extent to which they have been achieved. The final goal achievement account employs the weighted index of goal achievement to determine the preferred course of action.

To date, much of the work in the field of multi-criteria decision making has focused on devising mathematically consistent methods of handling weights and basic data. The major practical problem, however, is in devising the weighting scheme to be adopted; CBA may be seen as a special case of multi-criteria approach in this context, with monetary values being employed as weights. Despite the practical difficulties of evaluating intangibles and the problems of equity, the CBA method is possibly more readily accepted than some of the alternative schemes suggested for multi-criteria procedures (e.g. basing them on past decisions, political debates or direct questioning of individuals).

14

The remaining chapters

The common theme of the remaining chapters in this book is an attempt to come to terms with some of the practical problems encountered across a wide range of cost—benefit problems in the transport sector, many of which have been touched upon in this introduction. The first four contributions are all marked by a concern for the strong influence which institutional and political factors can have on the conduct of cost—benefit analyses in transport. In chapter 2, Peter Mackie is concerned with the appraisal of a proposal to expand one of the network of regional airports in the UK. He emphasises how different CBA in practice can be from the apparently clear-cut requirements set out in some of the more basic textbooks. The investment decision with which he is concerned must take place in a framework dictated by government policy on the strategy for regional airport development, the need to obtain planning permission for building work, and the existence of separate financial criteria laid down for general expenditure by local authorities, including local expenditure on airport provision. The exercise is far from being a straightforward piece of purely economic calculus.

Chapter 4, too, is much concerned with the role of government in influencing expenditure on transport. It is inevitable that a project as important and politically sensitive as the Channel Tunnel should bear the imprint of the (not necessarily consistent) views of successive governments. Political events, and the attitudes of major public bodies such as British Rail, have probably had more influence in determining the present situation regarding progress with the Channel Tunnel, than any of the pieces of formal economic work as yet performed on it. Nevertheless, Ken Gwilliam argues convincingly in this chapter for the importance to the final decision of both straightforward commercial and cost—benefit related economic considerations. The economic analysis undertaken thus far has certainly shed considerable light on what seem to be the more appropriate specifications of the scheme, and there is potential for further insight to be gained through appropriate economic work. Certainly, as the chapter concludes,

> . . . it is quite inappropriate to rely on the uncoordinated, and frequently conflicting, activities of a host of private and public institutions to bring [about] a timely and rational decision

on a project of such

> size and international institutional complexity.

Institutional attitudes and boundaries are also a matter for concern in two other chapters of the book. In chapter 3, David Gillingwater considers the relationship between transport investment appraisal and land-use policy decisions. He clearly identifies a number of critical differences between the two separate, but closely linked spheres of planning practice, and examines attempts to close the gap between them. Again, the important practical consequences for transport appraisal and society in general of topics which are far removed from textbook CBA are emphasised. David Hensher and his colleagues, in chapter 5, also point to the way in which administrative structures can have a significant impact on the way in which transport investment is appraised within the general CBA format. The appraisal exercise which they describe is one which attempted to put into practice a number of the new approaches to the implementation of CBA discussed in the previous section. Their comments about the experiences encountered and about the likely effects of this influential inquiry on transport planning in Australia are particularly of interest.

The remaining chapters are for the most part not accounts of experience with individual applications of CBA, but are more concerned with what can be done to make its use more appropriate in the light of particular problems frequently encountered in practice. Norman Ashford and John Clark concentrate on the use of CBA for appraising developments in transport technology. They identify a number of deficiencies, leading to divergence between the assumptions inherent in many recent studies and the real requirements of decision makers. One area where there has, until recently, been considerable divergence between the theory and practice of decision making is in the recognition of uncertainty. In chapter 7, Alan Pearman discusses the treatment of risk and uncertainty in road investment appraisal. He points to the inadequate analysis of such questions in much past CBA work and to the fact that transport infrastructure, with its high cost, long life and highly specific function, is specially prone to erroneous decision making if the full range of possible alternative futures in which schemes may have to operate is not properly taken into account.

Clifford Sharp's concern in chapter 8 is with one of the most thoroughly investigated, yet persistently controversial, inputs to transport CBA, the valuation of time savings. He juxtaposes the theory of time evaluation, with its roots in a carefully specified welfare economic framework, and the compromises which are forced on any practitioner. It is clear that many effectively intractable problems, both of theory and practice, are likely to persist for some time in this area. The same is undoubtedly true of the question investigated by Ken Button in chapter 9. Forecasting traffic levels is central to the appraisal process. If it cannot be done reliably, the foundations of conventional CBA as applied in transport investment appraisal are seriously undermined. Again, theoretical and practical arguments tend to point in different directions. In theory, traffic is generated by the interaction of highly complex social and economic forces, and to model and then forecast the consequences of such interaction requires highly sophisticated, not to mention complex, models of man and the society in which he lives. In practice, however, since we are concerned with forecasts twenty or thirty years into the future, the approach must be different. Nobody can forecast this far ahead the highly specific inputs required even for the present generation of behavioural models. Practicality dictates far cruder, aggregate models, with independent variables at least reasonably susceptible to reliable forecasting.

Finally, in chapter 10, John Holt explores a topic which may receive less attention in the professional literature than many of those previously discussed, but which in every way fits in with the overriding concern of this book, confronting the theory of CBA with the importance of being able to achieve worthwhile results in practice. Overseas trade is vital to many developing countries, and many have also suffered because of the inadequacy or inappropriateness of their port facilities. But the choice of alternative technologies is considerable and the interdependence between the country providing port facilities, the shippers and other trading nations is highly complex. In such circumstances both the question of whose costs and benefits to consider, as well as how to measure them, becomes very difficult. The fact that capital is so short that the opportunity costs of analytical errors are much compounded serves only to emphasise the importance of achieving a good marriage between theory and practice, and provides a highly appropriate theme for the conclusion of the book.

References

Barrell, D.W. and Hills, P.J., 'The application of cost–benefit analysis to transport investment projects in Britain' in *Transportation*, 1972, vol.1, pp. 29–54.

Department of Transport, *Report of the Advisory Committee on Trunk Road Assessment*, HMSO, London 1978.

Dupuit, J., 'On the measurement of the utility of public works' in *Annales des Ponts et Chaussées*, 1844, series 2, vol.8; English translation by R.H. Barback, *International Economic Paper*, 1952, no.2, pp. 83–110.

Hill, M., 'A goals achievement matrix for evaluating alternative plans', in *Journal of the American Institute of Planners*, 1968, vol.34, pp. 19–29.

Lichfield, N., 'Economics of Planned Development' in *The Estates Gazette*, 1956, part IV, pp. 253 *et seq.*

Minard, C.J., 'Notions élementaires d'économie publique appliquées aux travaux publics' in *Annales des Ponts et Chaussées. Memoires et Documents*, 1850, vol.14, pp. 1−125.

Navier, H., 'De l'execution des travaux publics, et particulièrement des concessions' in *Annales des Ponts et Chaussées. Memoires et Documents*, series 1, 1832, vol.1, pp. 1−31.

Parker, P., *A Way to run a Railway*, 1978, Haldane Memorial Lecture.

Pearman, A.D., *An Assessment of Multiple Criteria Decision Making Methods and their Potential Use in Comparability Studies between Trunk Road and Rail Investment*, report prepared for the British Railways Board, 1978.

Peters, G.H., *Cost−Benefit Analysis and Public Expenditure*, Eaton Paper 8, Institute of Economic Affairs, London 1968.

Prest, A.R. and R. Turvey, 'Cost−benefit analysis: a survey' in *Economic Journal*, 1965, vol.75, pp. 685−705.

Wildavsky, A., 'The political economy of efficiency: cost−benefit analysis, systems analysis and program budgeting' in *Public Administration Review*, 1966, vol.26, pp. 292−310.

2 Appraisal of regional airport projects — a case study

P. J. Mackie

Introduction

The aim of this chapter is to review the state of the art of appraising regional airport projects. The case to be studied is the proposed run-way extension and allied works at Leeds/Bradford Airport in West Yorkshire, though more general conclusions about the formation and execution of airports policy will be drawn

Project appraisal as described in textbooks sometimes appears deceptively clear-cut. Objectives are given or set, the project options are defined, the inputs and outputs associated with each option are forecast, and then evaluated against the objectives, and finally, the option with the highest return is selected and implemented. Indeed, this is an extremely useful framework for project appraisal, but there are numerous practical difficulties. The objectives of the investing enterprise may be unclear, the range of options for testing hard to define, forecasting subject to major uncertainty, and evaluation con-troversial. Whether to present the results in rate of return form, or as a planning balance sheet, showing the incidence of effects, has also been a matter for debate.

The need for clarity of objectives is paramount, for the objectives to be satisfied determine the nature and breadth of the appraisal. If the investing agency is a private firm, then the appraisal will be dominated by projections of the financial costs and revenues associated with each project option. For public sector projects, financial appraisal is relevant where the activity is regarded as commercial, but where prices fail to reflect costs, or where there are significant externalities or system effects, a broader approach is required in which the costs and benefits to all affected parties are considered — a social cost—benefit analysis.

Airport investment has been regarded as a suitable subject for cost—benefit analysis. The benefits to airport users are not necessarily fully represented by the landing charges which they (ultimately) pay. Aircraft noise is a classic externality, while airports are claimed to confer development benefits upon the local economy. Finally, airports are elements of an interdependent system: investment at one location may be expected to have consequences for demand, output and costs in the rest of the system. These effects can be considered within a cost—benefit framework, and of course, the Roskill Report on the Third London Airport did contain what is still the largest and most ambitious cost—benefit analysis ever undertaken (Commission on the Third London Airport, 1971).

Yet a mere seven years later, the main academic observer of airport economics wrote 'From the Government's point of view, it would certainly seem as if airport cost—benefit analysis is dead' (Doganis et al., 1978). This is not because there is a dearth of airport projects to appraise, quite the reverse. Aside from the long-running third London airport saga, the last couple of years have seen public inquiries into proposals for new terminals at Birmingham and Norwich, and runway extensions at East Midlands and Leeds/Bradford, while the rebuilding of the runway at Manchester has also taken place. If cost—benefit analysis is dead, what has taken its place?

So far, we have written as if there is a single point at which airport projects are subjected to appraisal. In fact, most major airport projects face something more akin to an obstacle course. First, their progress will be greatly eased if they fit in with national airports policy. Secondly, planning permission must be obtained for all significant developments. Thirdly, local authority capital expenditure is subject to financial control, and central government may need to be convinced that a project offers a good return before permission to spend is granted. Appraisal, then, is a multi-stage process, and we need to consider the procedures at each of the different stages.

National airport planning

Airport developments, like trunk road and power station projects, are difficult to deal with institutionally because they have both national and local consequences. While the local interest has always been clear, it was with the establishment of the Civil Aviation Authority in 1972 that the national interest in airport planning was explicitly recognised. Among the duties of the CAA are:

> to consider what aerodromes are in its opinion likely to be required from time to time in the United Kingdom in addition to or in place of or by way of alteration of existing aerodromes; and

> to make recommendations to the Secretary of State arising out of its consideration of that matter. (Civil Aviation Act, 1971)

The CAA acted promptly to carry out these duties. It commissioned a series of regional studies by consultants (Stratford, 1974; Metra, 1974; CAA, 1975a) and when the studies were completed, gave its advice to the Secretary of State for Trade (CAA, 1975b; 1975c; 1975d; 1976). Meanwhile, the Government had itself been reviewing airports policy following the abandonment of the Maplin project in 1974, and these two streams of work led to the Airport Strategy Consultation Document in 1976 (DoT, 1976). Then, in the light of comments received, and after further updating work, the 1978 *Airports Policy* White Paper emerged (Cmnd 7084). This in turn led to the establishment of the Advisory Committee on Airports Policy, whose first report on the need for a third London airport appeared at the end of 1979 (DoT, 1979).

The 1970s was therefore a decade of progress towards the formulation of a national airports policy and in the 1978 White Paper specific roles were assigned to particular airports in England and Wales. Thus Manchester was to be a Category A airport, providing for intercontinental, international and domestic traffic. Birmingham, East Midlands, Leeds/Bradford, Newcastle and Cardiff would be regional airports, providing some short-haul international services, domestic services feeding into the major hub airports at London and Manchester, and inclusive tour operations. Local airports, Category C, would cater for general aviation with some domestic scheduled services and charter flights. It was stressed in the White Paper that the categories needed to be interpreted flexibly.

The technical basis for the airports policy has been the subject of discussion elsewhere (Caves, 1980; Doganis et al., 1978). Briefly, the consultants analysed the strategic options for each region within a cost–benefit framework, and the CAA then reviewed the studies and reworked some of the analysis. Account was taken of airport capital and operating costs, airline costs, surface access costs for passengers, and noise costs. The broad conclusion which emerged was that, in cost–benefit terms, the best strategy was to concentrate development at a small number of airports, so as to gain the available economies of scale in airport and airline operations. For example, the CAA's reworking showed the best option for Central England to be a two-airport system (Manchester and Birmingham), compared with the existing six airports. However, the CAA stopped short of recommending the phasing out of operations at East Midlands, Leeds/Bradford, Liverpool and Blackpool. They concluded that 'where local communities are willing to carry the financial deficits involved, airports other than Manchester and Birmingham might be free to provide a range of services restricted to domestic flights, whole-plane inclusive tour and other charters, and general aviation' (CAA, 1975c, para.66). Licences for international scheduled services might not be granted until corresponding services from Manchester and Birmingham had become fully viable.

This conclusion is important because it formed the basis for subsequent policy. It is not clear, though, why the CAA rejected the analysis of its own officials. One argument used at the time was that some types of service exist for which convenient airport access is of particular importance, but the high values of business travel time used in the cost–benefit analysis should have reflected that. There remains the suspicion that unstated factors, such as regional political pride, were allowed to overrule the economic logic. Certainly, no quantified justification of the recommended strategy was ever published. It was with this, and similar stories, in mind that Doganis wrote his epitaph to airport cost–benefit analysis in 1978.

National airports policy is the top tier in the airport planning process, but it is not the last word. Airports are owned not by the Government but by the British Airports Authority or local authorities, either singly or in consortia. There is nothing to prevent a local authority from trying to promote developments not encouraged by national policy, or from deciding not to develop its airport in the way envisaged. However, in practice, national policy acts as a sieve. Where developments are consistent with the plan set out in the White Paper, the presumption will be in their favour. Where they are not, the Government has the instruments of finance, and through the CAA, of airline route licensing, to prevent unwanted development from occurring. Given that the Government has, rightly, a strong say in the pattern of development, it is regrettable that, despite the torrent of words, the intellectual basis of its policy is suspect.

Local airport planning

If a local authority decides that it wishes to extend the runway or expand the terminal facilities at its airport, then it must obtain planning permission. The planning application is likely to encounter objections, the Secretary of State for the Environment will 'call in' the scheme, and a public inquiry will be held. At the public inquiry, it is the task of the Inspector to weigh the pros and cons, and to make his recommendations to the Secretary of State accordingly. In principle, then, this is another point in the process at which a social cost—benefit analysis could be a useful aid to decision taking. With this in mind, we shall consider the nature of the evidence presented on behalf of the applicants at the public inquiry into the proposed runway extension at Leeds/Bradford airport (LBA) held in autumn 1979.

Some brief background may be helpful. The main runway at LBA is, at 1646 metres, the shortest of any major airport in the UK. It is suitable for turbo-prop aircraft, notably the Viscount, but does not allow modern short-haul jets other than one version of the Boeing 737 to operate at economic payloads over existing or projected routes. Furthermore, the runway lacks a Runway End Safety Area (RESA) at one end, and the CAA intends to require that this should be remedied. Because of physical restrictions at the site, with reservoirs at one end of the runway, and a main road at the other, the RESA could only be provided by reducing the length of the runway by 90 metres. This, it was generally agreed at the public inquiry, would mean the end of inclusive tour traffic at LBA.

The strategic choice, therefore, is between doing nothing, and extending the runway by some 600 metres, so as to cater for a wide range of jet aircraft. Extension of the runway requires the A658 road to be placed in tunnel. As well as the runway extension, the project includes improvements to the approach and runway lighting, and development of the terminal buildings to cater for the anticipated increase in traffic. The project appraisal, therefore, takes the form of a comparison between the future with the project constructed, and the future with the present runway, shortened by the 90 metres required to provide the RESA. It is clear that the administrative decision by CAA to impose the RESA requirement and thereby remove the inclusive tour traffic is absolutely critical to the result of the scheme appraisal.

In broadest outline, the case made by the applicants for planning permission was that the project was envisaged by, and was consistent with, national airports policy, that the costs of the airport would be covered by the revenues from users, that the project conferred economic development benefits upon the region, and that these merits outweighed the environmental costs. Since noise and other external costs are not traded in the market, it is difficult to know what weight or value should be attached to a worsening of the environment. However, this chapter focuses on the less well recognised pitfalls involved in evaluating the costs, revenues and benefits to airport operators and users.

At the public inquiry, the financial evidence focused on the question of the viability of the airport as a whole (Pollard, 1979a). It is easy to understand why, for the White Paper stated:

> Basic to the application of these guidelines will be the principle that air transport facilities should not in general be subsidised by the taxpayer or the ratepayer. (para. 41)

Indeed, but for this emphasis, the financial effect of the project might have been held to be irrelevant to the decision on the planning application. The Inspector reported:

> This [finance] is not a matter on which the Secretary of State asked to be informed further . . . In a strict planning inquiry one should normally put finance on one side. This, however, is not simply a planning inquiry, but is one which necessitates consideration of a Government White Paper wherein it is expressly stated that air travel generally should not be subsidised by either taxpayer or ratepayer. (Radmore, 1980, para. 387)

While the statement in *Airports Policy* ensures that the overall finances of airports are a relevant matter at planning inquiries, it does distract attention from the worth of the project itself. As things stand, a profitable airport could satisfy the test of overall financial viability, though the project it was proposing might be unsound. The proper test of a project's worth is the expected rate of return on the project itself. The next two sections examine the strengths and weaknesses of the commercial case for the runway extension project at Leeds/Bradford, and the following section questions whether projects which are justified on a test of financial profitability are automatically also justified in social cost–benefit terms.

The commercial case

In order to examine the commercial case for the project, it is necessary to forecast air traffic, airport revenue, and airport operating costs with and without the project. If the expected present value of the net revenue stream over the life of the project is sufficient, after discounting at an appropriate rate, to defray the capital costs, the project is commercially justified.

Since much local authority capital expenditure is for social projects where rates of return cannot usefully be calculated, no standard investment criteria are laid down. However, nationalised industries, including the British Airports Authority, are required to appraise their investment programmes formally, and to show that they yield a real rate of return higher than the social opportunity cost of capital, currently taken to be 5 per cent. The *Airports Policy* paper states:

> At publicly owned airports, the authorities concerned will be expected to relate the development of their airports to the Government's airports policy, *as well as to the criteria which may from time to time apply to public sector projects*. (Para. 18; author's italics)

It therefore seems reasonable to apply this same test in this case, and this was the approach adopted by the airport treasurer in his evidence (Pollard, 1979b).

The starting point is to forecast air passenger traffic with and without the project. Two different approaches were followed. The airport engineer made forecasts based on the expected national growth rates of air traffic, together with predictions of the share of the inclusive tour market which would be attracted to LBA, and of a number of new international scheduled services (Gaffney, 1979). The airport director built up a forecast on the basis of discussions with airlines currently using, or expecting to use, the airport (Seller, 1979). The traffic forecasts for 1987/8 are shown in table 2.1.

Table 2.1
Terminal air passengers at Leeds/Bradford ('000s)

Type of traffic	1978 Actual	1987/8 With runway extended		1987/8 With runway extended	1987/8 Without extension
		Airport engineer		Airport director	Airport director
		Low	*High*		
Domestic	211	285	353	305	94
International scheduled	65	162	210	141	32
Inclusive tour	55	262	354	354	—
Total	331	709	917	800	126

Source: Gaffney (1979), Seller (1979).

The airport engineer also made traffic forecasts for 1992 and 1997, and predicted the capital costs of the project (£14.6 million at September 1979 prices).

The runway extension would permit a much enhanced range of

25

inclusive tour services and a limited number of new scheduled services to be provided which, together with natural traffic growth, would more than double passenger traffic over the next decade (see table 2.1). Without the runway extension, inclusive tour traffic would disappear and, it was argued, scheduled services and traffic would atrophy.

Table 2.2 shows the predicted financial consequences for the airport. With the runway extended, the airport is shown to be in financial surplus after interest; if the runway is not extended, the airport is in deficit. The advantages of scale are clearly seen; the revenue per passenger at a throughput of 800,000 is £4.30 (September 1979 prices), while the incremental operating cost per passenger is less than £1.

Table 2.2
Forecast airport income and expenditure 1987/8

		With runway extension	Without runway extension	Net difference
	1978/9			
Volume of passengers ('000)	324	800	125	675
Income (£'000s)				
Fees and charges	1,010	3,080	660	2,420
Other	149	370	40	330
	1,159	3,450	700	2,750
Operating expenditure	720	1,350	820	530
Trading surplus	439	2,100	-120	2,220
Debt charges	158	1,700	90	1,610
Net surplus (deficit)	281	400	(210)	610

Source: Pollard (1979a)

Performing similar calculations for each year over a twenty-year period, the treasurer obtained a stream of incremental net revenues attributable to the project, which he could compare with the capital costs. Some results are shown in tables 2.3 and 2.4. All costs and revenues are at September 1979 prices, and are discounted to that date.

Table 2.3 shows the net revenue generated by the project in selected future years, based on the mid-point of the range of forecasts made by the airport engineer. Comparing the present value of the revenue stream with the present value of capital costs (table 2.4), we see that, even on

Table 2.3
Traffic and net revenue: forecast mean in selected years

Volume of passengers '000s

	With extension	Without extension	Net difference	Net revenue difference (£'000s)	5% discount factors	Present value
1987/8	800	125	675	2,220	0.677	1,503
1992/3	1,000	125	875	2,870	0.530	1,521
1997/8	1,200	125	1,075	3,520	0.416	1,464

PV (for years 1981–2000) = 26,391

Table 2.4
Present value and internal rate of return

	PV of net revenues (£m)	PV of capital costs* (£m)	NPV (5% discount rate) (£m)	IRR (%)
Forecast mean traffic	26.4	11.8	+14.6	18
Low traffic	21.8	11.8	+10.0	16

*Capital costs exclude some £0.5m incurred whether or not the project is undertaken.

Source: Pollard (1979b), supplemented by author's calculations.

the airport engineer's low traffic forecast, the project's internal rate of return is well above the assumed opportunity cost of capital of 5 per cent. Looking at the same results another way, if the central forecasts came true, the project would pay for itself by 1988, or, if the low forecasts occurred, by 1990.

Critique

The determinants of the financial return on the project are summarised in figure 2.1.

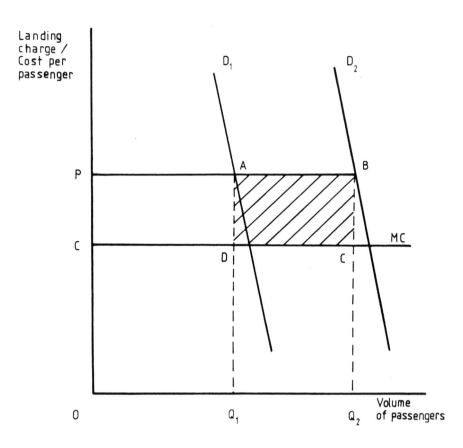

Figure 2.1   Determinants of the financial return on the project

D_1 and D_2 are the demand curves for travel from Leeds/Bradford in year X with and without the runway extension. If the landing charge per passenger is OP, and the marginal operating expenditure per passenger is OC, then $ABCD$ and its equivalent in other years, measures the incremental revenue which can be set against the capital costs. Clearly, the size of $ABCD$ depends upon the size of the shift in demand by, the level of landing charges, and the level of operating costs. Each of these elements was subjected to scrutiny at the public inquiry.

Traffic forecasts

The main determinants of the volume of air traffic at an airport are:

Real personal disposable income (leisure traffic)
Real GDP (business traffic)
Price of air travel
Range of services available
Quality of service (frequency, jets etc.)
Developments elsewhere in the airport system.

The income elasticity of demand for air travel is high, so that the growth rate of air traffic is extremely sensitive to the growth rate of disposable income and GDP. Leisure traffic, particularly inclusive tour traffic, is also price elastic, and is therefore sensitive to fluctuations in real fuel prices and exchange rates.

The airport engineer adopted the air traffic growth rates envisaged in the *Airports Policy* White Paper, but by the time of the public inquiry, the income growth assumptions on which these forecasts were based appeared over-optimistic. In addition, his forecast of international scheduled traffic assumed new direct routes to Brussels, West Germany, Switzerland and other European destinations would come into operation. Examination of the regional demand for travel to these destinations suggested that this, too, was over-optimistic. Taking these points together, the author's forecasts (see table 2.5) on behalf of a group of local objectors were some 15–20 per cent below the airport engineer's. With the benefit of hindsight, recent revisions to the national air traffic forecasts lend support to the author's forecasts (DoT, 1981).

Table 2.5
Forecasts of traffic in 1987/8 ('000s)

| | With runway extension | | Without runway extension | |
	Low	High	Low	High
Domestic	229	285	207	272
International scheduled	134	186	100	119
Inclusive tour	191	290	–	–
TOTAL	554	761	307	391

Source: Mackie (1979)

Forecasting the volume of air traffic without the runway extension is even more difficult and contentious. Scheduled services would have to be provided by some combination of Fokker F27s and F28s, HS 748s, Viscounts, until they are life-expired, and possibly the new BAe 146s. The question is whether second-level operators would be willing and able to continue supplying the market using this equipment. As mentioned earlier, the airport director's prediction, based on his discussions with the airlines, was that the services would decline.

An alternative view is that airlines would not be unduly inconvenienced in the short-haul scheduled market if the runway were not extended. On this view, the effective constraint on aircraft size, except on the London route, is not the length of the runway, but the size of the regional market. The small size of the market dictates that in order to provide services of commercially saleable frequency at profitable load factors, the operators must use small aircraft. A recent Government report puts the minimum market size for jet operation of short-haul scheduled services at 40,000 passengers per annum (DoT, 1979). Only the London (Heathrow) and Amsterdam services from Leeds/Bradford will have reached that threshold by 1987. This line of argument suggests that, with the important exception of the London route, scheduled services and traffic would be largely unaffected by the runway extension, because operators would be using the same equipment which they would choose to use anyway. This in turn implies that the airport director's forecast of traffic in the absence of the runway extension was unduly pessimistic.

To summarise, the applicants for planning permission expected that the runway extension would add some 700,000 passengers to the throughput at LBA in 1987. The objectors predicted that the figure would be about 300,000, while the independent CAA witness took an intermediate position. Not surprisingly, the return on the project is sensitive to which set of forecasts is right, as well as to the precise timing of traffic growth in the immediate future (Hill, 1979).

Revenue per passenger

The forecast of revenue per passenger is as important for the financial return as the forecast of passenger volume. The scale of fees and charges used at Leeds/Bradford was a standard scale established by the Joint Airport Charges Committee (JACC), and used by most local authority airports. This committee had come into being with the express intention of raising the level of real landing charges over the period up to 1981/82 so as to eliminate the financial deficits at some airports. As a result, while all costs were expressed at 1979/80 prices in the treasurer's appraisal, revenues were taken at 1979/80 prices plus 8.2 per cent, to allow for the implementation of this policy.

In terms of the financial appraisal of the project, this is a perfectly proper procedure. The only way to calculate the financial return on the project is to predict the unit revenue, and to apply it to the expected volume of traffic. The only criticism of the procedures followed is that demand may not be completely inelastic to landing charges — though since these are only a proportion of total airline costs, demand for air travel should be fairly inelastic to an all-round increase. The real criticism is of the financial criterion itself. It is unsatisfactory that the worth of an investment should be affected by a change in pricing policy quite unrelated to the investment itself, and we return to this below. In any case, under threat of reference to the Restrictive Trade Practices Court, the cartel pricing arrangements have now ceased, so it remains to be seen whether the forecast real revenue per passenger can be sustained in the face of price competition from other airports.

Operating costs

The prediction of the operating costs of the airport is another controversial matter. The forecast increase in operating expenditure was based on the airport director's prediction that 34 additional staff would be required in 1987/88 compared with the status quo, together with assumptions about property and equipment, local rates and other cost items.

Two independent checks suggest that the increase in operating costs which will be required to accommodate the increased passenger throughput was under-estimated by the airport director and treasurer. Doganis and his associates have calculated labour productivity statistics for all UK airports, including LBA, where the average labour productivity per employee was 4,880 work load units (wlu) in 1976/77 (Doganis et al, 1978). (One work load unit is one passenger or two hundred pounds of freight.) In order to achieve the forecast 1987/88 throughput of 800,000 passengers and 2,000 tons of freight at the forecast employment level, average productivity would have to rise to 6,820 wlu's per employee. This is much higher than any airport in the country, with the exception of Heathrow, Gatwick and Jersey. If LBA were to achieve the creditable level of 6,000 wlu's/employee, this would require an additional 50 staff compared with the present, and not 34.

A second check can be run using the cost model developed in the same work. The relationship between operating costs and passenger volume is of special interest in this context, particularly as Doganis's relationship succeeds in predicting LBA's operating cost level correctly

31

in 1974/75, and gives a good result for 1978/79. Doganis relates the level of operating costs at an airport to the volume of passengers, the proportion of international passengers, and whether or not CAA provides the air traffic control. Applying this relationship to an airport with 820,000 wlu's, 61 per cent international passengers, and providing its own ATC (that is, LBA in 1987/88), we find that compared with 1979/80, operating costs would increase by some £1.1 million, or £2.36 per additional passenger, rather than the £432,000 (£0.91 per additional passenger) predicted by the airport treasurer.

Sensitivity tests

It can readily be shown that the net present value of the project is sensitive to variations in traffic forecasts and operating cost assumptions. Table 2.6 shows what happens to the value of the project when given combinations of events occur, keeping all other assumptions as for tables 2.3 and 2.4. Since 20 years is a rather short period over which to appraise a project of this kind, the year in which the present value of the project reaches zero is also shown for each set of events. Air traffic is assumed to reach a plateau in 1997, and no allowance is made for major maintenance or reconstruction of the runway.

The sensitivity analysis shows that the financial return on the project is robust to the downward revision in air traffic which is now warranted, as long as the rest of the applicants' predictions are valid. If the applicants have been too optimistic about the incremental costs of handling the extra traffic, or too pessimistic about the air traffic volumes without the runway extension, the project begins to look marginal in financial terms.

It is sometimes argued that it is a weakness of investment appraisal that different people can obtain widely different estimates of the returns on the same project. In fact, that is a major strength, because if the returns are shown to be sensitive to variations in certain parameters, the attention of decision makers is focused on these parameters. Ultimately, which forecasts are most credible is a matter for considered judgement. In this case, the inspector decided that, overall, the applicants' evidence on traffic and finance was more convincing than the objectors' and, on the basis of this and other evidence, that the Secretary of State should grant planning permission for the project.

It may also be argued that planning inquiries are not appropriate venues for hearing complex financial evidence, and that the public interest in ensuring that taxpayers' money is properly spent can be satisfied elsewhere (Anderson, 1981). Traditionally, local authorities have needed specific Central Government permission when financing major capital projects by borrowing, and now, under the Local Government, Planning and Land Act 1980, they require specific permission

Table 2.6
Sensitivity analysis

| Event | Traffic forecasts 1987/88 ('000 passengers) | | | | Incremental value per passenger (£) | Incremental cost per passenger (£) | NPV (£m) | |
| | With runway extended | | Without runway extended | | | | | |
	Low	High	Low	High			Low	High
1 Baseline (as in tables 2.3, 2.4)	700	800*	125	125*	4.30	0.91	+10.0 Year 1990	+14.6* 1988
2 With extension traffic forecasts as in table 2.5	554	761	125	125	4.30	0.91	+ 6.0 Year 1992	+14.0 1989
3 With extension and without extension traffic forecasts as in table 2.5	554	761	307	391	4.30	0.91	– 2.0 Year 2004	+ 3.3 1995
4 With extension traffic forecasts as in table 2.5, and higher incremental operating costs	554	761	125	125	4.30	2.36	– 1.6 Year 2008	+ 3.0 1995
5 With extension and without extension traffic forecasts as in table 2.5 and higher incremental operating costs	554	761	307	391	4.30	2.36	– 6.2 not within 40 years	– 3.1 2008

*Central forecast

to spend on capital projects at airports, however the expenditure is to be financed (Longley, 1981). At this stage, then, the Government can ensure that the project offers an adequate return.

The main defect of considering the financial evidence at this stage is the lack of openness of the procedure. Increasingly, projects with significant land-use and environmental consequences do not merely have to be justified, they must be seen to be justified. One of the great virtues of the local planning inquiry is that it does provide a forum for transparent decision making.

The social cost—benefit case

The question which remains is whether the financial rate of return is a suitable test of the worth of this project or whether all the costs and benefits of the project, 'to whomsoever they accrue', should be considered. It is widely recognised that the consequences of airport projects for economic development, road traffic, and the environment must be taken into account. In this chapter, however, we concentrate on air traffic, revenues and operating costs.

There are three sets of interested parties when an airport expands – air passengers, airlines, and the airport owner/operator. Air passengers can be subdivided into those who would have used the airport regardless of the project, those diverted from other airports, and those induced to make journeys by air which they would otherwise have made by surface modes of transport or not at all. Some of the principal benefits and costs of the runway extension at LBA are set out in table 2.7.

Table 2.7
Impact of project on interested parties

1 Passengers	(a) Existing passengers	— higher quality of service (frequency, jets)
	(b) Diverted passengers	— lower access times/costs to airports
		— different airline fares
	(c) Generated passengers	— benefit attached to travel, net of fare and access costs to airport
2 Airlines	(a) Revenue	— additional revenue from diverted and generated passengers
		— revenue losses on other routes
	(b) Costs	— additional station costs
		— additional flying hours to meet demand
		— additional landing charges
3 Airports	(a) The investing airport	— additional revenue from landing charges etc.
		— capital costs of the project
		— additional operating costs
	(b) Other airports	— reduced revenues (diverted traffic)
		— reduced operating costs

34

The table shows how partial a calculation the financial rate of return on the project is. It takes account only of the revenue and cost effects at the investing airport, and ignores the impact on passengers, airlines, and the rest of the airport system. In four respects, the social cost—benefit return on the project is a more satisfactory measure of project worth than the financial rate of return.

Passenger benefits

A cost—benefit analysis would provide a more complete account of the user benefits from the project. It is true that the increased airport revenue is a reflection of the increased benefits to passengers. Airport revenue is generated from passengers who divert from other airports or decide to make new trips precisely because the project creates new, more beneficial opportunities for them. However, given that airports are not perfect price discriminators, the increase in revenue cannot possibly be an exact measure of the increase in passenger benefits, and a direct measure is therefore to be preferred.

A virtue of measuring the benefits to passengers is that it focuses attention on the demand forecasting methods used. Inclusive tour traffic at LBA was predicted by adopting the national growth rates for this traffic, assuming that the Yorkshire and Humberside regional demand would grow at the same rate as the national market, and assuming that LBA would attract 30 per cent of the regional demand in 1987/88. If we could understand, or replicate, the way in which people decide whether to take an inclusive tour, and which airport to fly from, then it would be possible to predict LBA's market share and revenue on a more scientific basis, and at the same time to measure the benefits of the new facility to users diverted from other airports. Indeed the airport traffic allocation model developed for the CAA was an attempt to do just this (DoT, 1976).

Pricing policy

As we have seen, the financial rate of return on a project is sensitive to variations in pricing policy which are quite extraneous to the project itself. A virtue of the cost—benefit measure is that it is much less sensitive, because a real price increase is primarily a transfer between one group of beneficiaries, the users, and another, the airport operator. If demand is totally price inelastic (figure 2.2(i)), then the revenue gain A from raising prices from OP to OP_1 is offset by an equal and opposite

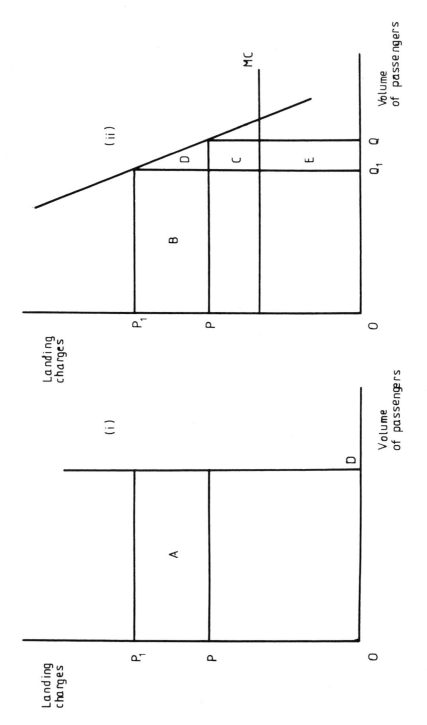

Figure 2.2 Effects of changes in airport pricing

loss of consumers' surplus. If demand is somewhat price responsive (figure 2.2(ii)), then the result is as follows:

Change in revenue	$B-(C+E)$
Change in consumer surplus	$-B-D$
Change in gross benefit	$-(C+D+E)$
Less Change in operating costs	$-E$
Change in net benefits	$-(C+D)$

Either way, the result is very different, and more sensible, than that given by the financial rate of return test.

System effects – revenue

Another virtue of a cost–benefit approach is that it concentrates attention on the impact of improvement at one airport on other airports within the system. Appraisal at the individual airport level carries with it the danger that the same air traffic is counted twice or more in different airports' traffic forecasts, which form the basis for their investment plans. To give an example, some 82,000 inclusive tour passengers from Yorkshire and Humberside used East Midlands airport in 1976, about one-quarter of East Midlands' IT traffic in that year. Presumably some of that traffic would now be captured by LBA. Yet, no mention is made of this prospective loss of traffic in the main air traffic evidence presented at the East Midlands runway extension inquiry (Poole, 1980). Since there appears to be a gentlemen's agreement among airport authorities not to object to one another's development proposals on grounds of abstraction of traffic, it is particularly important to adopt procedures which ensure that individual investment proposals are based on mutually consistent traffic forecasts.

System effects – operating costs

A system-wide appraisal also ensures that airport operating costs are treated correctly. There is a general consensus that airports are subject to economies of scale. To handle air traffic of a given class, a runway of given length, and a terminal building must be provided. Average costs per passenger fall as passenger volume rises, at least up to 'capacity', since these fixed outlays are spread over larger volumes. It is, therefore, important (see figure 2.3) to consider the effects of an expansion at airport A on the other airports in the system (airport B).

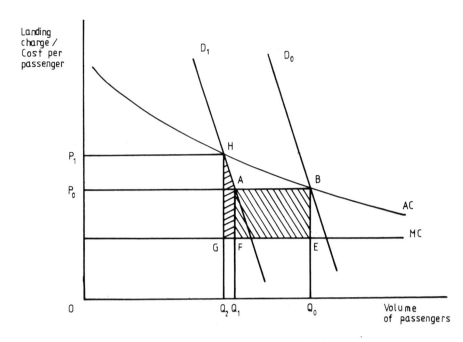

Figure 2.3   Systems effects of a change in demand for an airport

Suppose first that airport B's landing charges are fixed at OP_0. When airport A is improved, demand falls from D_0 to D_1, and the loss of revenue ABQ_0Q_1 is not matched by the reduction in operating costs FEQ_0Q_1. The net revenue loss $ABEF$ is a measure of the reduced efficiency in the rest of the airport system. If airport B is under a Government instruction to break even, then it must increase its landing charges to OP_1, shedding further traffic Q_1Q_2, and creating a further surplus loss $HAFG$. These losses should clearly be taken into consideration in determining whether to invest at airport A.

An objection to this line of reasoning might be that air traffic is growing secularly, and that the traffic abstracted from B will quickly be made good by natural growth. However, even in a growth climate, unless B is at or near capacity, it will be operating at higher average costs than would otherwise have been the case. Others have diagnosed an 'airport disease' — premature competitive expansion of capacity (Walters 1978; Doganis et al, 1978). The appropriate remedy for this disease is to ensure that the consequences for system costs and revenues are taken into account when appraising individual airport projects. When this is done, the social cost—benefit return to the airport system as a whole could easily turn out lower than the financial return on the project to the individual airport.

Conclusions

1   The consultants' studies of the early 1970s, and the CAA's re-working of these suggest that the most efficient and economic airport system for England and Wales would be a small number of large airports. However, the architects of airports policy have shied away from that conclusion, without being very explicit about their reasons.

2   No precise statement exists of the criterion by which regional airport projects are to be evaluated; in the case studied, the test used was the financial rate of return on the project.

3   The financial return on the runway extension at Leeds/Bradford is sensitive to the traffic forecasts with and without the extension, and to the prediction of future operating costs. On some plausible combinations of events, the project is marginal or sub-marginal before considering the environmental effects.

4   The financial return is not a good measure of the project's worth. It fails to reflect passenger benefits adequately, it is unduly influenced by the pricing policy of the airport, and it fails to take account of the impact of the development on operating costs and revenues in the rest of the airport system. A cost—benefit analysis of the project would be a better test.

5   The local planning inquiry provides a good forum within which to present and debate the costs and benefits of airport projects.

References

Airports Policy, HMSO, Cmnd 7084, London, 1978.

Anderson, E. *Investment Appraisal in the UK with Special Reference to Leeds/Bradford,* paper given to the Airports Economics course, Polytechnic of Central London, 1981.

Caves, R.E. 'Airport system planning — a UK study' in *Transportation Planning and Technology,* 1980, vol.6, pp. 117—30.

Civil Aviation Authority, *Airport Development Policy in South Wales and the South West Region of England*, CAP 377, 1975a.

Civil Aviation Authority, *The Development of the UK Airport System*, CAP 372, 1975b.

Civil Aviation Authority, *Airport Development in the Central England Region*, CAP 373, 1975c.

Civil Aviation Authority, *Future Airport Development in the Northern Region*, CAP 374, 1975d.

Civil Aviation Authority, *Future Airport Development in South Wales and the South-West*, CAP 380, 1976.

Commission on the Third London Airport, *Report*, HMSO, London, 1971.

Department of Trade, *Airport Strategy for Great Britain*, vols 1 and 2, HMSO, London, 1976.

Department of Trade, *Report of the Advisory Committee on Airports Policy*, HMSO, London, 1979.

Department of Trade, *Report of the Air Traffic Forecasting Working Party*, HMSO, London, 1981.

Doganis, R., Pearson, R. and Thompson, G.F. *Airport Economics in the Seventies*, Polytechnic of Central London, Transport Studies Group, Research Report No.5, 1978.

Gaffney, J.A. *Proof of Evidence, and Appendix*, Evidence to the Public Inquiry into the Proposed Runway Extension at Leeds/Bradford, 1979.

Hill, S.W. *Proof of Evidence*, Evidence to the Public Inquiry into the Proposed Runway Extension at Leeds/Bradford, 1979.

Longley, D. *The Effects of Central Government Control on Local Authority Airport Financial Practice*, paper given to the Airports Economics course, Polytechnic of Central London, 1981.

Mackie, P.J. *Proof of Evidence*, Evidence to the Public Inquiry into the Proposed Runway Extension at Leeds/Bradford, 1979.

Metra Consulting Group, *Central England Airport Study*, 1974.

Pollard, G.S. *Proof of Evidence*, Evidence to the Public Inquiry into the Proposed Runway Extension at Leeds/Bradford, 1979a.

Pollard, G.S. *Point Arising from Mr Pollard's Evidence*, Evidence to the Public Inquiry into the Proposed Runway Extension at Leeds/Bradford, 1979b.

Poole, M.A. *Proof of Evidence*, Inquiry into Proposed Runway Extension at East Midlands Airport, 1980.

Radmore, V.C. *Inspector's Report*, Public Inquiry into the Proposed Runway Extension at Leeds/Bradford, 1980.

Seller, G.P. *Proof of Evidence, and Appendix*, Evidence to the Public Inquiry into the Proposed Runway Extension at Leeds/Bradford, 1979.

Stratford, A. and Associates, *Northern Region Airport Study*, 1974.
Walters, A.A. 'Airports — an economic survey' in *Journal of Transport Economics and Policy*, 1978, vol.12, pp. 125—60.

3 Transport investment appraisal and land-use policy: the political strategies of planning practice

D. Gillingwater

When it's a notion
When it's still vague
It is praised.
When it looms big
When plans are in motion
Objections are raised.

Berthold Brecht
Poems of Reconstruction 1947–1953

Introduction

There can be little doubt that the relationship between planning for land use and the appraisal of transport investment projects and programmes is fraught with tensions. This state of affairs cannot be attributed to capriciousness on the parts of either land-use or transport planners; rather it can be argued that it reflects the very different traditions and structural constraints which have historically under-pinned and determined the practices of the transport planning and land-use planning fraternities. A critical examination of most published plans and a comparison with the literature generated by practitioners and academics alike yields numerous examples (Boyce, Day and McDonald, 1970; Hart, 1976; Rothenberg, 1974; Moseley, 1979).

At the level of appearances, however, the image which is conveyed is the precise opposite. The portrayal of a broad community of interests, based on a consensus of shared values, is more often than not presented: after all, the argument runs, in the final analysis both operate in the public sphere, both are concerned with attempts to bring about improvements in the organisation of society, and both share a common focus of attention – the planning of territorial space. Furthermore, it is contended, this consensus is found in the actual technical and organisational bases of transport planning and land-use planning. For example, students of transport planning take compulsory courses in land-use planning, and transport planning figures very strongly throughout the formal education of land-use planners; those public agencies with specific transport and land-use planning responsibilities more often than not share and integrate the technical expertise of transport and land-use planners (Cullingworth, 1980); and it is often a legal requirement that land-use policy statements and plans incorporate a specific transport planning dimension (Ministry of Housing and Local Government, 1970), and for transport policies and programmes to contain a land-use planning base (Department of the Environment, 1973).

A considered and more critical evaluation, however, suggests that this consensus is little more than a veil of tolerance (Healey, 1977) masking a deeper structure of mutual suspicion and fundamental differences (Simmie, 1974). These reflect specific dilemmas, paradoxes and contradictions within the technical bases, organisational arenas and political spheres of land-use and transport planning (Arctander, 1972; Van Gunsteren, 1976), as well as their situation within the broader public sphere of an advanced or late form of capitalist social organisation (Offe, 1975).

The purpose of this chapter is to explore the general issues raised by this type of analysis for the practice of land-use and transport planning, by focusing specifically on the function of transport investment appraisal. In order to do this it will be necessary to present an outline of the *modus operandi* of transport planning and land-use planning practices. A comparison of these somewhat generalised accounts or typifications should begin to tease out some of the critical differences which, it could be contended, characterise their problematical relationship. This constitutes the first part of the chapter.

The second part examines the basis of strategies which have attempted to 'close' the gap between the conflicting demands of transport planners and land-use planners noted above. Particular attention is paid to a critical review of the traditional strategy which has been adopted: the conventional land-use and transport planning study (Black, 1981). This is compared with 'alternative' approaches based on principles of land-use structure (Albers, 1974) and 'planning guidelines'

(Self, 1977). All three are found to be seriously wanting in one or more respects.

The final part builds on the argument that orthodox attempts which seek to integrate land-use considerations into conventional transport planning practices are, with respect to investment appraisal at least, of limited relevance and unnecessarily limiting in scope. The chapter concludes with an account of the implications of continuing this 'politics of compromise' approach for investment appraisal, and an alternative predicated in *political* economy is suggested (Taebel, 1978; Habermas, 1971).

Transport planning and land-use planning

Although this chapter is primarily about land-use and transport investment appraisal, it is contended that an examination of this relationship cannot be separated from the broader questions as to who is doing the appraising and on what basis? Historically, such questions have been the prerogative of the transport planning fraternity. The notion that land-use planners should have a determining role is a comparatively recent phenomenon (Hart, 1976; Starkie, 1973). This begs the more general question as to who constitutes these planning fraternities? 'Transport planners' are those who have undergone some formal training in one or more core areas of planning for transport. In very general terms they include those primarily with a civil engineering or applied economics (including statistics and quantitative methods) background. This categorisation would therefore exclude 'transport managers' and 'transport operators'. 'Land-use planners' on the other hand are those who have had some formal training in the general area of environmental planning which has been 'professionally approved', for example by the Royal Town Planning Institute.

This categorisation is by no means exhaustive, but it is important to the general argument for two reasons: because it is contended, firstly, that the traditional *modus operandi* – or instrumental ideology (Habermas, 1979) – of transport planners differs significantly from that of orthodox land-use planners; and secondly, that although ultimately such a distinction is unimportant, it may reinforce and assist in the creation of artificial barriers resistant to critical reflection and self-criticism. There is a vital assumption which runs through the argument of this chapter, albeit largely implicitly, to the effect that the principal dilemma or threat confronting the appraisal of transport investment is not posed by land-use planners casually assuming away rational judgements about economic efficiency on equity or 'planning' grounds (like the siting of major airports), nor of transport economists blocking desirable schemes of social relevance proposed by land-use planners (like 'free' public transport). The normative cutting-edge of the argument is based on the need to improve the present practices of planning-in-general, of which specific planning formations, e.g. transport and land-use, are just a part. In many respects this means the realignment and reconstruction of the very foundations of such specific planning formations, if not the entire reconstruction of planning itself. Following Habermas (1979, p.95), this reconstruction signifies the taking apart of the specific practices of, for example, land-use and transport planning, and putting the whole back together again in a revamped form 'in order to attain more fully the goal it has set for itself'.

If the specific practices of transport planning and land-use planning (and, may it be said, other forms too) are examined in quite general terms, it is possible to discern a number of common, visible attributes. For example, both are concerned with attempts to anticipate the future. Whether this involves a veneer of technical sophistication in attempting, for example, to predict levels of car ownership at time $t + n$, or simply the application of rule-of-thumb methods in, for example, estimating the 'knock-on' effects of industrial closure, there is a shared concern for anticipating the future. Parallel to this activity are attempts by both transport and land-use planners, as Benton MacKaye (1928) has put it, to wage a determined visualisation of the future; that is, not only to anticipate what the future might hold, but what it could hold if we so wished it. Examples are legion, but attempts to work out a 'desirable' modal split between public and private transport is one, together with the concern of land-use planners to, for example, adopt conservation measures for the protection of historic town centres. However, both sets of planners are not only concerned with speculation, determined or otherwise, since both have a normative cutting edge in seeking ways of bringing about that more 'desirable' state of affairs. Hart (1976) refers to this activity as the process of attempting to 'order change', such that the original intentions of planners at time $t + 0$, for time $t + n$, are translated into actual impact at time $t + n$. For example, transport planners attempt to design comprehensive road networks and attach specific time horizons to their desired implementation, but they also endeavour to get them into the road building programme. Land-use planners, especially those engaged in the 'total' planning of large, new communities like new towns constantly strive to ensure that development occurs in step with their master plan phasing programme.

These three practices — of anticipation, visualisation and ordering change — correspond to the future oriented, progressive dimension which is associated with both types of planning activity. They are therefore integral parts and instances of the instrumental ideologies which support both transport planning and land-use planning, albeit at the level of appearances.

However, there is another side to this particular equation. Planners not only concern themselves with the future, but they are also heavily constrained by the past and the present. Situations arise where they must respond to current crises. For example, land-use planners have become increasingly concerned with the problems presently facing inner cities; and transport planners have specific legal responsibilities with regard to the present crisis facing the provision of public transport services in rural areas. However, not only is 'firefighting' a characteristic of both modes of planning, but operating under severe constraint is another. A particularly topical example is the constraint imposed on public expenditure through the operation of 'cash limits' on inner city programmes and transport supplementary grants to local authorities, irrespective of the merits of the individual cases (Carvel, 1981). This means that the aspirations of both land-use and transport planners can never be geared towards the creation of schemes which are substantially unconstrained, either in terms of their demands upon scarce resources, for example, free public transport, or which correspond to a form of utopian idealism, for example, creating a 'perfect' urban structure. Both planners share a concern for attempting to understand the present structure of the world as they find it and how it is changing. Hart (1976) has aptly termed it the comprehension of how order itself is changing — economic, political, spatial and temporal.

These three additional practices — of responding, being constrained and comprehending changing orders — correspond to the present-oriented, conservative dimension which is so typical of both land-use and transport planning. They are in turn integral parts and instances of the instrumental ideologies which support both modes of planning practice.

Although this account has been essentially descriptive, it begins to point to some interesting issues and dilemmas facing the present practices of land-use and transport planning. Indeed it is possible to argue that there are internal paradoxes, if not contradictions, which can be identified in this account. On the one hand it has been argued that both transport and land-use planning share in the future-oriented and progressive practices of anticipating change, of visualising the future, and of attempts to order future change. On the other hand both are engaged in the present-oriented and conservative practices of responding to current crises, where actions are hemmed in on all sides by constraints, and pondering about the ways in which the world is changing. Whether or not it is possible to reconcile these apparent differences in emphasis will not be explored at this stage (Gillingwater, 1978). However, two points are worth consideration: firstly, although

46

this account has been largely descriptive and ahistorical, it is possible to periodise the actual practices of contemporary British land-use and transport planning. In very general terms it is possible to argue that, for the three decades until the early 1970s, the dominant mode was characterised by future-oriented and progressive planning practices. From the mid-1970s, this changed quite dramatically, and the prevailing emphasis is dominated by a present-oriented and conservative mode of planning. Secondly, this change has been wrought within both land-use and transport planning, suggesting perhaps that there are other deeper, more structural, reasons for the tensions between them. It is this aspect which will occupy much of the last part of the chapter.

Having derived a broad description of similarities between the respective instrumental ideologies of land-use and transport planning, it is important to the overall argument that their significant differences are also explored. There are a number of ways in which this can be examined, and at four different levels. The first is the 'technical' level or dimension. This consists of those practices, usually clearly visible, which typify the expertise and skills associated with transport and land-use planners. Of particular interest here are the control devices which planners attempt to deploy, together with the form which this intervention takes and the notion of space which dominates their strategic approach. The second is the 'administrative' dimension. The technical expertise and skills noted above cannot be divorced from the broader and less visible administrative context of which they form a constituent part. These administrative practices form both the platform and the delivery system by which transport and land-use planners contrive to seek legitimacy for their technical interests. Of interest here are the orientation of the administrative strategies which are engineered, the administrative objectives which are pursued, and the organisational output which typifies these strategies and objectives.

The third general level or dimension is the 'political'. Both, indeed all, forms of public planning share the simple *raison d'être* of intervention in society's affairs. Both are therefore concerned with the less visible processes which typify the exercise of political power and influence (Lukes, 1974), if only in the narrower technical sense of arbitration and negotiation, or of mobilising bias (Bachrach and Baratz, 1962). Transport planners and land-use planners pursue particular policy objectives within a given image of the sorts of problem which typify their respective technical interests, thus ensuring their technical–political involvement. Since both modes of planner engage in attempts to make policy, it is not surprising that both share a political commitment which seeks to implement policy and to ensure its eventual impact. This political sphere incorporates both the aforementioned administrative arenas and technical domains or, put the other way round, the technical domains and administrative arenas are situated within this broader and deeper political sphere.

The fourth dimension is 'ideological' and concerns those instrumental assumptions which provide the very foundations for the practices of the institutions of transport and land-use planning. These, it has been contended, are rarely if ever visible or opened up for critical scrutiny (Healey, 1977; Simmie, 1974). This dimension, arguably the most significant of the four, relates to the critical assumptions which underpin the technical interests of planning; in particular those assumptions concerning the evaluation of the impacts and efficacy of schemes and programmes (both proposed and effected), within the context provided by the prevailing institutional orthodoxy. This ideological dimension provides the *modus operandi* as well as the institutional basis for the production and reproduction of transport planning and land-use planning. It determines, and is determined by, those practices which typify the political spheres, the administrative arenas, and the technical domains of transport planners and land-use planners. Nothing more and nothing less.

The transport planning mode

The dominant characteristics which have moulded the shape and hence practices of contemporary transport planning reflect a shared concern for the need to develop financial or budgetary instruments and programmes to control and influence the patterns of movement across territorial space. In Britain the evolution of the transport policies and programmes package (TPP) illustrates this development most dramatically. The relationship between strategic policies for transport, infrastructure proposals within a framework of a rolling programme of capital and revenue spending, and proposals relating to public transport provision and funding, are all brought together within the one umbrella of an annual review statement at a local authority level. These are submitted to the Department of Transport/Department of the Environment for approval as bids for central funding in the form of Transport Supplementary Grants. According to Circular 104/73, the emphasis of the TPP process is 'more on resource allocation, "value for money", and operational measures' (Department of the Environment, 1973). The technical emphasis throughout this process tends to be dominated by the administrative requirements associated with the management of central government—local authority relations; administrative space assumes a dominance over territorial space.

There can be little doubt that this orientation, typified by the TPP process, is rooted in an administrative strategy concerned with the management of existing policies and programmes for transport (Hall,

1980). This is reflected in the general administrative priority which can be discerned: the strengthening of existing policy, and the stress on efficiency criteria to be applied in the allocation of, for example, block grant. It would appear that, in terms of organisational output at least, the principal thrust of contemporary transport planning is to be found in the generation of specific projects and schemes, which are increasingly dominated by small-scale infrastructure improvements and public transport financing schemes (cf. Nottinghamshire County Council, 1979).

In policy terms, it is becoming increasingly clear that the problems concerning contemporary transport planners remain largely specific and sectoral. For example, the traditional concern for a myriad of specific highway improvements, and a multiplicity of limited infrastructure projects relating to traffic management, still represent the core activities of professional practice and account for the lion's share of capital programmes. The increasing concern for the public transport sector remains largely unintegrated, except in the administrative setting of financial programmes (White, 1976). The overwhelming impression which is created from even a cursory perusal of, for example, TPPs and Public Transport Plans is a dominant concern for the present and immediate future; a political strategy which it would seem is dominated by the need to generate immediate or short-run payoffs, and which is highly fragmented and largely ameliorative in nature; and finally where the policy objective is to intervene directly, either by building new or upgrading roads, or by subsidising public transport operations with cash subsidies.

This strategic concern for the strengthening of existing policy for transport through a complex system of administrative planning — where the emphasis is on financial instruments, budgetary programmes and efficiency considerations — reflects, it is contended, the deeper interests and motivation of orthodox transport planners. Three aspects of this strategic concern in particular merit attention. First, there can be little doubt that the principal technical interest of contemporary transport planners is to be found in the generation and evaluation of specific projects, i.e. in terms of engineering a design and appraising its efficiency. This reflects, not unsurprisingly, the dominant professional orthodoxy of the two main strands which characterise the practitioners of transport planning — civil engineers and applied economists. Secondly, it reflects a deeper structural emphasis, or ideological stress, on matters of concern to transport planners which are very specific and selectivist; where the dominant concern is with the details, the minutiae and the particulars of a given problem, such as stemming the decline in public transport patronage by experimenting with changes in the levels of cash subsidy to public transport operators (Trench, 1975;

Hillman, Henderson and Whalley, 1976). Finally, it reflects a very technical–administrative–rational approach to the resolution of often highly-charged political problems (Van Gunsteren, 1976). A corollary of this is that the evaluation in political terms, in the broader political sphere, of the impact of the kinds of projects and programmes which are the traditional fayre of transport planners is problematical, because much of the impact is opaque and hidden, and very difficult to identify let alone specify (Commission on the Third London Airport, 1971). Strategies to counter the problems which this opaqueness creates have become apparent in at least two quite different respects: firstly, transport planners have developed special skills in project evaluation (notably variations on the theme of cost-effectiveness or cost–benefit analysis) (Pearce and Nash, 1981). Secondly, much of what is undertaken by transport planners is in turn hidden from direct public scrutiny. For example, much of the transport planning process, typified by the whole of the TPP process, is essentially a technical exercise initiated and evaluated by technical experts in the privatised sphere of a very complex system of administrative planning. For example, TPPs are not statutory documents, they are not the subject of any form of statutory approval, and there is no formal requirement for a sustained and reasoned review in the public sphere.

It is possible to codify the general characteristics of transport planning, based on this summary account and related examples. Broadly these characteristics are concerned with the four related dimensions outlined earlier: the technical, the administrative, the political, and the ideological. These are illustrated in table 3.1.

Table 3.1
The transport planning mode

Explanatory level	Transport planning characteristics
1 Technical dimension	
Control devices	Financial instruments
Intervention format	Budgetary programmes
Spatial bias	Administrative planning
2 Administrative dimension	
Administrative strategy	Strengthen existing policy
Administrative priority	Efficiency criteria
Organisational output	Specific project packages
3 Political dimension	
Problem image	Sectoral
Policy objective	Direct price effects
Policy impact	Short-run payoffs
4 Ideological dimension	
Technical interest	Project evaluation
Ideological stress	Selectivist
Impact evaluation	Opaque
Example	Transport policies and programmes

The dominant characteristics which have moulded the shape and hence practices of contemporary land-use planning have been usefully explored by Regan (1978). Building on his analysis, it is possible to argue that the traditional approach to land-use planning in Britain is based on the development of technical skills and expertise to influence, if not control, land use by the production of general planning schemes. The principal device which underpins these schemes is a statutory development plan, in the form of a suggested locational pattern for the future provision of social overhead capital. Examples include the planning of wholly new communities, such as the free-standing British new towns like Harlow, as well as the major expansion of existing towns and cities, like Peterborough and Milton Keynes. The focus for such attention has been unequivocal: to plan for the use and development of territorial space, primarily land.

In Britain the vehicles designed for delivering these general planning schemes have been either regional strategies (cf. South East Joint Planning Team, 1970) or structure plan written statements and key diagrams (cf. Hertfordshire County Council, 1980), or local plans (cf. Newark District Council, 1976), or combinations of such plans. The technical emphasis throughout all of these schemes is broadly similar: as Circular 4/79 has stated, 'a broad and open consideration of planning problems taking account of physical, economic and social aspects [and indicating] the relationship between . . . policy and general proposals for the development and other use of land on the one hand and social needs, problems and opportunities on the other' (Department of the Environment, 1979).

The almost universal response by land-use planners to these kinds of issue has been to devise a strategy whereby the making of substantially new policy is seen as the principal administrative requirement. Indeed this view is one which has been fostered and developed, albeit implicitly, by the Department of the Environment. For example, in Circular 4/79, those local authorities responsible for the production of structure plans were effectively instructed to focus attention on three key issues: the location of housing, the location of centres for employment, and transport requirements. Furthermore, they were instructed to stress the relationships between these three policy areas (Department of the Environment, 1979). For most local authorities, these were issues which had not previously been explored, and the emphasis on policy relationships was interpreted as a requirement to assume responsibility for the co-ordination of existing policy areas, like housing, employment and transport (Jowell and Noble, 1981; Steeley, 1978).

It is also perhaps unsurprising, given the overall tenor of Circular

4/79, to detect an overarching concern for considerations of equity in these general planning schemes. The administrative priority reflects this concern, stressing notions like 'local needs', 'community interests', 'social impact' and other similar less than tangible policies. In terms of organisational output, the principal product of this land-use planning activity has almost universally taken the form of future-oriented strategic policy statements. For example, in the structure plans produced by local authorities, considerable weight in the written statement is given to an account of the overall strategy (usually a key diagram structuring future land use), and a statement of proposed policies together with their 'reasoned justification'.

There can be little doubt that this orientation, typified in this case by the process of producing local authority structure plans, is rooted in a political strategy which is attempting to assist in the long-term restructuring of territorial space according to some notion of an 'ideal urban form' (Mingione, 1981; Kirk, 1980; Albers, 1974; Self, 1977). For example, most structure plan policies and key diagrams, although in principle subject to review every five years, are supposed to have a life of at least fifteen years. In policy terms, the brief which land-use planners have tended to adopt has been very widely drawn indeed, again reflecting advice from the 'centre'. It is clear that the problems which they have concerned themselves with have global manifestations, that 'physical planning policies should be based upon a clear understanding of the social structure of the area, the ways of life of significant social groups and the needs which arise from them' (Department of the Environment, 1973). Given this social orientation, it is perhaps not surprising to find that a significant part of the land-use planners' political strategy is, to all intents and purposes, the pursuit of policies designed to achieve in the long-run an indirect and redistributive effect on the level of real income in an area.

This strategic concern for the creation of substantially new policy areas for land use, through a system of territorial planning — where the emphasis is on the location and distribution of social overhead capital, in the form of general planning schemes dominated by equity considerations — reflects, it is contended, the deeper interests and motivation of orthodox land-use planners. Three aspects of this strategic concern merit further attention. First, there can be little doubt that the prevailing technical interest of land-use planners is in their attempts to propose and evaluate, in quite general and purposefully loose terms, very broad, global policy options. These relate to the future structuring of land uses, which reflect the key issues of housing, employment and transport. Secondly, it reflects a deeper structural emphasis, or ideological stress, on matters of concern to land-use planners which are universalist in origin and aspiring to a rational

52

comprehensiveness (Gillingwater, 1975). The dominant concern is with the development of a tangible strategic thrust, which by definition walks the tightrope between being regarded as too general and abstruse, and therefore impracticable, and being too specific and inelastic, and therefore too inflexible (Langley, 1979).

Finally, it reflects an essentially technical—administrative—rational approach to the resolution of often heavily-politicised problems (Van Gunsteren, 1976). The technical domain and administrative arena of land-use planners is identified as the legitimate origin of and destination for land-use planning practice (Friend and Jessop, 1969), with often unfortunate consequences. For example, the whole structure and orientation of structure plan written statements reflects and reinforces the technical interests of land-use planners, in the sense that it becomes very problematical indeed to evaluate, in political terms in the broader political sphere, the impact of these kinds of broad, strategic policies. This is not because they are hidden or opaque; rather the reverse. The policies and proposals emanating from land-use planners are clearly visible and transparent. After all they are published, and more often than not in the form of statutory documents. Nevertheless a problem of major proportion remains. What do the policies and proposals really mean, in terms of the ability of land-use planners to control the future pattern of land use? This problem is compounded in no small way because the general planning schemes are open to public scrutiny, at quasi-judical proceedings such as inquiries in public. But it would appear that the general form which most schemes take militates

Table 3.2
The land use planning mode

Explanatory level	Land-use planning characteristics
1 Technical dimension	
Control devices	Overhead capital planning
Intervention format	General planning schemes
Spatial bias	Territorial planning
2 Administrative dimension	
Administrative strategy	Create new policy
Administrative priority	Equity considerations
Organisational output	Strategic policy statements
3 Political dimension	
Problem image	Global
Policy objective	Indirect income effects
Policy impact	Long-term restructuring
4 Ideological dimension	
Technical interest	Policy evaluation
Ideological stress	Universalist
Impact evaluation	Transparent
Example	Structure plan written statements

against the ability to offer a sustained and reasoned review in the public sphere (Darke, 1980; Kemp, 1980; Habermas, 1974). For example, structure plans may be statutory documents carrying the force of law, they may be subject to statutory approval, and they may have been scrutinised in public, but it does not guarantee that they are necessarily the most appropriate vehicles for the delivery of strategic policies for the structuring of future land uses.

These general characteristics of orthodox land-use planning and related examples can be codified with respect to the four dimensions outlined previously: the technical, the administrative, the political, and the ideological (see table 3.2).

The modes compared

The previous two sections have attempted to map out in broad outline the principal characteristics of orthodox approaches to contemporary transport and land-use planning practice. They are clearly generalisations which are of a provisional nature; they are not the result of exhaustive empirical case studies. Nevertheless they represent a limited attempt to construct typifications of the present practices, or instrumental ideologies, of transport planning and land-use planning, in order to facilitate comparisons between their respective technical, administrative, political and ideological dimensions.

With regard to the first of these dimensions, it is clear that the dominant interests in the two technical domains differ significantly. For transport planners the concern with financial instruments and budgetary programmes is paramount; administrative planning reigns supreme. For land-use planners the priority lies with the territorial planning of social overhead capital; the production of general planning schemes is paramount. There would appear to be little in common between these technical domains.

A review of the dominant characteristics of the two administrative arenas indicates similar significant differences. For transport planners the dominant concern is with the strengthening of existing policy, principally by generating and evaluating specific projects, on the basis of efficiency criteria within a given policy framework. For land-use planners the priority lies with the creation of substantively new policy areas, primarily by moulding together strategic policies which have been based on equity considerations.

In their respective political spheres, the differences between the two modes are equally significant. For transport planners the dominant interest would appear to be in devising specific strategies for tackling given problems by direct intervention, the objective being to generate price effects which yield immediate or short-run payoffs. For land-use planners, the reverse would seem to be the case. Here primary concern is with the identification of more global problems, together with the devising of strategic policies to assist in the restructuring of an area; the objective being to generate income effects in the longer term by indirect intervention.

Finally, it would appear that there are also differences of some significance in their respective ideological practices. For example, the technical interest of transport planners is dominated by a concern for the use of efficiency criteria in project evaluation; for land-use planners the concern is with a broader notion of equity considerations in policy evaluation. The ideological stress underpinning transport planning is therefore inherently selectivist in orientation, whereas for land-use planning a more universalist approach reigns supreme. But, more importantly, both seek an ideological base from which to gain legitimation for their respective practices. For land-use planners this has presented a problem of similar proportion to that facing transport planners. Whereas for the latter the problem of the source for legitimation is tied up with the broader problem of a political strategy whose effects are essentially hidden and difficult to specify, for land-use planners the problem is the reverse: the political strategy is clear, in the sense that it is well documented, but its comprehension by the public is shrouded in mystery. This amounts to arguably the only problem which is shared between the two modes of planning, and is one which strikes at the very heart of their respective institutions: the fundamental inability to seek a total legitimacy for their practices, and hence a basic incapacity to produce and reproduce their practices without let or hindrance (Lukes, 1974).

To further facilitate this generalised comparison, table 3.3 illustrates the characteristics of transport planning and land-use planning on the basis of the twelve explanatory levels employed previously.

One further point is worth emphasising at this stage. The two typifications presented here are not intended to be faithful descriptions or critical analyses of how transport and land-use planners actually operate (an empirically-informed approach). These typifications are attempts to construct the instrumental ideologies which dominate orthodox transport and land-use planning practices; they are attempts to outline the sources and structures of their technical legitimacy, based on the kind of arguments which transport and land-use planners employ when they seek to justify their respective practices. In themselves these typifications do not constitute the actual practices of transport or land-use planning.

Table 3.3
The modes compared

Transport planning characteristics	Explanatory level	Land-use planning characteristics
	1 Technical dimension	
Financial instruments	Control devices	Overhead capital planning
Budgetary programmes	Intervention format	General planning schemes
Administrative planning	Spatial bias	Territorial planning
	2 Administrative dimension	
Strengthen existing policy	Administrative strategy	Create new policy
Efficiency criteria	Administrative priority	Equity considerations
Specific project packages	Organisational output	Strategic policy statements
	3 Political dimension	
Sectoral	Problem image	Global
Direct price effects	Policy objective	Indirect income effects
Short-run payoffs	Policy impact	Long-term restructuring
	4 Ideological dimension	
Project evaluation	Technical interest	Policy evaluation
Selectivist	Ideological stress	Universalist
Opaque	Impact evaluation	Transparent
Transport policies and programmes	Example	Structure plan written statements

The politics of transport and land-use planning

This approach glosses over, or rather assumes as given, any notion of history, i.e. the material conditions which have shaped the social and cultural production and reproduction of the instrumental ideologies of transport and land-use planners. The account thus far has focused attention mainly on the institutions and formations of planning, together with their organisational characteristics. What is also required is an account of their social relations and capacities for responsive change, or as Raymond Williams (1981, p.29) has put it:

> those dynamic actual states and works within which there are not only continuities and persistent determinations but also tensions, conflicts, resolutions and irresolutions, innovations and actual changes.

According to Williams, any attempt to address these kinds of issue requires an examination of (a) the relationships between, for example, transport and land-use planning as social activities, and (b) the material conditions which give rise and signify meaning to their practices, and which ensure their continuity. This requires a critical examination of at least four situations within which such 'tensions, conflicts, resolutions and irresolutions, innovations and actual changes' can be socially, and therefore historically, related: (i) the rise of new social and political alignments in the practices of transport and land-use planning, which bring in new kinds of knowledge-producer and interest; (ii) the redefinition, by an existing social and political alignment in the practices of transport and land-use planning, of its conditions and relations, or of the general order within which these exist and are changing, so that new kinds of practices are necessary; (iii) the changes in the means of social and cultural production in the practices of transport and land-use planning, which provide new formal possibilities (which may or may not be initially linked with (i) and (ii)); and finally (iv) the recognition, by specifically social and cultural movements in transport and land-use planning, of the rise of new alignments and/or the redefinition of existing alignments, 'at a level preceding or not directly joined to their articulate social organisation'.

Williams' argument provides a form of analysis which may be brought to bear in an evaluation of the production and reproduction of transport and land-use planning as essentially social practices, rooted in a deeper material structure of political economy (Garnham, 1977). It is perhaps of interest to note that, to date, no such work specifically on transport and land-use planning has been undertaken; further, that in this chapter little can be done other than to note it as a major deficiency.

However, it is possible to make a comparison between attempts by other authors to periodise the contemporary history of transport and land-use planning. Button (1977), for example, identifies four phases characterised by the particular priorities and political judgements of the government in power, and by the methods of control and regulation governments have adopted. For Button the crucial signifying determinant is 'external': the way in which the political authority of the formal State has changed. This leads him to suggest an initial period from about 1918 to the late 1950s, what he calls 'the age of the highway engineer'; another from the late 1950s to the middle 1960s, what he refers to as 'the era of the Buchanan doctrine'; a third from the middle 1960s to the early 1970s, quite specifically referred to as 'the 1968 Transport Act'; and finally, the period from the early 1970s onward, what he calls 'the reforms of the 1970s'.

Healey (1977, pp. 203—6), on the other hand, argues from a very different perspective: the role which sociologists have played in transport planning practice — a perspective which focuses on organisational and professional constraints. For Healey the signifying determinants are essentially 'internal' to transport planning, and based on four stages characterised by 'paradigm tension', which he contends are located in the postwar period. The first he calls the 'description stage', where the market-oriented consensus model of the road planner was the lynchpin of professional acitivity. In this phase the planner was typically the engineer, aided latterly by the economist. The second stage he calls the 'prescriptive stage', where the whole planning system was geared towards the production of a long-term rational plan for the optimum transport system. Although he is not explicit about when this phase dominated, it would appear that he is referring to a period from about the early 1950s to the middle 1960s. During both of these phases, he suggests, the planning establishment was dominated by a hierarchist ideology rooted in a 'one-way causal paradigm'; this stressed the importance of consensus-seeking strategies and the undesirability of diversity and conflict.

The third stage was the 'phase of rejection', characterised by the development of popular opposition to the basic principles of prescriptive transport planning; this was not simply a dispute over technical issues, but was a profound rejection of the political and social assumptions which underpinned the functional rationality of the planning process. Significant professional responses to this crisis, which he periodises from the middle 1960s to the early 1970s, were the concerted attempts to adopt a systems approach to planning, and the introduction of applied social scientists — primarily sociologists — into transport planning practices. The emphasis of concern during this period shifted to a broader examination of the social impact and distributive effects of transport policies and schemes, together with an attempt to incorporate this popular opposition by the formal institution of 'public participation'. According to Healey, this was an accommodation strategy: these changes were introduced by transport planners to allow them to continue without altering fundamentally their political strategy and planning practices.

The fourth and final stage is what he calls the 'phase of restudy' — a period characterised by a search for new directions and radical departures from orthodox practices, where the major issues facing transport planners were perceived by them as being political. This phase he periodises as beginning in the middle 1970s and, he suggests, is typified by the work in the book of which his chapter formed one part — David Hensher's edited volume on *Urban Transport Economics*, published in 1977.

Whereas Button emphasised the history of transport policy and Healey transport planning, Hart (1976) attempts a more sophisticated periodisation based on the interrelation of transport policy, transport planning and land-use planning. His seminal study of strategic planning in London proposes an evaluation of the competing instrumental ideologies, or what he calls 'policy modes', which have dominated strategic planning practices. The first of these is the 'cohesive policy mode', which he contends was the dominant signifying determinant of the period from the 1930s to the late 1950s. Here the emphasis was on the formulation of grand, consensus-based strategies which were complete in themselves; these consisted of bringing applied imagination together with an organic concept of spatial organisation, and which culminated in comprehensive design packages for whole cities. He cites Abercrombie's *Greater London Plan* of 1944, together with the 1947 Act *Development Plans*, as examples of this period.

Hart's second period, from about the late 1950s to the very late 1960s, he calls the era of the 'factored policy mode'. Here the emphasis was placed on the steady refinement of concepts, techniques and their application, in attempts to increase the efficiency of spatial organisation in operational terms. This factored approach stressed a fundamental concern for the way in which spatial organisation works, and how its 'performance' could be improved in structural terms. The solutions put forward as a result of this type of planning activity, and in response to presently-perceived and anticipated problems of the day, were extruded continuously. These extrusions became increasingly specific and detailed as they progressed from the planning authority to the various implementing agencies involved. He cites the primary road network, as set out in the *Greater London Development Plan* of 1969, as a concise example of this era.

The third period runs from the very late 1960s to the present. This, what Hart refers to as the era of the 'diffused policy mode', has been characterised by an intense politicisation of planning: where there is some degree of conflict among various organised groups, and where the planning authority itself acts as a leading contestant. Attention is focused on those planning proposals which are particularly contentious, and which cannot be contained within the bounds of traditional party political methods of dealing with disputes. As Hart puts it, the struggle may assume an adversarial character in political terms, and administrative co-ordination becomes as a result more piecemeal and fragmented. He cites the Greater London Development Plan Inquiry, which lasted from 1970 until 1972, as an example.

These three accounts, by Button, Healey and Hart, represent considered attempts to grapple with the ways in which the contemporary practices of transport and land-use planning have changed. Neither Button's nor Healey's contributions are totally convincing, because of their fairly narrow assumptions about what constitutes the signifying determinants of planning practices; for Button these were about political authority, whereas for Healey, professional and organisational constraints were paramount. Hart's account, on the other hand, represents a fundamental attempt to interrelate the technical, administrative and political dimensions of transport and land-use planning, where their instrumental ideologies are seen as important signifying determinants. But it is also clear that Hart's account is not complete. Reference back to Raymond Williams' argument, about the need to situate the kind of social activities specified by Hart in the material conditions which gave rise to and signified meaning to the practices of transport and land-use planners in London, suggests that such instrumental ideologies need to be situated in the material conditions of a political economy *per se*. This Hart's account fails to do. But whatever the limitations, it represents an important first step towards a political economy of transport and land-use planning.

In many respects the periodisations of Healey and Hart are complementary; for example, both stress the rise and apparent demise of what Van Gunsteren (1976) has called the rational-central-rule approach to transport and land-use planning. There are also similarities in their actual time periods; for example, Healey's 'phase of rejection' appears to parallel Hart's era of the 'diffused policy mode', as indeed does Healey's later 'phase of restudy'.

However, what is perhaps their most important correlation concerns the similar ways in which they describe earlier attempts to confront the 'internal' crisis of the relationship between transport planning and land-use planning. As both Healey and Hart point out, during the late 1950s and early 1960s, transport and land-use planners derived a common and shared approach to their respective tasks, by bringing land-use matters into transport plans and transport matters into land-use plans. With a recognition that transport and related problems were increasing in scale, complexity and magnitude faster than the ability to resolve them, and coupled with a belated awareness that the organisation of transport influenced land-use patterns and vice versa, it was hardly surprising to find that both transport and land-use planners were searching for a common approach, if not panacea, which could be taken on board by both fraternities. This technical consensus arose in the shape of the land-use transport study. At a stroke, as Duhs and Beggs (1977, p.228) have put it, 'the preparation of metropolitan transportation plans became something of a boom industry during the 1960s, with many large cities commissioning comprehensive transportation plans charged with the responsibility for devising appropriate transport arrangements for some twenty to thirty years into the future'. It would seem that the transport and land-use planning dilemma had been resolved once and for all.

History, however, belies this attempt at resolution. As both Healey and Hart have more than adequately confirmed, the seeds of its own destruction were sown within the operationalisation of the instrumental ideologies of both transport and land-use planning. For all the apparent differences in their technical domains, administrative arenas, and political spheres, there was a profound and 'deep' structural complementarity in their ideological practices; as noted earlier, the only correspondence of significance would seem to be in their fundamental inability to seek a total legitimacy for their practices. In the era of Healey's 'prescriptive phase' and Hart's 'factored policy mode', both transport and land-use planners thought they had achieved precisely this — an 'end of ideology'. This was predicated on the view that in the final analysis both land-use and transport planners were working towards a similar end: the transformation of western society into a post-industrial society based upon a global consensus and its corollary, an 'end of ideology'. There was almost universal subscription to this view, and it was argued that both land-use and transport planners were to play their part (Meyerson and Banfield, 1955). It was assumed that a combined approach would contribute to this overall consensus-seeking activity, in that a comprehensive long-term plan for a transport system and land-use pattern could be designed on a rational basis, and would produce an overall net benefit which could be justified in terms of the 'public interest' or 'general social welfare'. When combined with the immanent rise of the quantitative imperative, the lure proved to be totally irresistible (Altshuler, 1965; Lee, 1973).

At the very heart of this technocratic solution was a rational—comprehensive model of decision-making processes, systematised by Herbert Simon (1947) in one of the most influential publications of the

61

1950s, *Administrative Behavior*. Stated baldly, this model consists of working through a specified number of sequences: firstly, the problem to be tackled is specified; secondly, the objectives to be achieved are determined; thirdly, all possible combinations, or alternatives, which would solve the problem and achieve the objectives are established; fourthly, these alternatives are evaluated and prioritised; fifthly, the alternative which is 'best' is selected; and finally, this preferred alternative is implemented (March and Simon, 1958). It is no exaggeration to claim that without exception every land-use transport study published in the 1960s adopted this rational decision model as an organising principle; indeed, many academic texts have elevated this method, which after all is only a procedural model, to a status which makes it almost substantive theory (Button, 1977; Duhs and Begg, 1977).

It remains a very dubious foundation indeed, and has been the subject of and subject to some withering criticism (Gillingwater, 1975; Van Gunsteren, 1976; Hart, 1976). For example, as Healey (1977, p.205) has described it:

> Planning organisations are hierarchical and inegalitarian, with a decision-process which is élite oriented, and planning procedures based upon the concept of the expert. The community is viewed as ignorant, incapable, lacking expertise, and limited in scope, and therefore to be kept uninformed, or only sufficiently informed to ensure agreement.

Far from 'ideology ending', it is now becoming clear that this attempted synthesis was itself a concerted attempt to produce and reproduce a dominant ideology of instrumentalism which reflected a 'deeper' set of conservative tendencies — the search for a continued legitimacy. However, the problem did not disappear, neither was it appropriated; rather it was transformed into a further technical argument. The 'failure' of these first generation plans, it was argued, could be attributed to a combination of circumstances: lack of technical expertise, too few resources, insufficient time, lack of data, poor quality of information, insufficiently-specified models, information out of date, etc. Failure was attributed to technical procedures rather than to ideological structures, thus enabling those very planning practices and their implicit assumptions to go unchallenged and remain intact. The solution was therefore crystal clear: improve the procedures and the task of consensus-building strategies can be resumed.

This, it could be contended, corresponds to the emergence of Healey's 'phase of rejection' and Hart's era of the 'diffused policy mode'. As a result of this apparently critical reassessment, the relationships between transport and land-use planning were restructured. In terms of Williams' argument, this resulted in the rise of a new social and political alignment and a change in the means of social and cultural production. For the first time, the alignment was broadened with the formal introduction of other specialists, such as sociologists and applied social scientists, into the land-use transport planning task. As Healey notes, this additional dimension was intended to assist in the incorporation of social impact studies into the technical domains of the transport and land-use planners. This 'internal' function was also to be complemented by an attempt to incorporate and institutionalise the kind of popular opposition to, for example, the construction of urban motorways, which was beginning to pose a major threat to the very institutions of transport planning and land-use planning. Sociologists were supposed to bring their social science skills to bear on formalising the problem of how to 'allow' the public to engage in the preparation of land-use transport planning policies and proposals.

The change in the means of social and cultural production reflects this realignment. Not only were sociologists supposed to provide the means by which 'public participation' could be incorporated, but they were also to introduce a new technical dimension into the evaluation of alternative strategies: as 'identifiers' of the so-called 'intangible' costs and benefits and distributional issues arising from such an evaluation exercise, by undertaking social impact analyses. As Healey (1977, p.207) puts it, 'an attempt to introduce social welfare considerations into physical planning decisions'.

The second change in the means of production was a shift away from a dominant concern for the making of rational—comprehensively constituted decisions towards a wider 'systems' orientation. The second generation of land-use transport studies and plans are therefore quite different from their forebears (Hutchinson, 1974; Black and Salter, 1975).

It would be no exaggeration to claim that in practice systems approaches have been adopted by transport and land-use planners as a means of resolving the kinds of procedural or methodological problems indicated above. As Black (1981, pp. 15 and 21) puts it, 'the methods or procedures of urban transport planning can be organised conveniently using the systems approach, a conceptual tool widely used in the study of physical and social systems which enables complex and dynamic situations to be understood in broad outline'. And further, 'transport planning, as a professional activity, can be justified to the community only if problems and solutions are considered in a rigorous way, including a detailed analysis of all relevant factors . . . . The systems approach provides the planners with a suitable framework for pursuing these ideals'.

For land-use planning this meant the application of operations research-based techniques to land-use problems. According to one protagonist, Chadwick (1971), this would then lead to an optimisation of the performance of the land-use system, whilst at the same time contributing to the optimisation of the social system as a whole.

This concern for interaction between one sub-system (i.e. transport) and another (i.e. land-use) and the general system (i.e. society), and the planners' role in forging the links, is a basic feature of the systems-theoretic view. For example, Rimmer (1977, p.198) states that it provides:

> a deeper understanding of the transport decision-making process and the complex world it is designed to structure and control in the progress towards a super-system capable of subsuming transport and other divisions of interest into an integrated framework.

Hutchinson (1974) takes this argument one stage further, when he suggests that the systems-theoretic approach may be viewed as an extension of a simple framework of interaction between 'government' and 'the community'.

But the relevance of systems approaches is not unproblematical; like the earlier rationality-grounded studies and plans, those based on systems-theoretic assumptions have also been subject to and the subject of withering criticism (Van Gunsteren, 1976; Vickers, 1970; Habermas, 1971). As Habermas has described it, such an approach, when elevated to the level of social organisation, as a solution to its problem-solving capacities, serves as an ideology for a new type of political strategy, which is concerned more and more with technical problems (like forecasting car-ownership growth) and less and less with practical questions (such as mobility problems of minority groups). Van Gunsteren develops this theme further, and levels seven major criticisms at the proponents of what he calls 'systems-rational planning'. Generalising his case, he argues that such systems approaches require a degree of comprehensiveness, with respect to scope, which is total, in order to inject certainty into planning decisions; it is a holistic approach, aimed at the technical control of a complex social system or part of that system, which in this case is the transport and land-use pattern and its social organisation. The conditions necessary for this degree of comprehensiveness and control simply do not exist and, therefore, as the famous Heisenberg principle suggests, is a conception which however desirable can never be fully operationalised. But the most relevant criticism he makes, in the sense that it has profound implications for the present and future organisation of transport and land-use planning, merits an outline in full:

Systems-rational planning ignores or suppresses rationalities other than its own (e.g. political rationality) which are essential for our living together in (relative) peace and dignity, without providing functional equivalents for those other rationalities. The deeper cause of this mistake is the failure to appreciate the meaning and character of tradition, commonsense understandings and forms of life, which constitute the given basis for any form of rationality and interaction. (Van Gunsteren, p.138)

In the light of this level of criticism, it is rather disturbing to find those who advocate its adoption, defending it in the final analysis solely on the grounds of its apparent simplicity and utility in application. For example, Black (1980, pp. 215–6) argues:

Above all, the systems approach provides a very *convenient framework* by reducing the intricate details of the transport planning process to *a few major steps* such as problem definition, data collection, analysis and forecasting, plan evaluation and implementation. (Emphases added)

Furthermore, that if transport planning as a whole has not contributed to what Chadwick refers to as 'optimisation of system performance', then Black suggests that this 'is a failure not of the systems approach but of *the way that it has been applied*' (emphasis added).

The moral is clear: failure can be attributed to technical procedures rather than ideological structures; improve the procedures and the task of consensus-building strategies can be resumed. But was not this precisely the same argument put forward following a supposedly critical assessment of the first generation of land-use transport studies? The question must therefore be raised as to whether or not the 'failure' of transport and land-use planning can be redressed by yet more modifications to technical procedures, of the kind which Black (1980, p.221) would have us adopt. For example:

future transport policy will be based on more sophisticated techniques of data collection and analysis, better information, and a truer appreciation (sic) of the wide-ranging implications of alternative courses of action. The systems approach should prove adaptable to this new challenge.

Whether or not further modifications to technical procedures will improve the quality of land-use transport planning is perhaps not a central issue. What is demonstrably clear is that to date the production of land-use transport policies and plans has 'failed' to provide either a vehicle for the delivery of consensus-building strategies or a delivery system for the integration of transport policies and land-use plans. The more fundamental question is therefore not so much about the rise of new social and political alignments, nor of changes wrought in the means of social and cultural production. Rather, to pursue Williams' arguments, the question is more about the effectiveness of land-use and transport planners, and their ability to redefine their social and political alignments and recognise the broader social and political movements which are apparent in the actual ideological practices of transport and land-use planning.

The contemporary history of attempts to bring together the practices of transport and land-use planners is littered with examples of the broadening out and tightening up of social and political alignments. Attempts to introduce social impact analysis, 'public participation', and systems-theoretic practices are exemplifications of this, as well as providing examples of the ways in which the means of production of land-use transport planning have changed. But when it comes to an examination of the ways in which transport and land-use planners have attempted to confront the problematic of redefinition and recognition of these alignments and movements, then the overall picture changes quite dramatically. Far from struggling with the issues which these raise, both fraternities have, or so it would appear, attempted to pursue a political strategy which assumes reified proportions; this strategy, predicated as it is on an attempt to generate on the one hand a consensus view of what constitutes transport and land-use issues, and on the other a source of legitimation for the production and reproduction of their respective technical practices, becomes rather like the Sorcerer's Apprentice — with its own internal dynamic, immovable and unyielding to threats posed from the outside (Gillingwater, 1975).

It could be contended that both planning fraternities, far from pursuing their professed task of confronting problems of the present and future, have actively been engaged in trying to resurrect or at least reconstitute the past. Their actual history reads more like a litany of special pleading (e.g. the need for more resources) and of being distracted from the cause (e.g. 'the need for public participation and the distractions of inquiries' (Black, 1981, p.219)), whatever 'the cause' might be. The general impression which has been created is that both fraternities have a developed sense of what constitutes 'the cause', a consciousness about what it is they are engaged in; and both sets of consciousness are deeply embedded in some historically determined sense of commitment to a body of knowledges and practices which are relatively 'closed' and 'technical', and ultimately 'false'.

Following an argument initially proposed by J. Foster (1974), it would seem that there has been no fundamental 'internal' challenge to the ideological presuppositions underpinning transport planning and land-use planning, which have been carefully built up over many years, because the potential for it has been effectively blocked out. One example of this thesis in particular merits attention: the manner in which a political challenge or threat (for example, arising from the popular protest against urban motorway plans in the late 1960s) can be reconstituted by simply rephrasing it in technical terminology as a technical problem, thus allowing it to be incorporated and accommodated into the existing body politic of orthodox planning practice. The threat posed by, for example, popular protest becomes internalised, is reconstituted, and takes the form of 'social impact analysis', to be accommodated by 'public participation' exercises. The original and material base of planning practices remains untouched. Rephrasing the Rowntree Research Unit's (1974) argument, the main purpose of this political strategy is to persuade the community to accept a certain range of policies and assumptions about policy, and to mobilise to achieve these aims in a socially comprehensive way on a technical rather than on an area, political party or interest basis. The significance of this approach lies in alternative approaches which have been, in all probability not consciously, repressed. In emphasising the technical, attention is directed away from the social. The causes of legitimate grievances are displaced from the arena of political debate in the public sphere to the arena of purely technical argument (Habermas, 1974). The contemporary debate over 'technical' factors affecting car ownership provides a particularly good example, especially when it comes to drawing-out 'political' implications for transport policy (Bates et al., 1981).

The importance of this part of the overall argument should not be overlooked, because it suggests that a critical examination of the actual practices of transport and land-use planning bears only a passing resemblance to the intentions on which those practices have been supposedly based. On the one hand it is possible to discern a political strategy which emphasises a progressive orientation, trying to open up the transport and land-use planning fraternities to developments in society at large; and on the other an ultimately self-defeating conservative orientation, mediating at a more intense level, as J. Foster puts it, defending its traditional identity and particularly the objective rights and standards used to define it against other practices and threats. In the case of land-use transport studies and plans, the progressive thrust has witnessed more flexible attempts to incorporate, for example, popular protest and political issues to ensure that the schemes and programmes proposed are eventually implemented. But at the same time, the conservative bias in both fraternities have ensured that such changes have only been incorporated within the terms dictated by their traditional identity of objective rights and standards. In the case of land-use transport studies and plans, this has been incorporated at the cost of rephrasing existing and potential political conflict into abstract technical problems and systems-theoretic structures.

In all probability, Black's contention that future transport policy will be based on more sophisticated techniques within an adaptable systems-theoretic framework is all too plausible, reflecting as it does the traditional identity of the objective rights and standards of the transport and land-use planning fraternities. But whether it will also result in a 'truer appreciation' of the wide-ranging implications of alternative courses of action is much more problematical (Apgar, 1978). This requires a resurgence of interest in and ultimate domination by the immanent progressive thrust in transport and land-use planning. It would appear that contemporary history does not augur too well for this to be brought about — unless, or perhaps until, the traditional identity of these objective rights and standards is somehow transformed.

The politics of capital investment planning in transport

The power of this tension can be illustrated quite clearly with reference to the specific problem of the planning of capital investment in transport schemes and programmes. On the one hand, the tension is posed in strictly traditional and technical terms: in planning such capital investment, should the pattern of future land uses proposed by land-use planners determine transport provision, or should an integrated plan for the future transport pattern dictate land uses? (Hansen, 1959.) This tension is vividly illustrated in proposals for the planning of new cities and the significant expansion of existing urban areas (Llewellyn-Davies et al., 1970), as well as in planning for major metropolitan areas like London (Greater London Council, 1969). This tension would appear to have been accommodated in the *Master Plan for Milton Keynes*, but for the *Greater London Development Plan* it meant to all intents and purposes the incorporation of two quite separate schemes in one submission document (Hart, 1976).

On the other hand, the tension is often posed as a professional problem: should the specific and 'hard' technical skills of the transport planner in economic evaluation be deployed as the ultimate test of the overall validity of any scheme or programme, or should the more general and 'soft' planning guidelines associated with land-use planners be applied at the end of the day? A particularly vivid example of the manner in which this tension has been elevated into a substantively political issue is provided by the deliberations of the Roskill Commission on the siting of a third London airport (Commission on the

Third London Airport, 1971). For one transport economist, Roskill provided evidence that 'considerable quantification is possible which should greatly improve the basis for decision-making' (Foster, C., 1974, p.184). For an advocate of planning guidelines, nothing could be further from the truth: 'It struck me at the time as strange that so many intelligent people should apparently accept "trial by quantification"' (Self, 1975, p.ix). Ten years on, and the ghost of political dissent is still haunting centre stage: in 1981, Pearce and Nash (1981, pp. 4 and 17) are prepared to argue that:

> In short, CBA seemed to be out of step with political pressures and changing values; yet CBA should have reflected those changing values.

Furthermore, that:

> The difficulty . . . is that it is very far from clear what . . . 'planning guidelines' are and whether or not they fit the very simple requirement for rationality . . . , namely a balancing of advantages with disadvantages.

It is therefore of more than passing interest to note that in September 1981, a public inquiry was convened to consider an application by the British Airports Authority for planning permission to make Stansted Airport the *de facto* third airport for London. Stansted was rejected by both sets of professionals at the time of the Roskill Commission, according to the application of both narrow economic criteria and the more general planning guidelines.

There is at least one further point of interest to note here. Whether or nor the tension between transport and land-use planners is resolvable depends upon the degree to which either fraternity, or both in concert, can achieve a measure of autonomy over 'internal' disputes about technical problems and professional responsibilities. In the former case, it is clear that technical problems are at least capable of resolution, and it has been forcefully argued that the application of systems-theoretic approaches offers this opportunity. Professional disputes, however, are clearly in a different political arena, primarily because the objective bases of the transport and land-use planning fraternities are apparently in a state of tension.

But this conclusion must be open to some measure of doubt. At the level of appearances it would seem that the objective bases are in conflict, but it was argued earlier that in terms of the deeper prevailing political strategies there is little to differentiate them. It is the contention here that what is in a state of tension is not the separate and specific practices of transport and land-use planners, but whether their respective progressive interests dominate their immanent conservative practices; that is, the ways in which the articulation of the objective rights and standards — which characterise the traditional political strategies of the two fraternities — are mobilised.

In this sense the tensions relating to the specific problem of planning capital investment in transport schemes and programmes reflect these deeper, more structural conditions: for transport planners it could be contended that their traditional political strategy is dominated by a prevailing conservative interest which has a progressive cutting edge, for example, to bring the most sophisticated techniques of economic evaluation yet devised to bear on a politically contentious issue — the siting of a third London airport; for land-use planners, their traditional political strategy is dominated, partly for historical reasons, by a prevailing progressive interest which has a contemporary conservative cutting edge, for example, to apply general planning guidelines to a technical planning problem — the siting of a third London airport. In both instances, neither political strategy is aimed at challenging the material basis of such proposals (Sandbach, 1980). In the case of the Roskill Commission, the necessity of a four-runway airport was assumed as given, on the basis of air traffic forecasts which had been prepared earlier; in its terms of reference the Commission was required to inquire only into 'the *timing* of the need for a four-runway airport . . . , to consider the various *alternative* sites, and to recommend *which site* should be selected' (emphases added) (House of Commons, 1968). The importance of this argument in this particular context has been well stated by Mishan (1970): in the case of the Roskill Commission, its work was by definition incomplete and partial, precisely because it assumed uncritically what was arguably the most critical part of its appraisal — the perceived institutional need for such a massive capital investment project. A cost–benefit analysis can be vindicated only by what he calls a 'social judgement', that is where 'an economic rearrangement which *could* make everyone better off is "a good thing" . . . (and) in order to be a valid judgement, the criterion adopted must be independent of existing institutions. This is far from being an esoteric refinement' (Mishan 1970, p.222). Clearly the work of the Roskill Commission was not independent of existing institutions, economic, political or legal. Perhaps more importantly, it did not recognise this dependence as constituting its material base. And this raises a far more fundamental question: is it even remotely conceivable that such exercises can ever be independent of existing institutions? The argument thus far suggests otherwise.

The tension between progressive and conservative interests in the two planning fraternities is, it has been argued, indicative of a shared political strategy which has at its base a quest for a practical ideology of consensus seeking, combined with ensuring that the conditions for a continued existence are met. But what of the material base to this strategy? How do the transport and land-use planning fraternities engage in the pursuit of their respective tasks? And what is the source of their legitimacy? These questions are by no means esoteric, nor do they imply a simplistic response; if the tensions in transport and land-use planning are not located in either the way technical problems are posed, or in different professional practices and orientations, or in differences in political strategy, then they must be located in the 'deeper' realms of the material base — those conditions which actively constitute and reconstitute transport and land-use planning practices.

At one level it is possible to argue a case that the process which creates these conditions is located in the very basis of the social organisation of contemporary society. This argument suggests that the tension in the material base is engendered by a struggle for dominance between the practices of a market-oriented economy and the perceived need for some planning intervention in those practices. In terms of transport planning, the implication is that such practices are constituted, reconstituted and legitimated on the basis of the application of market-oriented criteria to the planning of capital investment projects and programmes: the 'need' for such investment is seen and evaluated in terms of 'project appraisal' or 'multiple-objective analysis', where notions of optimising performance, economic efficiency, internal rates of return or net present value, pricing mechanisms and market failure, in the form of shadow pricing exercises and calculation of consumer surplus, are all instrumental to the process of reaching decisions about the balance between capital projects and revenue programmes, for example, new roads versus subsidies to public transport, taxation of private car users, and licensing schemes. The rules are those of the market-place, the yardstick is essentially whether or not a project or programme is cost effective; and potential returns are judged in the light of prevailing anticipated rates of return in the private financial markets (Department of Transport, 1978). Such exercises reflect the 'reality' of the financial and economic situation of the day (Harrison, 1974); what Healey (1977, p.207) has referred to as 'the dominance of the market in setting goals and evaluating alternative courses of action'. This dominance is therefore essentially one of conservatism, of a risk-aversion, uncertainty-minimising strategy; 'do nothing' strategies loom large (Sharp and Gibson, 1979).

For land-use planning, the implication is that its practices are constituted, reconstituted and legitimated on the basis of the adaptation and manipulation of market-oriented criteria to the planning of capital investment projects and programmes. The 'need' for such schemes is seen and evaluated not in terms of 'project appraisal' but with more

71

generalised criteria: what Self (1977) has referred to as the general physical-cum-social effects of proposals, where skills of imaginative synthesis attempt to dominate decisions arrived at on the basis of first-, second-, or even third-best criteria; where the broader, longer-term and more abstract notion of the 'public interest' looms large, and considerations of equity outweigh a narrower-based concern for efficiency; where subjective assessments as to the social desirability of schemes outweigh the criterion of internal rates of return; and where it is possible to justify proposals politically on the grounds of 'appreciative judgements' about the provision of public or collective goods, potential external effects, the problems generated by demands for 'lumpy' investment, and the promotion of public welfare in general (Gillingwater, 1975).

All these propositions are wrapped up, or ordered, according to the application of principles of what Albers (1974, pp. 213–5) calls models of 'planned urban structure'. Albers argues that land-use planners exercise some choice in their attempts to restructure territorial space in the long term. They pursue planning guidelines which stress either the concept of a compact concentric city, or that of a linear city based upon a transport 'backbone', or a dispersed settlement structure. All three are essentially and consciously geometric designs which emphasise point, area and line patterns. All three rest on the assumption that future settlement structures need to be ordered relative to some index of concentration-dispersal, and which recognises the concept of a hierarchy of centres as a basic organising device.

The land-use planner's principal task is to evaluate the policy implications of a set of alternative settlement structures proposed for time $t + n$. These are based on a limited number of concentration-dispersal patterns, modified in turn by alterations to the proposed hierarchy of centres. The criteria employed in this evaluation process are dominated by attempts to determine the general physical-cum-social effects of each alternative, which are generated by the interaction of the dominant land users – the location of homes, workplaces, and transport and communication. In more specific terms, this means for example for transport, the identification and location of deprived groups and their accessibility problems; the social and spatial distribution of notional anticipated costs and benefits of investment decisions; and the social and spatial consequences of deconcentration and settlement strategies (Muller, 1976; Albers, 1974; Sutton, 1981). Issues such as 'compensation' and 'betterment' also gain significance, where according to Self (1977, p.170):

Only the guiding 'appreciative judgements' which may cause new problems to be viewed through old lenses, or alternatively may introduce new intellectual and social perspectives, cannot be . . . differentiated. Innovation here may come from any participant in the policy process, and the most technically proficient expert may never be able to change his spectacles.

The dominance which Self is arguing for in defence of a planning guidelines approach is therefore essentially a progressive orientation to the problem of the planning of capital investment projects and programmes: a risk-exploiting, uncertainty-capitalising strategy. 'Do something' strategies are an imperative.

According to this argument, the apparent tension between transport and land-use planners is based therefore not so much on differences in technical expertise or professional abilities, nor in their respective political strategies, but rather in the emphasis which each gives to the dominance, acceptance and acceptability of market-oriented criteria. For the orthodox transport planning fraternity, the application of such criteria creates and sustains the process which constitutes, reconstitutes and legitimates transport planning as a social practice. For the orthodox land-use planning fraternity, the adaptation and manipulation of market-based criteria is central, which in turn creates, sustains and legitimates land-use planning as a social practice. In the case of transport planning, the conservative interest dominates; for land-use planning the progressive interest dominates. What is common to both is the general acceptance and acceptability of the market as, as Healey (1977, p.207) puts it, 'a mechanism for the identification of social priorities and the distribution of resources and opportunities'. In this sense, the political strategies of the transport planning and land-use planning fraternities are similar, since neither challenge this crucial assumption; rather they seek to incorporate, accommodate and turn it to their eventual mutual advantage. It is a crucially important source of legitimation.

The material base, that is the existing social organisation of contemporary society, provides both the conditions necessary for the practices of transport and land-use planning and the sources of their political strategies (Offe, 1975). Contemporary society is in turn characterised by a dominant political strategy emphasising the privatised ownership of socially-produced wealth — which is, to quote Mishan again, 'a social judgement' deemed to be 'a good thing'. A corollary tumbles out of this analysis, with respect to the planning of capital investment projects and programmes in transport; in whose interests then are these schemes being proposed and disposed? Are these projects and programmes intended to supplement and complement the political strategy of 'privatisation'? Or are they intended to assist its further development and consolidation?

It is clear that the dominance, acceptance and acceptability of market-oriented criteria is to be found in the material base of these political strategies. Underpinning this in turn is a tacit acceptance of private property rights as a principle of contemporary social organisation (Roweiss and Scott, 1981). Translated into issues facing the relationship between land use and transport investment appraisal, this means that the sanctities of 'consumer sovereignty' and 'individual preferences', often translated as 'we get the transport system we deserve, because it reflects what we are prepared to pay for', provide political constraints against which it is deemed inappropriate to challenge. And so transport and land-use planners focus on essentially descriptive so-called 'behavioural determinants' of firms and households, as reflected in their private locational decisions. The basic task of transport and land-use planners is to accommodate the general trends which a sum of these individual decisions indicates. In this sense transport becomes a commodity, a 'good', albeit an intermediate one arrived at on the basis of derived demand, and land becomes a 'factor of production'. The key to both is seen in terms of an understanding of the way the respective markets for transport and land use operate. Technically sophisticated models of urban structure and transport networks are produced to aid this understanding (Taebel, 1978; Cordey-Hayes and Varaprasad, 1980).

To accommodate the problems which arise as a result of developing such sophisticated models, both transport and land-use planners have taken flights into fantasy. For example, two transport planners have recently professed that:

> Despite the intrinsically dynamic character of the processes being modelled, most of our thinking and theories in urban studies have been based on linear equilibrating chains of monocausality (monofunctional thinking) . . . Almost all previous approaches to studying the land-use/transport interaction have been concerned with compiling large data inventories of trip-making in terms of land-use and using derived empirical relationships to obtain highly specific transport output at a fine spatial scale. There has been little concern with the subsequent reciprocal interactions between transport supply and land-use, and of the impossibility of specifying detailed population and employment inputs for some decades ahead. In spite of their size and spatial complexity, *existing models pay no attention to the underlying processes of change.* (Emphasis added) (Varaprasad and Cordey-Hayes, 1980, pp. 3—4)

Both transport and land-use planners have, or so it would seem, lurched into some form of positivistic idealism: for transport planners, data manipulation and fine-tuning have been and remain at the centre of their orthodox practices; for land-use planners, the design and evaluation, in policy terms, of so-called 'alternative' settlement strategies has prevailed. This positivistic and idealistic orientation becomes clearer when the technical assumptions behind these respective practices are examined in more detail. Of more than passing interest are those assumptions which are common to both forms of planning practice. In the first place, both fraternities base their practices on highly abstract interpretations of how presently-constituted social formations are organised. Both appeal to a sense of social organisation which appears to be governed by a set of 'natural laws' or at least 'norms' of social behaviour, and which manifest themselves in everyday life. For example, Albers (1974, p.214) would have us believe that:

> the concentric settlement structure . . . is a *typical corollary* of the agrarian society characterised by the dependence of the town on its agricultural hinterland. The *fear* of *overconcentration* . . . has done much to nourish the idea of decentralisation . . . . The idea of a dispersed settlement structure owes much to the socio-cultural ideal of reconciling the *natural* tensions between town and country. (Emphasis added)

What precisely Albers means by 'typical', 'fear', 'overconcentration' and 'natural' in this context is unclear and not explored by him; what is clear is that these terms are so ambiguous, politicised and value-laden that to leave them unqualified is at best to tempt providence, and at worst to appeal to 'commonsensical interpretation', and hence to run the risk of elevating prejudice into 'fact'. What, for example, in this context is commonsensical about 'fear'?

In the second place, both transport and land-use planners base their practices on very idealistic and simplistic notions of land-use/transport interaction. A general example is the espoused relevance of systems-theoretic methods for transport planning practice. A more specific example is in the transport modelling sequence, a necessary prerequisite to investment appraisal, where trips are generated and distributed according to origins and destinations, and a 'modal split' exercise undertaken. As Button (1977, p.120) has described, what this means in practice is that when the focus of attention is on, for example, private car travel, public transport becomes treated as a residual. This leads him to suggest that no really satisfactory modal choice model has been developed to date. It is tempting to add here that any such exercise, if based on traditional assumptions about transport modal split, is doomed to the inevitability of failure.

In the case of land-use planning, this idealism and simplicity is both particularly stark and naive. For example, the models of settlement structure which Albers (1968) has codified bear little resemblance to existing settlement structures. They are essentially geometrical designs which exhibit an internal nested symmetry; above all they are technical solutions to technically-perceived problems which are 'pure' in form, and by definition unsullied by the practical—political and messy traits which so characterise the presently-constituted social life world. What is so naive about them is not so much their impracticability, which is demonstrably obvious (unless settlements are being created wholly from scratch, such as Chandigarh or Brasilia), but that their designation as optimum patterns of settlement structure is so implausible. This raises the much broader issue of relationships between social formations, their potential for transformation, and their spatial organisation. For example, is it conceivable to have an optimum form of spatial organisation which is independent of an optimum form of social organisation? Is not an optimum spatial organisation coterminous with an optimum social organisation? Does not spatial organisation reflect social organisation, rather than the other way round?

These kinds of question, which apply to all models of spatial structure which have at their roots, or are derived from, classical 'central place theory' (cf. Paterson, 1977), raise another set of issues for planning practice. How are these 'desirable' models of planned urban structure to be translated into actual practice? How are they to be created in a material sense, or are they to remain at the level of ideas? Are they 'models' which are to be aspired or approximated to as heuristic devices, or are they 'blue prints' which should be imposed on existing settlement structures? In no way can these sorts of political question be resolved purely within the technical realm of land-use planning practice, because, as Varaprasad and Cordey-Hayes have so cogently stated, these various models pay no attention to the underlying processes of change. It is precisely these underlying processes which present and raise issues which are to be found at the very core of the public sphere of civil society, and which both transport and land-use planning fraternities ignore at their peril.

It is in this process of understanding the underlying dynamics of change that 'reality' seems to get lost, in the sense that 'transport' becomes treated as a thing and a vehicle, literally, which, it is argued, can be modelled in its own right, and independently of those changes occurring in the material base of civil society. If, however, transport is comprehended in relation to the material base, then this transforms the orthodox picture of 'reality'. Transport now becomes part of a process which is just one component of the unstable and contradictory nature of the complex dynamics which characterise a capitalist form of economic development. The use of, for example, orthodox static equilibrium modes of economic thought somehow hinders this sort of under-standing (Smith, 1981). It is therefore perhaps hardly surprising to encounter what is in effect an increasingly familiar litany of criticisms which are levelled against transport and land-use planning practice as a result. (Banister, 1980; Sutton, 1981). For example, in a study under-taken by Leveris (1975) (cited in Black 1980, p.217), it was found that six major weaknesses were identified by planners themselves, which when ranked according to frequency of response, corresponded to:

1   The uncritical acceptance of a given land-use pattern and the failure to analyse alternatives.

2   A low degree of implementation.

3   Lack of public participation.

4   Inadequate treatment of public transport.

5   Too costly and time-consuming modelling.

6   Neglect of social and environmental impacts.

The first of these weaknesses is a damning indictment of orthodox transport planning practices. Land uses are the result of the imperatives which give shape to social organisation; in themselves they are a relatively unimportant and abstract phenomenon, unless related back to the set of social and political relationships which give land-use a practical signifying meaning — that is, the forms of ownership of and control over land, as vested in private property rights. Any single pattern of future land use proposed by planners presupposes forms of ownership and control, and in so doing presents the danger of reifying the existing set of social and political relationships which create those very conditions for ownership and control. To date, both transport and land-use planners have a poorly developed understanding of these relationships (cf. Hansen, 1959; Vickerman, 1974; Gillespie, 1980).

It is perhaps unsurprising to learn that the implementation of transport-related projects and programmes presents problems, especially since the majority of proposals have concerned infrastructure schemes (mainly road-building and fixed track installations) which are both costly, in political and resource terms, and problematical (potential public opposition). It is still far from clear that road-building projects contribute to a more 'effective' transport system *per se* (Foster, C., 1974; Moseley, 1979; Muller, 1976), especially since most schemes are aimed at managing the peak-time problem. But what does this problem of the peak actually mean? Essentially, it is about accommodating journeys-to-work and problems of capacity arising from those very social and political relationships which give land-use a practical signify-ing meaning, i.e. those forms of ownership and control not solely of land but of the privatisation process itself: the phenomenon of urbanisation, and the resulting spatial concentration of economic activities. It would appear that both transport and land-use planners have a poorly developed sense of this process (Harvey, 1981).

Given these kinds of problem, which threaten the very core of the practices of orthodox transport and land-use planners, it is hardly surprising to learn that quantification and modelling have become dominant concerns. For example, Voorhees et al. (1966) examined, on the basis of 23 cities in the United States, the assertion that trip lengths are influenced by city size and travel costs, given a constant distribution of activities. As a result they arrived at the following equation:

$$\bar{L} = 0.003 \, P^{0.20} \, S^{1.49}$$

where $\bar{L}$ is average trip length in miles, P is population of the urban area, and S is average network speed. According to Paterson (1977, p.168):

> This suggests that work trip lengths increase with population size, but at less than the fourth root of population, so that a 1 per cent increase in population leads to an increase of only 0.2 per cent in the work trip length . . . . This is evidence of adaptive response or economising behaviour within a city, which produces a structural change to a more economical pattern as city size increases.

What explanatory power does this statement actually convey? It is above all a descriptive statement of aggregate work trips and population size. But what meanings can be attributed to average network speed and trip length? And on what basis were the urban areas delineated? The key link appears to be 'through a process of a progressive dispersion of work places'. So is not the more central issue, why firms are progressively dispersing? In other words, the equation and its implications convey descriptive power only; the more significant question relates back to the spatial expression of the set of social and political relationships which give land use a practical signifying meaning, i.e. the forms of ownership and control not solely of land, nor of the privatisation process itself, but more importantly of the material basis of production which characterises those relationships. It appears that transport and land-use planners also have a poorly developed conception of the material base (Harvey, 1981).

Given the scope and range of these six weaknesses, it is tempting to ask the rhetorical question: what has planning for transport actually achieved? One response, by Muller (1976, pp. 212–3), has suggested quite unequivocally that:

> in most instances the existing metropolitan transport network is ill-equipped to serve the changing needs of its residents in the mid-1970s.

Muller goes on to argue that the contemporary organisation of metropolitan areas is in the process of undergoing a rapid restructuring, largely attributable to the great increase in suburbanised employment trends. As a result, he argues, contemporary society faces an accessibility crisis, which is surprisingly complex:

> job openings are . . . largely confined to the suburbs, and . . . job searches in outlying areas are next to impossible for the autoless to undertake . . . . For the hardy who nevertheless choose to reverse commute between the inner city and the few suburban employment centres which are accessible to bus and rail routes, work trips are usually arduous experiences in terms of extra time, higher cost, and the inconvenience of using two or more public transport modes.

Muller concludes with a plea for a general redirection of planning effort and priorities into what he calls 'social transport provision'. Moseley (1979, p.163) echoes this theme:

> Part of the problem is undoubtedly political: there is not yet sufficiently widespread acceptance that neither rising car ownership nor the gradual relocation of the . . . population by migratory movements will ensure levels of accessibility for the whole population which might be termed 'reasonable' by today's standard.

Muller's and Moseley's arguments begin to convey the 'reality' facing the planning of capital investment projects and programmes in transport provision. Both argue from the position of accessibility problems rather than the more conventionally specified problem of mobility. Both imply that the conventional practices of transport planning, in the form of models of trip generation and distribution, modal split and network assignment, leave something to be desired, primarily because of their inbuilt bias towards private car ownership mobility patterns, even when public transport compensations are incorporated. They largely ignore the transport problems of, for example, major disadvantaged groups — the poor, the elderly, the handicapped, the young, and women. In other words, the conception of rationality which underpins conventional planning methodologies, including project appraisal techniques, is a narrow functional form of rationality (car ownership, trips, modal split, freight transport etc); the accessibility approach demands that social groups and interests (the elderly, transport co-ordination etc.) be the focus of attention rather than abstract categories. The requirement here is for an explicitly political form of rationality to underpin planning practices. It would seem that transport and land-use planners have a poorly developed conceptualisation of the implications of this orientation. What it does suggest is that the dominance, acceptance and acceptability of a market-oriented criteria approach to the planning of capital investment in transport provision is found to be wanting out in the margins — spatially, in the centres of metropolitan areas and rural hinterlands; and socially, in the neglect of an increasing proportion of the population which is disadvantaged in transport terms (Gillespie, 1980; Hall, 1980; Banister, 1980).

A political economy of transport

These intensely political issues are guaranteed to generate much heat and light among the two planning fraternities whenever they are raised. Yet they must be raised, if only because of their problematical nature and implications for future planning activity. Leach (1969, p.4) has articulated this view particularly cogently, albeit in a different but planning-related context:

> What I am suggesting . . . is not that there should be no planning, but that when there is planning it must be justified by quite arbitrary principles such as aesthetic fashion or religious dogma or even military convenience. The 'needs of society', which it is now fashionable to invoke, won't work at all. No plan can ever be defended on the grounds that it represents 'the only sociological solution', because sociological solutions are infinitely adaptable.

It is not stretching Leach's argument too far to suggest that appeals to improve the application of technical skills of project appraisal or of planning guidelines represent further examples of 'quite arbitrary principles', evoking latterday equivalents of the 'needs of society' approach. This chapter so far has attempted to develop an argument which suggests that the problem of the planning of capital investment projects and programmes in transport is greater than the sum of the apparent differences between transport planners and land-use planners at the levels of their respective technical domains, administrative arenas, political spheres and ideological practices. If there is a tension permeating planning for transport, then it has to be sought at an altogether different and 'deeper' level, within the material base of existing society.

Two implications present themselves immediately. The first concerns the nature of the organisation of the material base, and the place which transport as a social activity occupies in that organisation, and its relationship to the imperative of 'privatisation' (Friedman, 1977); the second concerns the relationship of transport and land-use planning, as examples of planning-in-general, to that imperative. The first means that there is a need to develop a sustained and critical account of the *political* economy of transport, i.e. of the material conditions which determine the production and reproduction of transport, as a time-space constituted social process, and its necessary infrastructure, political and historical as well as physical (Marx, 1857). By definition this should also include the second: the relationship of planning interventions in transport to the social organisation of transport itself, which in turn requires a systematic treatment of transport and land-use planning as specific modes of intervention by agencies of the State — if only because the bulk of capital investment projects and programmes in transport are undertaken by or with the specific assistance of agencies of the State. To date there has been no systematic attempt to produce a sustained account of the political economy of transport along these lines (Taebel, 1978; cf. Gough, 1979).

One of the purposes of this chapter has been to illustrate the point that what passes for the study of the practices of land use and transport investment appraisal is far from complete; furthermore, that what is available is exceedingly partial, creating the impression that the historical relationship is essentially a technical and administrative exercise, reflecting the different technical interests and professional expertise of transport planners and land-use planners (Aldcroft, 1975). At the level of appearances this is demonstrably true, but it is at best only a description of the relationship; it conveys precious little in the way of explanatory power. It is the contention here that if the relationship between transport planning and land-use planning is to be radically 'progressive' in the sense implied by Bouchier (1978), then it is both important and necessary to explore critically the present basis of the relationship. One part of this exploration is an essentially intellectual task: to provide a political economy of transport. In itself it is not the single most important task facing the global practices of transport and land-use planning, but it would represent a significant step towards a more critical and reflective enterprise.

References

Aaronovitch, S. and Smith, R. (eds) *The Political Economy of British Capitalism*, McGraw-Hill, Maidenhead, 1981.

Albers, G., 'Toward a Theory of Urban Structure' in *Town and Country Planning Summer School Report*, Town Planning Institute, London, 1968.

Albers, G., 'A Town Planner's View of Urban Structure as an Object of Physical Planning' in Rothenberg, J. and Heggie, I. (eds) *Transport and the Urban Environment*, MacMillan, London, 1974.

Aldcroft, D., *British Transport since 1914: An Economic History*, David and Charles, Newton Abbot, 1975.

Altshuler, A., *The City Planning Process*, Cornell University Press, Ithaca, 1965.

Apgar, M., 'Next Steps in Planning: From Systems to Strategy' in *Town and Country Planning Summer School Report*, Royal Town Planning Institute, 1978.

Arctander, P., 'The Process is the Purpose' in *Journal of the Royal Town Planning Institute*, 1972, vol.58, pp. 313–5.

Bachrach, P. and Baratz, M., 'Two Faces of Power' in *American Political Science Review*, 1962, vol.56, pp. 947–52.

Banister, D., *Transport Mobility and Deprivation in Inter-Urban Areas*, Saxon House Studies, Farnborough, 1980.

Bates, J., Roberts, M., Lowe, S. and Richards, P., *The Factors Affecting Household Car Ownership*, Gower Press, Farnborough, 1981.

Black, J., *Urban Transport Planning*, Croom Helm, London, 1981.

Black, J. and Salter, R., 'The Modelling Achievements of British Urban Land-Use/Transport Studies Outside the Conurbations' in *Journal of the Institution of Municipal Engineers*, 1975, vol.102, pp. 100–5.

Blonk, W. (ed.) *Transport and Regional Development*, Saxon House Studies, Farnborough, 1979.

Bouchier, D., *Idealism and Revolution*, Edward Arnold, London, 1979.

Boyce, D., Day, N. and McDonald, C., *Metropolitan Plan Making*, Regional Science Research Institute, University of Pennsylvania, Philadelphia, 1970.

Button, K., *The Economics of Urban Transport*, Saxon House Studies, Farnborough, 1977.

Cameron, G. (ed.) *The Future of the British Conurbations*, Longman, London, 1980.

Carvel, J., 'The Big Spenders Who are Most at Risk' in *The Guardian*, Monday, 19 October 1981.

Chadwick, G., *A Systems View of Planning*, Pergamon Press, Oxford, 1971.

Commission on the Third London Airport, *Minutes and Proceedings*, HMSO, London, 1971.

Cordey-Hayes, M. and Varaprasad, N., 'A Dynamic Urban Growth Model for Strategic Transport Planning', CTS Research Report 16, Cranfield Institute of Technology, Cranfield, 1980.

Cullingworth, J., *Town and Country Planning in Britain*, Allen and Unwin, London, 1980.

Darke, R., 'Public Participation and State Power: The Case of South Yorkshire' in *Policy and Politics*, 1979, vol.7, pp. 337—55.

Dear, M. and Scott, A. (eds) *Urbanization and Urban Planning in Capitalist Society*, Methuen, London, 1981.

Department of the Environment, 'Local Transport Grants', Circular 104/73, HMSO, London, 1973.

Department of the Environment, 'Social Aspects of Development Plans', Structure Plans Note 7/73, mimeo, Department of the Environment, London, 1973.

Department of the Environment, 'Memorandum on Structure Plans and Local Plans', Circular 4/79, HMSO, London, 1979.

Department of Transport, *Report of the Advisory Committee on Trunk Road Assessment*, HMSO, London, 1978.

Duhs, L. and Beggs, J., 'The Urban Transportation Study' in Hensher, D. (ed.) *Urban Transport Economics*, Cambridge University Press, Cambridge, 1977.

Foster, C., 'Transport and the Urban Environment' in Rothenberg, J. and Heggie, I. (eds) *Transport and the Urban Environment*, MacMillan, London, 1974.

Foster, J., *Class Struggle and the Industrial Revolution*, Methuen, London, 1974.

Friedman, A., *Industry and Labour*, MacMillan, London, 1977.

Friend, J. and Jessop, W., *Local Government and Strategic Choice*, Pergamon Press, Oxford, 1969.

Garnham, N. 'Towards a Political Economy of Culture' in *New Universities Quarterly*, 1977, vol.31, pp. 341—57.

Gillespie, A., *Transport and the Inner City*, The Inner City in Context Series No.3, Social Science Research Council, London, 1980.

Gillingwater, D., *Regional Planning and Social Change*, Saxon House Studies, Farnborough, 1975.

Gillingwater, D., 'Regional Planning: Policy, Control or Communication?' *Trent Papers in Planning 78/5*, Trent Polytechnic, Nottingham, 1978.

Gough, I., *The Political Economy of the Welfare State*, MacMillan, London, 1979.

Greater London Council, *Greater London Development Plan Statement*, Greater London Council, London, 1969.

Habermas, J., *Toward a Rational Society*, Heinemann, London, 1971.

Habermas, J., 'The Public Sphere' in *New German Critique*, 1974, no.3, pp. 49—55.

Habermas, J., *Communication and the Evolution of Society*, Heinemann, London, 1979.

Habermas, J., 'Toward a Reconstruction of Historical Materialism' in Habermas, J., *Communication and the Evolution of Society*, Heinemann, London, 1979.

Hall, P., 'Transport in the Conurbations' in Cameron, G. (ed.) *The Future of the British Conurbations*, Longman, London, 1980.

Hansen, W., 'How Accessibility Shapes Land Use', *Journal of the American Institute of Planners*, 1959, vol.25, pp. 73—6.

Harrison, A., *The Economics of Transport Appraisal*, Croom Helm, London, 1974.

Hart, D., *Strategic Planning in London*, Pergamon Press, Oxford, 1976.

Harvey, D., 'The Urban Process under Capitalism: A Framework for Analysis' in Dear, M. and Scott, A. (eds) *Urbanization and Urban Planning in Capitalist Society*, Methuen, London, 1981.

Healey, P., 'The Sociology of Urban Transport Planning: A Socio-Political Perspective' in Hensher, D. (ed.) *Urban Transport Economics*, Cambridge University Press, Cambridge, 1977.

Hensher, D. (ed.) *Urban Transport Economics*, Cambridge University Press, Cambridge, 1977.

Hertfordshire County Council, *Hertfordshire Structure Plan Written Statement*, Hertfordshire County Council, Hertford, 1980.

Hillman, M., Henderson, I. and Whalley, A., *Transport Realities and Planning Policy*, PEP Broadsheet 567, Political and Economic Planning, London, 1976.

House of Commons, *Official Report*, 20 May 1968, cols 32—9.

Hutchinson, B., *Principles of Urban Transport Systems Planning*, McGraw-Hill, New York, 1974.

Jowell, J. and Noble, D., 'Structure Plans as Instruments of Social and Economic Policy' in *Journal of Planning and Environment Law*, July 1981, pp. 466—80.

Kemp, R., 'Planning, Legitimation, and the Development of Nuclear Energy: A Critical Theoretic Analysis of the Windscale Inquiry' in *International Journal of Urban and Regional Research*, 1980, vol.4, pp. 350—71.

Kirk, G., *Urban Planning in a Capitalist Society*, Croom Helm, London, 1980.

Langley, P., 'The Social Impact of Structure Planning Policies', Proceedings of the PTRC Summer Annual Meeting, Seminar D, PTRC, London, 1979.

Leach, E., 'Planning and Evolution' in *Journal of the Town Planning Institute*, 1969, vol.55, pp. 2—8.

Lee, D., 'Requiem for Large-Scale Models' in *Journal of the American Institute of Planners*, 1973, vol.39, pp. 163—78.

Leveris, B., 'Australian Transportation Studies: An Appraisal Using the Delphi Approach' in *Australian Road Research Board Internal Report 2*, Vermont, Victoria, 1975.

Lindberg, L., Alford, R., Crouch, C. and Offe, C. (eds) *Stress and Contradiction in Modern Capitalism*, Lexington Books, London, 1975.

Llewellyn-Davies, Weeks, Forestier-Walker and Bor, *The Plan for Milton Keynes*, Milton Keynes Development Corporation, Wavendon, 1970.

Lukes, S., *Power: A Radical View*, MacMillan, London, 1974.

MacKaye, B., *The New Exploration: A Philosophy of Regional Planning*, University of Illinois Press, Illinois (1962 edition), 1928.

March, J. and Simon, H., *Organisations*, John Wiley, New York, 1958.

Marx, K., 'The Method of Political Economy' in Marx, K., *Grundrisse*, Penguin Books, Harmondsworth (1972 edition), 1857.

Meyerson, M. and Banfield, E., *Politics, Planning and the Public Interest*, Free Press, Glencoe, 1955.

Mingione, E., *Social Conflict and the City*, Basil Blackwell, Oxford, 1981.

Ministry of Housing and Local Government, *Development Plans: A Manual on Form and Content*, HMSO, London, 1970.

Mishan, E., 'What is Wrong with Roskill?' in *Journal of Transport Economics and Policy*, 1970, vol.4, pp. 221–34.

Moseley, M., *Accessibility: The Rural Challenge*, Methuen, London, 1979.

Muller, P., 'Social Transportation Geography' in *Progress in Geography*, 1976, vol.8, pp. 208–31.

Newark District Council, *Western Area Plan*, Newark District Council, Newark, 1976.

Nottinghamshire County Council, *Transport Policies and Programme*, Nottinghamshire County Council, West Bridgford, 1979.

Offe, C., 'The Theory of the Capitalist State and the Problem of Policy Formation' in Lindberg, L., Alford, R., Crouch, C. and Offe, C. (eds) *Stress and Contradiction in Modern Capitalism*, Lexington Books, London, 1975.

Paterson, J., 'Transport and Land-Use Determinants of Urban Structure' in Hensher, D. (ed.) *Urban Transport Economics*, Cambridge University Press, Cambridge, 1977.

Pearce, D. and Nash, C., *The Social Appraisal of Projects*, MacMillan, London, 1981.

Regan D., 'The Pathology of British Land-Use Planning' in *Local Government Studies*, 1978, vol.4, pp. 3–23.

Rimmer, P., 'Transport Decision-Making and its Spatial Repercussions' in Hensher, D. (ed.) *Urban Transport Economics*, MacMillan, London, 1977.

Rothenberg, J., 'Introduction' in Rothenberg, J. and Heggie, I. (eds) *Transport and the Urban Environment*, MacMillan, London, 1974.

Rothenberg, J. and Heggie, I. (eds) *Transport and the Urban Environment*, MacMillan, London, 1974.

Roweis, S. and Scott, A., 'The Urban Land Question' in Dear, M. and Scott, A. (eds) *Urbanization and Urban Planning in Capitalist Society*, Methuen, London, 1981.

Sandbach, F., *Environment, Ideology and Policy*, Basil Blackwell, Oxford, 1980.

Self, P., *Econocrats and the Policy Process*, MacMillan, London, 1977.

Sharp, C. and Gibson, M., 'Transport and Regional Policy in Great Britain' in Blonk, W. (ed.) *Transport and Regional Development*, Saxon House Studies, Farnborough, 1979.

Simmie, J., *Citizens in Conflict*, Hutchinson Educational, London, 1974.

Simon, H., *Administrative Behavior*, Free Press, Glencoe, 1947.

Smith, R., 'Introduction' in Aaronovitch, S. and Smith, R. (eds) *The Political Economy of British Capitalism*, McGraw-Hill, Maidenhead, 1981.

South East Joint Planning Team, *Strategic Plan for the South East*, HMSO, London, 1970.

Starkie, D., 'Transportation Planning and Public Policy' in *Progress in Planning*, 1973, vol.1, pp. 313–89.

Steeley, G., 'Strategic Local Planning' in *Town and Country Planning Summer School Report*, Royal Town Planning Institute, London, 1978.

Sutton, J., 'Minority Modes of Transport: The Planning of Social Transport Services around a Provincial City', mimeo, Department of Town and Country Planning, Trent Polytechnic, Nottingham, 1981.

Taebel, D., *The Political Economy of Urban Transport*, Kennikat Press, New York, 1978.

Trench, S., 'Economic Criteria and Transport Subsidies' in Wilmers, P. and Moseley, M. (eds) *Rural Public Transport and Planning*, Regional Studies Association, London, 1975.

van Gunsteren, H., *The Quest for Control*, John Wiley, London, 1976.

Varaprasad, N. and Cordey-Hayes, M., 'A Dynamic Urban Growth Model for Strategic Transport Planning', Regional Science Association First World Congress, Cambridge, Massachusetts, 1980.

Vickerman, R., 'Accessibility, Attraction and Potential: A Review of Some Concepts and their Use in Determining Mobility' in *Environment and Planning*, 1974, vol.6, pp. 675–91.

Vickers, C., *Value Systems and Social Process*, Penguin Books, Harmondsworth, 1970.

Voorhees, A., Bellomo, S., Schofer, J. and Cleveland, D., 'Factors in Work Trip Lengths' in *Highway Research Record*, 1966, no.141, pp. 24—39.

White, P., *Planning for Public Transport*, Hutchinson Educational, London, 1976.

Williams, R., *Culture*, Fontana, London, 1981.

Wilmers, P. and Moseley, M. (eds) *Rural Public Transport and Planning*, Regional Studies Association, London, 1975.

4 Appraisal of the Channel Tunnel

K. M. Gwilliam

Introduction

The history of the Channel Tunnel is a cautionary tale in public decision making. It is a hundred years since the first attempt to construct a tunnel. The entrance to the original shaft can still be seen at Sangatte, near Calais. In more modern times, it is over fifteen years since the French and British Prime Ministers announced their joint decision that the tunnel should be built 'subject to finding a solution for the construction work on mutually acceptable terms'. And yet, in early September 1981, M. Mitterand and Mrs Thatcher reappeared almost at square one with a public agreement to undertake joint studies of the project.

The purpose of this chapter is to examine the nature of the judgements that have to be made and to explore the extent to which the indecision of past years might have been avoided by more thorough and perceptive cost—benefit analyses.

Some recent history is a necessary prelude to this discussion. Serious modern considerations of the project recommenced in 1957 when an Anglo-French Channel Tunnel study group was set up, comprising British Rail, the French railways (SNCF) and other financial interests. Three years later, a competing, but French dominated, Channel Bridge study group was set up in Paris. Separate proposals were submitted to the two governments who convened a joint official working group to examine them. In July 1963 this group reported in favour of a rail tunnel (Cmnd 2137) and, after further investigations had confirmed the technical feasibility of the tunnel, the two governments announced their joint intention to proceed with the building of a tunnel in July 1966.

Arrangements for the financing and construction of the tunnel proceeded very slowly. Tenders were considered and a successful group, consisting of separate British and French Channel Tunnel companies, selected. Initial agreement was reached in October 1972 to authorise phase I, covering the main technical, economic and financial studies and to provide the framework for completion of the project (Cmnd 5256). An Anglo-French treaty was signed in November 1973 authorising a second phase, including trial borings which began a year later.

Following the publication of a White Paper (Cmnd 5430), a Channel Tunnel (Initial Finance) Bill in late 1973 provided Treasury guarantees for loans raised in connection with phase II and it was expected that a hybrid Channel Tunnel Bill would be enacted during 1974 enabling the Anglo-French treaty to be ratified by 1 January 1975. The construction of a double-track, large-bore rail tunnel with high capacity both for classic rail traffic and for road vehicle ferrying (the 'rolling motorway') seemed assured.

It was at this very late stage that things began to go wrong. The Channel Tunnel Bill was given a second reading in December 1973, and sent to a select committee. Proceedings were interrupted by the dissolution of Parliament and the already substantial parliamentary difficulties of passing a hybrid bill were exacerbated by the two general elections of 1974.

These technical difficulties were compounded by the decision of the new Labour Government in April 1974 that 'a full and searching reassessment of the project should be carried out before any decision is taken to embark on the main works'. A Channel Tunnel advisory group was set up under Sir Alec Cairncross, to report by Spring 1975. Inevitably this meant that the British government was unable to ratify the treaty on 1 January and so it was formally conceded, on 20 January 1975, that the project had been abandoned. Ironically, the Cairncross Committee reported very soon afterwards in terms which were broadly in favour of proceeding.

The timetable difficulties were, of course, only the consequence of a loss of commitment to the project. The *immediate* causes of the hesitancy were associated with the proposed high speed rail link from London to Folkestone which had been subject to fierce environmental opposition. The new government also appeared to have an underlying concern about the environmental opposition to the terminal provisions necessary for the ferrying of road traffic through the tunnel.

The form in which the Channel Link project re-emerged was a direct response to these concerns. In February 1979 BR submitted a preliminary proposal for a single-track small-bore railway tunnel without any new links to London, the primary function of which would be to link the British and Continental rail networks. The Minister of Transport appointed Sir Alec Cairncross to advise him on the proposals and in March 1980 opened up the discussion of alternatives by announcing in Parliament that he looked forward to receiving any specific proposals for a tunnel or other fixed link across the Channel. In the next year he received a host of proposals ranging from a single-bore tunnel, even more modest than the BR scheme, to a combined road/rail, bridge/tunnel scheme estimated, at £5,300 million, to cost about 8 times as much.

The role which will be played by formal economic appraisal in coming to a decision has yet to be seen, but several attempts at such formal appraisal have been made. In the early 1970s the British and French Channel Tunnel companies commissioned economic and financial studies to be undertaken jointly by Coopers and Lybrand Associates and the French firm SETEC-Économie. The British Department of the Environment later commissioned a cost—benefit study by Coopers to be based on the traffic and revenue forecasts of the joint study. This was published in June 1973 (DoE, 1973b) and was in the process of being updated as part of the phase II studies when the project was abandoned. The work was, however, made available to the Cairncross Committee and used as the basis of their subsequent analysis (DoE, 1975).

In 1979 Coopers and Lybrand were again engaged by the Commissioners of the European Economic Communities to report on the assessment of 'community interest' in transport projects, the Channel Link being used as a working example. The traffic forecasts were once more revised, and applied in the appraisal of four alternative forms of link including the new BR scheme, the original two-bore wide-gauge tunnel scheme, a road bridge and a combined road bridge and rail tunnel scheme. British Rail have also undertaken detailed traffic and economic appraisals. These appraisals were reviewed in the context of the Inquiry of the House of Commons Transport Committee into the Channel Link schemes, and further analysis is currently being undertaken in the Channel Study Unit within the Department of Transport.

Formally the most ambitious of the appraisal efforts so far is that undertaken for the EEC (Commission of the European Economic Communities, 1980). Four alternatives are appraised, in financial and cost—benefit terms, on alternative economic parameter assumptions, using a wide range of discount rates, and alternative time horizons. The results of the financial appraisal on a fifty-year time horizon are shown in table 4.1.

Table 4.1
Financial analysis of alternative Channel Link schemes

	Bridge	Bridge plus single rail tunnel	Double 7 metre rail tunnel	Single 6 metre rail tunnel
Net present value (£ million)				
%				
Low growth case 3	1,725	2,999	4,215	2,162
Low growth case 5	282	901	2,074	1,131
Low growth case 10	-739	-863	280	213
High growth case 3	5,202	6,512	6,631	2,265
High growth case 5	2,070	2,698	3,335	1,183
High growth case 10	-283	-245	612	223
Internal rates of return (%)				
Low growth	5.7	6.8	12.6	14.3
High growth	8.7	9.1	14.9	14.3

Source: Commission of the European Economic Communities (1980)

This appraisal showed that, within the range of assumptions explored, the double-track rail tunnel dominated the other alternatives for all scenarios except the low growth/high discount rate situation in which circumstances the single rail tunnel might be preferred.

Extending the range of benefits and beneficiaries in a cost–benefit analysis did not substantially alter this conclusion. The returns rose on all schemes. The only additional situation in which the double rail tunnel might not be preferred was in the high growth/low discount rate case where the net present value of fifty years of a bridge plus a single rail tunnel just exceeded that of the double rail tunnel (see table 4.2).

Such calculations, of course, are only as valid as the cost and revenue calculations on which they are based and have already been subject to wide-ranging criticism. The capital cost estimates were in all cases those made by the project sponsors. The House of Commons Transport Committee came to the conclusion that the technical feasibility of the bridge proposals had not been adequately demonstrated; the implication is that if problems arose, the capital costs would be much higher. On the benefit side, Professor C.D. Foster conceded, in evidence to the Transport Committee, that the estimates of rail tunnel freight traffic might be too high whilst shipping interests argued that the competitive performance of the ferries had been seriously underestimated.

Table 4.2
Cost—benefit analysis of alternative Channel Link schemes

	Bridge	Bridge plus single rail tunnel	Double 7 metre rail tunnel	Single 6 metre rail tunnel
Net present value (£ million)				
%				
Low growth case 3	2,642	5,125	5,898	2,645
5	759	2,090	3,084	1,435
10	-573	-345	643	330
High growth case 3	6,977	9,013	8,948	3,092
5	3,183	4,433	4,770	1,713
10	135	486	1,172	443
Internal rates of return (%)				
Low growth case	6.5	8.6	15.7	16.2
High growth case	10.9	11.8	19.2	18.2

Source: Commission of the European Economic Communities (1980)

It is perhaps significant that, in their definitive proposal in 1981, the railway operators themselves only now forecast a financial internal rate of return of 9.5 per cent (BR/SNCF, 1981).

The benefit criterion — financial or social surplus appraisal

In a statement to Parliament in March 1980, the Minister of Transport declared that the government could not contemplate public funding of the Channel Link, but was keen to receive and examine any proposal capable of attracting genuine risk capital. The potential commercial viability of schemes was thus crucial, and both the EEC study and BR's own appraisal of their scheme included a financial appraisal.

Given this precondition of private finance, it would seem that selection of the preferred alternative could proceed along two different lines. On the one hand, the governments might impose constraints limiting any adverse external effects (such as impacts on the local environment), but subject to these conditions being met, accept that scheme which offered the highest financial return. Selling a franchise might have been a way of implementing this selection process. On the other hand, an acceptable financial return might have been treated as the entry condition to a selection process of a cost—benefit kind using some social surplus criterion. The two procedures would not necessarily yield the same conclusion.

In the event, a rather different problem has emerged. Despite the early appraisals suggesting real financial returns of an acceptable order, the merchant banking world does not seem to be impressed and, to date, no firm proposals for genuine risk financing have come forward. To some extent, this may result from the abnormally high current rates of interest which, unless bonds can be indexed, make the borrower very vulnerable. To some extent, the explanation of the paradox must lie in the peculiar nature and magnitude of the commercial and political risks involved, to which we shall return. The consequence of it is that it appears increasingly unlikely that the private sector will generate a range of alternative packages between which the governments can subsequently choose, unless the governments first take steps and give commitments which limit the private risk to those more normally borne in the private sector. For example, a very minimum precondition would seem to be guarantees against politically inspired cancellation or limitation of returns. Even more controversially, some minimum throughput guarantee might be required as evidence of adequate commitment to a rail tunnel.

If such guarantees were provided, and were to be the basis for the generation of alternative privately financed proposals, an interesting issue in cost—benefit analysis arises. In selecting between alternatives which had passed some prior test of financial viability, and for which no sectoral budget constraint applied, the correct decision criterion would seem to be to select the project with the highest net present value. If, however, the nature of the guarantees which the government had to give in order to stimulate the private financing of projects was such as to lead the investment to be treated as essentially equivalent to government borrowing, then it would seem appropriate to treat it as budget constrained. The appropriate criterion then would be the NPV/C ratio. Table 4.3 shows the appropriate calculations (all derived from the data of table 4.2) on which to base a decision.

Table 4.3

NPV/C ratios for cost—benefit analysis of alternative schemes

			1) Single rail track 6 metre tunnel	2) Double rail track 7 metre tunnel	3) Increment (2)−(1)	4) Bridge plus single track rail tunnel	5) Increment (4)−(2)
		%					
Low growth	at	5	2.32	2.36	2.38	0.68	−0.57
	at	10	0.53	0.49	0.45	−0.11	−0.57
High growth	at	5	2.77	3.65	4.42	1.45	−0.19
	at	10	0.72	0.90	1.05	0.16	−0.20

Source: House of Commons (1981)

Viewed in this way, the options seem to narrow considerably. The incremental NPV/C of the road bridge plus rail tunnel option is always negative in the range of discount rates likely to be used, whilst the incremental NPV/C ratio of going from the single tunnel to the double tunnel is similar to, but usually greater than, that of the single scheme alone. This suggests that if anything is worth building, it would be the larger scheme if these are the proper alternatives to have under consideration, and if they do not differ substantially in dimensions outside the CBA calculations.

The range of options

By the openness of the Minister of Transport's invitation of proposals for a link, the range of options was inevitably extended. The proposals forthcoming differ in three main dimensions, namely:

(a) type of structure;
(b) operating system;
(c) capacity.

Three main *types of structure* have been proposed. The bored tunnel, the preferred option in 1973 studies, was the most common. It has the advantage that the technology is well developed and, as a result of preparatory work for the scheme abandoned in 1975, there is considerable detailed knowledge of a preferred route through the lower chalk strata. The main disadvantage of this technology is that there are no significant economies of scale in tunnel dimension. This creates enormous difficulties as far as the provision of road facilities is concerned (House of Commons, 1981, Annex D), which effectively ties such a structure to a relatively low capacity and a rail operating system. The corollary of the absence of scale economies, however, is that this type of structure is most suitable for a phased expansion of capacity.

An alternative tunnel technology, which gets over the problem of the cross-section dimension, is the submerged tube. The bulk of the construction work, including the fitting out, can be carried out away from the site and this technology has been used for major road tunnels such as the Hong Kong cross-harbour tunnel. But the ventilation, driver fatigue and fire risks associated with long road tunnels remain; in addition, there appears to be considerable uncertainty as to how quickly, or at what cost, suitable equipment could be developed for dredging the sea-bed in mid-Channel and positioning the tubes.

The bridge alternatives are even more risky. Both during construction and operation, the bridge would be an additional hazard in a congested shipping channel. The combination of main span lengths at least 50 per cent greater than anything yet constructed with the requirement of multiple piers requiring protection from collision yields uncertainty both about immediate technical feasibility and cost which led the House of Commons Transport Committee to conclude that 'it would be irresponsible of the governments to contemplate a bridge project until the technical feasibility of such a project has been conclusively demonstrated'.

Thus, the first dimension of choice of option, that of type of structure, though implicitly economic, appears to have been decided fairly conclusively on grounds of safety and technical feasibility.

The selection of a rail *operating system* is already implicit in the choice of a bored tunnel structure. However, there still remains the choice between a pure rail system, catering only for the classic rail traffic, and the rolling motorway concept in which a high frequency road vehicle ferry is operated through a rail tunnel. There are some differences between the types of tunnel required for the two operating systems. A 6.02 metre internal diameter tunnel, as proposed by BR, would not be capable of ferrying a very large proportion of the current cross-Channel road freight vehicle movement. For this purpose, an internal diameter of at least 6.85 metres would be required (hereafter referred to as the 7m tunnel). The construction costs increase approximately linearly with the diameter of the bore.

The selection between these options appears to be very closely linked to the issue of choice of *capacity*, as the immediate market for a vehicle ferry tunnel would obviously be much greater than that for a traditional rail tunnel.

Where the choice lies between alternatives involving different capital costs, an incremental appraisal is appropriate. A form of incremental appraisal is possible using the EEC analysis as we have shown in table 4.3. But where traffic volume is expected to vary over time, and where the alternatives are of differing capacity, received wisdom would also require the phasing of capacity increases to be considered. In this particular case, the combination of alternative operating systems (6 metre or 7 metre tunnel) and capacity (single bore or double bore) renders the appropriate incremental analysis very complicated.

For safety and maintenance reasons the proposers of a single-bore running tunnel also include in their scheme a smaller bore (4.5 metre) parallel service tunnel, which would just as adequately service two running tunnels as one. A second running tunnel could be added whenever required, so that single and double tunnel schemes of the same diameter are not mutually exclusive. The same is not true of the choice between 6 metre and 7 metre tunnels. Increasing the bore would be impractically disruptive and expensive so that, for a single bore, they must be regarded as mutually exclusive.

Given the constraints on availability of capital, and the desire to limit the gestation period of any scheme chosen, it seems inevitable to choose the completion of a single-bore scheme in the first instance. The validity of that conclusion, and the justification of a phased programme could, of course, be demonstrated in a formal cost–benefit appraisal.

If a phased construction is acceptable, the immediately dominating question would then seem to concern the choice of diameter, and hence of operating system. Unfortunately, the analysis so far undertaken is not directed in this way. In 1975, the Cairncross Committee considered only a twin-bore 7 metre tunnel. BR, in 1979–80, have considered only a single-bore 6 metre tunnel. The EEC-commissioned work, comparing the two, misses the crucial comparison. Whilst a twin 7 metre tunnel might be preferable to a single 6 metre tunnel, it does not follow that it would be better than a twin 6 metre scheme suitably phased, or a single 7 metre tunnel, or a dual 7 metre tunnel suitably phased, or a combination of an initial 6 metre followed by a subsequent 7 metre tunnel.

On the basis of the work already done, it would be possible to make a reasonable estimate of the capital costs of any of these alternatives. It might not be too difficult to make estimates of the performance of the alternatives and hence the costs of traffics under different schemes.

The real complication in the analysis is that much of the traffic assigned to the BR scheme is, on BR's own admission, quite sensitive to the relative performance of alternative modes. Hence, in order to appraise the alternative schemes with any confidence it is necessary to obtain separate traffic forecasts for each of them. That has not yet been done.

A very serious problem in appraising a new fixed link concerns the performance of the 'do minimum' alternative. In the absence of a single institutional supporter the merits and capabilities of the conventional service may be ignored by default. The House of Commons Transport Committee commented on this possibility. In order to make this case the Dover Harbour Board has now organised a working party of shipping interests which produced an interim report in June 1981 (Dover Harbour Board, 1981).

There has never been any doubt that an augmented ferry service could handle any foreseeable level of cross-Channel traffic. The Dover Harbour Board claim that five new vessels of 400 passenger car unit (pcu) capacity, costing £17 million each at current prices could carry all the road vehicle traffic expected to divert to the tunnel by the year 2000. Even more significant than the claimed difference in capital costs, which has been conceded previously, is the claim that the new vessels could even be operated more cheaply than a tunnel, thus completely eliminating the advantage that the fixed link has been argued to possess.

These figures are themselves disputable. They imply a number of vehicle crossings per capacity pcu about three times the present number and costs less than 40 per cent of current costs. Although it is clear that the newest generation of vessels is substantially more efficient than the majority of vessels currently in use, the forecasts appear excessively optimistic in view of both usage and price trends in the 1970s. The rapid growth of freight traffic during the decade has reduced peakiness of traffic substantially but the midsummer traffic remains nearly twice the midwinter load and such a disparity inevitably limits overall load factors. Moreover, discriminatory pricing has already been extremely used to increase average load factors and to iron out the peak so that no entirely new use profile is likely to arise on this account. What is clear, however, is that the rates of return claimed in the BR and Coopers and Lybrand appraisals are likely to be too high, and that uncertainty about prospective ferry performance is a serious impediment in the search for 'genuine risk capital'.

The environmental issues

We have already noted that the downfall of the earlier scheme, in 1975, was closely associated with the widespread environmental opposition to the construction of a new railway through Kent, and to the local environmental impact of the terminal facilities. Further, more intense channelling of road freight traffic on inadequate roads to the terminal also offended. The new BR scheme omits the new rail link, requires very limited terminal facilities and, if anything, takes traffic off the local roads. Moreover, in so far as it increases the rail share of the international traffic with the continent, it offers a diffused reduction in road traffic. For these reasons, the BR scheme has achieved the acquiescence of the Kent County Council (which was a stern opponent of the previous scheme), and the positive support of such groups as the Council for the Protection of Rural England. In their environmental analysis (which was a qualitative appraisal of the effects of the alternative schemes on the visual environment, road noise, air pollution, aircraft noise and accidents), Coopers and Lybrand concluded that the single-track rail tunnel (the BR scheme) scored more highly than the alternatives.

Although the environmental lobby is currently less vociferous than five years ago, it may again be on this front that the political issue is fought if, as seems possible, an attempt is made to provide for the rolling motorway concept of operation of a rail tunnel. Whilst (with the exception of the Maidstone–Ashford section of the M 20), the motorway links now complete or planned for completion before any fixed link could be commissioned are adequate to keep road traffic off sensitive local roads, and the rolling motorway would be unlikely to generate much new road traffic, Kent County Council are still vigorously opposed to the larger terminal facilities required. The issue of the trade-off between this environmental impact and a financial or economic benefit may thus re-emerge.

The spatial distribution of costs and benefits

One of the ironies of a scheme which the appraisals suggest to yield substantial net benefits is that none of the regional bodies appears very enthusiastic in its support. There appears to be little confidence, either in Kent or the Nord/Pas de Calais region of France concerning employment or other local benefits, and both appear to be most concerned to obtain adequate compensation for the adverse effects that the fixed link might have on their port interests. In contrast, other interest groups, such as the Campaign for the North, presume that the benefits will accrue predominatly to the South East, and are con- cerned at the least to mitigate this effect.

These regional effects have been the subject of some study. In 1973, the government commissioned an investigation of the economic and social impacts of a Channel Tunnel on Kent (Department of the Environment, 1973a) which concluded that the local employment effects would not be great, though there might be some need for a contingency plan to deal with short-term problems arising from redun- dancies in shipping and ports.

In their 1980 EEC study, Coopers and Lybrand also examined the likely regional effects. In the construction phase, the commodities most in demand would be concrete and steel, though in proportions not yet established. Some of the increased demand for steel for the link would be offset by the reduced demand for steel for shipping. Overall, how- ever, it was concluded that the lower activity regions in the UK would suffer. An interesting variation on this theme was played by Redpath, Dorman Long whose gigantic scheme for a combined road/rail, bridge/ submerged tube scheme was partly justified on the grounds that it would generate economic activity in those regions (the North East) and industries (steel) which were most in need of support.

In the operating phase, Coopers and Lybrand showed that user benefits fall sharply with distance from the facility, although less so in the case of a classic rail tunnel than for any of the other alternatives. It was not believed, however, that the fixed link would significantly change the distribution of spatial advantage.

One of the most interesting conclusions reached by Coopers and Lybrand concerned the national distribution of benefits of the tunnel. Having examined both the user benefits and the multiplier effects of the construction expenditures, they concluded that 47 per cent of the net benefits of the scheme would accrue to France, 29.5 per cent to the UK, 9 per cent to other EEC member countries and 14.5 per cent to other countries.

Institutional difficulties and risks

The constraint that the fixed link should be capable of attracting private risk capital produces some substantial institutional difficulties when the project concerned is an international link joining the rail systems of two nationalised industries.

The first point to note about the private finance requirements is the curious market structure which it implies. A fixed link would, because of its large indivisible capacity, be a monopoly provision. If the sole customers were also monopolists in the provision of rail transport, then we have a bilateral monopoly. Inevitably, a financier would be looking for some guarantees to reduce the risk attached to a very large investment of such little versatility. The railways could not afford any such guarantee to be solely a throughput guarantee irrespective of price, hence any kind of commitment would inevitably be to produce a minimum revenue. Once this revenue is set at such a level as to ensure anything like a reasonable return on the capital invested, the effective risk has been transferred from the terminal proprietors to the users. But without it, the proprietors would themselves be very vulnerable. The British government thus appears to have put itself in a box. Private finance requires some revenue guarantee; but a revenue guarantee given by a nationalised industry cannot easily be disguised as being consistent with the requirement for private risk finance. Until this hurdle is overcome, further progress is unlikely.

The inseparability of government support and the commercial prospects of a rail-based scheme goes further than this however. BR have estimated a total freight market of 5.28 million tonnes in 1992, rising to over 6 million tonnes in 2000. This implies a very substantial capture of traffic from the roads, the achievement of which is very dependent on the quality of rail service provided. Their own forecasts presume that private sidings will become available in the UK as suitable traffic opportunities are identified; that wagons of the required type will be readily available; and that an adequate supply of containers is forthcoming. All of these imply the availability of investment finance which might not be forthcoming if the domestic rail freight sector were in deficit or in decline.

Commercial risks

Some of the risks of a Channel link are of a more normal commercial kind. The risk on capital cost seems to attach mostly to the bridge and submerged tube options, on account of a range of technical uncertainties. The bored tunnel options look much more secure in this respect. On the benefit side, considerable risk attaches both to the estimation of the total market for which the link would cater and about the market share which it might achieve.

Over the last decade, passenger traffic on the main cross-Channel services has grown on average by 8.3 per cent per annum, and unitised freight traffic between Britain and the French, Belgian and Dutch ports by an average of 13.7 per cent per annum. This rate of growth has exceeded that forecast in earlier studies and has so far shown little sign of falling off, despite recession in the Western European economies. The rates have also substantially exceeded the rate of growth of domestic traffic during the same period. On that basis, the Coopers and Lybrand forecasts of a total freight market growth of about 3 per cent per annum and a total passenger market growth of less than 2 per cent per annum over the rest of the decade look relatively modest.

The high recent growth rates are largely a result of British entry to the EEC. At best we must expect them to taper off as the adjustment of the European economy is completed. At worst one may foresee some reversal of the pattern in the event of any British withdrawal from the EEC. Given that the major opposition party is committed to UK withdrawal from the EEC, there is a major political uncertainty surrounding all forecasts.

The introduction of a new mode inevitably also produces great uncertainty about the share of the total traffic which that mode can attract. The share will depend on the performance of the fixed link, the competitive response of existing modes, and on the consumers' response to the alternatives offered.

In the passenger market, it is possible to predict the performance of the link with some degree of confidence. The BR scheme would provide through service from London to Paris in 4 hours 30 minutes and London to Brussels in 4 hours 10 minutes. This compares with the present rail/sea time of 7 hours to Paris and with an air centre-to-centre time of about 3 hours. This performance could be prejudiced somewhat if dual voltage locomotives and through running of stock cannot be agreed between BR and SNCF, or if it proved impossible to agree on train customs and immigration arrangements.

The requirement to operate in 'flights' of trains in a single tunnel means that, with a three-hour cycle, there would be a rather less regular service on the fixed link than that provided by air, but it should still be possible to give a high average frequency, and schedules at the appropriate times. A double tunnel would give the same centre-to-centre timings but allow a regular hourly frequency to be maintained.

The BR forecast is that a single rail link would attract 80 per cent of the current rail-connected classic passenger market and 20 per cent of that which is road connected. In addition they expect to gain 12 per cent of the air traffic to the 'tunnel zone countries'. There are some elements of conservatism in their estimating procedures — for instance no new traffic generation or capture of car accompanied traffic and a model based solely on rail travel time with no additional attraction assumed to arise from the elimination of the interchanges. But there are also some optimistic assumptions; relatively high values of time were used in the modelling and on-train immigration arrangements were assumed.

Dominating these potential sources of error, however, would appear to be the risks associated with the response of competing modes. No allowance is made for any reduction in the real fares for the short-haul air routes despite recent trends in air fares. As BR project that about 20 per cent of the passengers on the single-rail link would be diverted from air, the single-track tunnel is vulnerable to air competitive pricing. The traffic on a double-rail tunnel, because it would carry a large proportion of accompanied cars, would be proportionately less vulnerable from this direction. Moreover, in recent years, car accompanied traffic has been growing more rapidly than air traffic, which is contrary to the Coopers view of future trends.

Competition from the ferry operators seems even more chancy. Coopers and Lybrand (whose estimates of the BR single-rail link traffic were broadly consistent with BR's own forecasts) assumed that the link would be able to charge a premium for non-car passengers of 20 per cent above the ferry rate. However, Coopers believe that fare cutting by the ferries to attract the foot passenger is quite likely as the marginal cost of the foot passenger on a vehicle ferry is very low. They considered that if ferry rates fell to 70 per cent of their original level it might reduce the link traffic by 25 per cent. In cost–benefit terms, the effects of such a rate war would be to redistribute welfare between operators and users with little effect on overall budget; the financial returns to the fixed link operator would fall. Again, curiously, a double-rail tunnel, because it would be competing in the accompanied car market and would therefore be able to launch a retaliatory war on the basic ferry traffic, would appear to be less vulnerable to competitive attack from competing modes wishing to fill spare capacity by discriminatory pricing.

High commercial risk similarly appears to exist in the freight market, for the single-bore rail tunnel. BR forecast a freight traffic of over 5 million tonnes in 1990 and over 6 million tonnes in 2000. Coopers and Lybrand were even more optimistic. These conclusions had been reached in different ways − BR by a pragmatic market survey of the main traffics, Coopers by the application of a freight modal split model. The Department of Transport are less sanguine. In their most recent published estimates they forecast only 4.5 million tonnes rail freight, of which 1.7 million tonnes is diverted from rail ferry, 0.8 million tonnes is from container and 2.0 million tonnes from RoRo (Cmnd 8561). The composition of this forecast traffic is shown in table 4.4.

Table 4.4
Composition of BR estimated rail tunnel freight market
(million tonnes)

	Containers	Wagon load	Train load	Cars	Total
1992	2.86	0.75	1.27	0.39	5.28
2000	3.47	0.80	1.46	0.39	6.14

Source: House of Commons (1981), Annex C

The vulnerability of the forecasts is apparent from table 4.4. Only 25 per cent of the traffic falls into the category of train load traffic which has been the most secure and rapidly expanding category of domestic freight. Wagon load traffic is 13−14 per cent, a category which has been declining both relatively and absolutely in recent years, and the future of which must be in some doubt. Container traffic accounts for 55 per cent. This traffic is very sensitive to the quality of service provided and thus depends on adequate infrastructure and mobile equipment being available both in the UK and on the Continent. We have already referred to the political risk attaching to the supply of capital for BR. But there is also an international dimension to the uncertainty as the continental railways are far less committed to containerisation, and more interested in piggybacking road vehicles, than BR. The absence of an adequate continental infrastructure for containers could severely damage the freight potential of the 6 metre rail tunnel.

Postscript on economic viability

It is interesting to note that the very recent forecasts of the joint UK/ French study group (Cmnd 8561), which take into account a number of the points mentioned, show lower returns than previously. The use of French values of time adds 1–1.5 per cent to the IRR and the range of returns has widened as between scenarios. The expected rate of return on the larger schemes, and on those involving direct road traffic are shown to be highest, but the bridge and composite schemes were still considered to have a much higher technological risk (see table 4.5). The group therefore considered that the balance of advantage lay with bored track rail tunnels with vehicle shuttle, constructed, if necessary, in phases.

Table 4.5
Resource cost comparison: internal rate of return of fixed link (%)

	Single 6m	Single 7m no shuttle	Single 7m with shuttle	Double 7m	Road bridge	Road bridge and rail tunnel	Composite scheme
Scenario A							
UK time values	9.1	8.5	6.1	12.3	13.9	12.0	10.2
French time values	10.7	10.0	7.0	13.4	15.0	13.2	11.2
Scenario B							
UK time values	5.4	5.0	4.0	7.3	8.4	7.1	5.3
French time values	6.8	6.2	5.1	8.1	9.1	8.0	6.1
Scenario C							
UK time values	1.6	1.2	1.0	2.4	0.3	0.0	0.0
French time values	2.5	2.0	1.7	3.0	0.7	0.6	0.0

Source: Cmnd 8561 (1982)

Conclusions

Our avowed objectives in this chapter were to identify the crucial judgements which have to be made before a Channel link project can proceed and to consider the extent to which earlier, more thorough, cost– benefit analysis would have enabled the issue to be resolved earlier and more satisfactorily.

If there is to be a fixed link, it now seems fairly clear that it will be a deep bored tube, initially for a single-track railway, and probably of an internal diameter leaving at least the possibility that it can be used for ferrying of cars and heavy goods vehicles. The questions which remain crucial, and much more open, concern whether there is to be a link at all at the one extreme and how any link should be operated and phased at the other. Doubt about the overall viability of a fixed link arises from uncertainty concerning the potential performance and costs of the sea ferry alternative. Until that is fully and independently explored, it will undermine both commercial and political confidence in the link.

Doubts concerning the operating system mainly relate to the questions whether or when to make the ancillary provisions for vehicle ferry operation. An initial phase with the classic rail facilities at Saltwood, and the Cheriton site left for subsequent road–rail transfer facilities, offers great flexibility in the timing of such a decision. The necessary judgements to resolve the matter concern the relative attractiveness to traffic of the alternative types of operation which in its turn depends in part on the future of rail freight, and particularly containerised rail freight in Western Europe. Lack of commitment to rail freight on the British part, or to the proposed style of container operation on the part of European railways could ensure an early transfer to the rolling motorway style of operation.

Dominating all of these technical uncertainties is the uncertainty of finance. We have argued that the governments' interest in the issue is so close that private finance without any form of guarantee is extremely unlikely. Further clarification, which may now need to be in the form of an agreed Anglo-French position, is absolutely essential to further progress.

It is rather more difficult to decide to what extent these remaining impediments to reaching a decision might have been overcome by better and more timely analysis. Looking back to 1975, there appear to have been three elements contributing to abandonment at such a late stage:

1   By insisting so strongly that the tunnel would not be feasible without the high speed link to London, BR prevented a thorough and timely examination of all the alternatives. When the Cairncross Committee eventually reported, it was (too late, of course) in terms of a tunnel without the link.

2   The environmental impact of the scheme did not appear to have been explored sufficiently thoroughly to offer justification for accepting, or attenuating, those effects.

3   The heavy dependence on government finance made the scheme particularly vulnerable to pressures on government financial capability.

It might be argued that the appropriate lessons have been learned. BR have now proposed a minimum scheme, with little environmental impact, hopefully capable of attracting private finance, so that none of these ingredients remain. The danger is that this new strategy has been developed and pursued in an equally blinkered way so that any change in circumstances or attitude will again undermine the project because it is not based on a full enough appraisal of the relevant alternatives and therefore not capable of adjustment.

BR have shown great resistance to consideration of anything but their own scheme, so that there is no adequate examination of the operating characteristics of the rolling motorway scheme, nor any market-research based forecast of its traffic potential. Most promoters of other schemes appear to be equally limited in their appraisal. Both BR and Kent have concentrated their detailed design interest in the location of the terminal for the 'mousehole' and together set their face against planning for any larger terminal facility.

In this rather unsatisfactory situation it is interesting to record the conclusion reached by the House of Commons Transport Committee in their examination of the link proposals. In view of the uncertainties attaching to the commercial prospects of a classic rail tunnel, but recognising environmental and other advantages of a rail only facility, the committee recommended that serious consideration be given to a single-bore, 6.85 metre tunnel. This tunnel would be designed in such a way to facilitate duplication and to allow a rolling motorway service to be provided eventually if so wished, but would only be provided initially with the terminal facilities and statutory powers to be operated as a classic rail tunnel. The committee recognised that neither BR nor the environmental interests would be wholly satisfied with a scheme which leaves the door open for a rolling motorway operation in due course, but it felt that such a scheme was versatile at relatively low incremental cost. The railway system would have the possibility to establish a service which would attract enough traffic to be viable and the time in which to develop that potential. It would be a low risk solution in that it would be viable with low growth of traffic but expandable with high growth, and would find a sensible place in either a rolling motorway or classic rail type of operation.

This arrangement has much to commend it. Even if it were intended from the outset to go on to a rolling motorway basis, it would allow the first bore to be put to immediate use and the costs of the ancillary investment of the full scheme (about £150 million on terminals and link roads) to be postponed. It might also reduce the commercial risk to BR by dissuading the ferry operators from abstracting the classic foot passenger by discriminatory pricing for fear of precipitating a retaliatory provision of vehicle ferry services.

There are clearly some economic questions which remain to be asked of this strategy, in particular whether, once built, it would not inevitably be more sensible to use the facility to provide whatever mix of classic rail and vehicle ferry services was most profitable or most economic. There are also the political doubts as to whether the environmental opposition would be at all defused by this device. What is clear is that there are intermediate strategies between the simple rail 'mousehole' and the full rolling motorway which deserve careful attention. There are also different pricing and operating régimes which might affect both the traffic levels and the commercial viability (Glaister, 1978). Cost–benefit appraisal could certainly shed some further light before the inevitable political dimension of the problem supervenes.

If the need for detailed appraisals is so obvious, one may finally ask why this has not already been done, given that the present bout of interest in the link has been going on for over twenty years. That is an institutional question to which one must give an institutional answer, or rather three answers. Firstly, there is the confusion introduced by the British government requirement for private finance. Given that requirement, it is unclear what status any cost–benefit appraisal would have, or who should do it. Perhaps the publication of Sir Alec Cairncross's advice to the government will resolve the matter. Secondly, and associated with this, the wide invitation to make proposals means that much of the effort has so far gone into persuasive advertising of promoters' schemes rather than into detached co-operative assessment. The role of BR is particularly awkward in this sense. Thirdly, there is a confusing international dimension. The British effectively killed the previous scheme unilaterally; the French are, not surprisingly therefore, unwilling to commit themselves now until they have some firm commitment from the British. With quite different views about the role of public finance of such projects and different priorities in containerisation strategy it is not clear what kind of agreement may be forthcoming.

If a moral has to be drawn it must surely be that in a project of this size and international institutional complexity, it is quite inappropriate to rely on the unco-ordinated, and frequently conflicting, activities of a host of private and public institutions to bring the matter to a timely and rational decision.

References

British Rail and SNCF, *Cross Channel Rail Link*, Joint Report, 1981.
Cmnd 2137, *Proposals for a Fixed Channel Link*, HMSO, London, 1963.
Cmnd 5256, *The Channel Tunnel Project*, HMSO, London, 1973.
Cmnd 5430, *The Channel Tunnel*, HMSO, London, 1973.

Cmnd 8561, *Fixed Channel Link:Report of UK/French Study Group*, HMSO, London, 1982.

Commission of the European Economic Communities, *The nature and extent of a possible Community interest in the construction of a fixed link across the Channel*, a presentation of some of the results of a study undertaken for the EEC by Coopers and Lybrand Associates, London and SETEC-Économie, Paris, EEC, Brussels, 1980.

Department of the Environment, *The Channel Tunnel: its economic and social impact on Kent*, report presented to the Department of the Environment and Kent County Council, Economic Consultants Ltd, HMSO, London, 1973a.

Department of the Environment, *The Channel Tunnel: a United Kingdom cost—benefit study*, report presented to the Secretary of State for the Environment by Coopers and Lybrand Associates Ltd, London, 1973b.

Department of the Environment, *The Channel Tunnel and alternative cross-Channel services*, a report presented to the Secretary of State for the Environment by the Channel Tunnel Advisory Group, HMSO, London, 1975.

Dover Harbour Board, *Channel Study Working Party, Interim Report*, Dover, 1981.

Glaister, S., 'Peak load pricing and the Channel Tunnel' in *Journal of Transport Economics and Policy*, 1976, vol.10, pp. 99—112.

House of Commons, *The Channel link*, Second Report of the Transport Committee Session 1980—81, HC 155—1, HMSO, London, 1981.

5 The appraisal process in transportation: an Australian experience

D. A. Hensher, D. S. Kirkby and M. E. Beesley

Introduction

In September 1978 the New South Wales (NSW) Government issued a commission to inquire into and report on the need for a major regional road link, or combination of road links, between the central industrial area and the western and south-western sub-regions of the Sydney metropolitan area. The terms of reference included the environmental and social impact of any proposal, the economics of transport, especially goods movement, and possible development of alternative transport modes in existing corridor reservations. While this may appear to be yet another public sector technical assessment of a very ordinary road project, its importance in Australia is not ordinary. The Commission of Inquiry into the Kyeemagh—Chullora Road (henceforth the 'inquiry') is the first independent inquiry in Australia into a major road proposal.

It provided an opportunity to implement the 'new' approaches to transport appraisal, which view comprehensiveness of evaluation studies as public involvement from the initial goal formulation stage (or 'social' evaluation) (Stanley and Nash, 1977; Wachs, 1977). Lessons learnt from this inquiry should help in future deliberations provided this first inquiry can convince the many sceptics of the value of investing in an

---

1 The comments of Peter Abelson and others who for various reasons must remain anonymous have been helpful in the writing of this chapter.

inquiry process.

The appraisal method used by the Road Authority was heavily influenced by the Leitch Committee in the UK (Department of Transport, 1978). This committee recommended inquiries to adopt a 'framework' of an appraisal of options consisting, first, of conventional elements in cost—benefit analysis, e.g. road users' time costs, fuel costs, accident losses and road producers' costs. (e.g. construction and maintenance). These items were considered to be measured in pounds sterling. To them were added other quantifiable effects on interests affected, e.g. householders inconvenienced by noise or other nuisances. 'Unquantifiable' effects, such as losses of landscape amenities, were also to be noted. The ambition was to cover the interested parties, and the wider community, in one statement. The approach owed much to the 'planning balance sheet' devised by Professor N. Lichfield several years before. This framework did not add any new impacts, rather it emphasised presentation of impacts in terms of groups affected. Good practitioners had been including the impacts for some years.

Accordingly, cost—benefit analyses were made for the four routes thought of as options, adopting much the same approach as Leitch had advocated — road users' and producers' costs, households affected etc. — but with less comprehensive coverage (see table 5.1). The calculations and accompanying explanations for the four, assessed against a fifth, or do-nothing, option, comprised the principal material initially supplied to those who proposed to give evidence. (The 'options' and calculations are further referred to below).

If the basic documents owed much to UK practice, the form of the inquiry itself was different in significant ways. Each 'option' was, in principle, given equal analytical attention. There was an exceptionally wide canvass of opinions. About one thousand parties, including local councils, expressed interest and secured copies of the background document. Much was done to enable interested parties to formulate opinions — by setting up information centres, displays, interpreters for those with language difficulties, and clerical assistance to those unused to formulating a submission. Thus, there was exceptional concern for the inarticulate. Over fourteen hundred written submissions were received, and one hundred and eighty appearances were made at the public hearings (see figure 5.1). In contrast, UK canvass of options is probably wider if statutory public consultation is included, which comes before the inquiry in most road schemes. The number of opinions canvassed, however, is typically less.

Though consultants were employed to advise the Commissioner, the wide-ranging process to stimulate criticism was not incorporated formally in the models used or options considered. There was no attempt, as in the UK Roskill and other airport inquiries, to feed back

109

Table 5.1
The initial appraisal of options, made available as part of the source document

Criteria	Cooks River option	South-Western option	Bexley Road option
TRANSPORT			
Accessibility improvements:			
Length of route	13.0 km	16.7 km	14.6 km (Harrow Road) 13.3 km (Bestic Street)
Congestion	Some at ends only	Constraint on King Georges Road section	Capacity constraint along route
Traffic levels and congestion:			
Effects on other routes	Widespread reductions on parallel minor routes; congestion remaining on radial major routes; increased traffic in south Marrickville	Reductions south of Cooks River, but none west of Canterbury Road; reductions on parallel routes; increased congestion on King Georges Road and in south Marrickville	No significant reduction of traffic on parallel routes or access roads
Traffic in residential areas:	Widespread reduction on minor routes and local streets; some trucks likely to remain on minor routes but fewer on local streets	Similar to Cooks River option	Few improvements except near the Rockdale and Campsie by-passes
Traffic in shopping centres:	Significant reductions in total traffic in Bexley North, Belmore, Rockdale, Earlwood, Canterbury, Ashfield, Marrickville, and in truck traffic in Earlwood, Ashfield, Bexley North, Canterbury and Rockdale	Significant reductions in total traffic in Marrickville, Earlwood, Rockdale, Kingsgrove, Beverly Hills, Bexley, Bexley North, and in truck traffic in Ashfield, Earlwood and Rockdale	Significant reductions only in Bay Street, Rockdale and Beamish Street, Campsie, with large increase in Bexley North
Bus operations:	Little improvement to bus operations due to reduced congestion; only 2 minor changes to bus routes	Some improvements to a few bus operations but worsening on Ring Road 3; only 2 minor changes to bus routes	Improvements in Rockdale and Campsie centres; worsening on Bexley Road unless bus priority given

ECONOMIC

Economic efficiency:

Total capital cost	$49.7 mil (min. prop. effect) $51.3 mil (max. open space)	$52.1 mil	$15.2 mil (Harrow Road) $17.8 mil (Bestic Street)
Benefit/cost ratio	1.41	1.16	1.78 (Harrow Road) 1.83 (Bestic Street)
Net present value	$9.5 mil	$3.7 mil	
Internal rate of return	17%	14%	
Early economic benefits:	Possible to construct independent and usable stages	Limited opportunity to construct independent and usable stages	Construction could be staged, with benefits derived from each stage
Equity of costs and benefits:	Not yet assessed	Not yet assessed	Not yet assessed.

SOCIAL

Exposure of pedestrians to accidents:

Access from residential, commercial, industrial or open space land to			via Harrow Road or Bestic Street	
(a) new road or existing minor roads	4610 m	670 m	3270 m	4930 m
(b) existing major roads	700 m	8600 m	5800 m	3670 m
Kerbside parking	Not yet determined	Not yet determined	Not yet determined	
Overall risk to pedestrians	Lowest	Higher than Cooks River option	Highest	

Exposure of motorists to accidents:

Median separation of	median: no median	median: no median	median: no median
(a) new road or existing minor roads	5.5 km:4.6 km	2.9 km:8.6 km	1.7 km:12.9 km (Harrow Road)
(b) existing major roads	2.3 km:0.4 km	6.9 km:0	1.5 km:11.8 km (Bestic Street)

Table 5.1 (cont.)

Criteria	Cooks River option	South-Western option	Bexley Road option	
			Harrow Road	Bestic Street
SOCIAL (cont.)				
Exposure of motorists to accidents:				
Number of intersections on				
(a) new road or existing minor roads	26	17	10	11
(b) existing major roads	12	46	67	67
Uncontrolled intersections	14	12	58	61
Lane widths	3.4 m	3.4 m	3.2 m	
Vehicular access control	8.7 km	11.1 km	None	
Overall risk to motorists	Lowest	A little higher than Cooks River option	Highest	
Disruption of local access:				
Houses with more difficult pedestrian or vehicular access	215	147	Very few	
Pedestrian separation	Moderate separation of several localities by heavy traffic	Physical separation of housing and open space along Wolli Creek Valley	Separation of some residential areas by increased traffic on existing local streets in the route	
Residential areas:				
Dwellings displaced	190 (minimum property effect) 212 (maximum open space)	158	49 (Harrow Road) 91 (Bestic Street)	
Properties partially acquired	115 (minimum property effect) 134 (maximum open space)	51	80 (Harrow Road) 86 (Bestic Street)	
Dwellings with amenity of adjacent land affected	305 (minimum property effect) 346 (maximum open space)	64	440 (Harrow Road) 534 (Bestic Street)	
Brick clad dwellings	57%	79%	76% (Harrow Road) 85% (Bestic Street)	

Open space and recreation facilities:

Total open space lost	6.6 ha (minimum property effect) 4.0 ha (maximum open space)	36.0 ha	2.0 ha (Harrow Road) 0.9 ha (Bestic Street)
Major impacts	Intrusion into linear open space along Cooks River	Loss of open space and natural character of Wolli Creek Valley	None
Recreation facilities disturbed	9 local parks or play areas partly resumed	8 local parks or play areas partly resumed	Access to 1 playground made difficult
Schools and community facilities:			
Schools displaced	None	None	None
Effects on high school catchments	Minor	Minor	None
Effects on primary school access	Pedestrians cross additional traffic to 4 schools	Pedestrians cross additional traffic to 2 schools; long detour needed in Beverly Hills	Pedestrians cross additional traffic to 4 schools (Harrow Road) or 6 (Bestic Street)
Community buildings displaced:	1 memorial hall 1 cinema	None	1 church (Bestic Street)
Effects on historic or notable features:			
Natural	Major impact on Cooks River Valley	Major impact on Wolli Creek Valley	None
Manmade, of regional significance	None	None	None
Manmade, of local significance	Not yet assessed	Not yet assessed	Not yet assessed
Development changes:	Possible redevelopment of industrial land at Bankstown/Canterbury and Arncliffe/Tempe; little effect on commercial centres; recreation oriented development along Cooks River and Botany Bay; some higher density residential possible along route	Industrial and recreation development similar to Cooks River option; could encourage expansion of Roselands and Bexley North shopping centres; higher density residential possible at Arncliffe and Earlwood, as with Cooks River option, but unlikely alongside Wolli Creek Valley	Reduced traffic in Rockdale centre could encourage development; little residential redevelopment likely

Table 5.1 (cont.)

Criteria	Cooks River option	South-Western option	Bexley Road option
SOCIAL (cont.)			
Business and employment:			
Jobs displaced	90	79	32 (Harrow Road) 65 (Bestic Street)
Construction jobs created	280 for 5–6 years	250 for 5–6 years	110 for 3 years
Need for land used by industry	1.25 ha	4.5 ha	2.2 ha (Harrow Road) 0.6 ha (Bestic Street)
Jobs attracted to the area	Not known	Not known	Not known
ENVIRONMENTAL			
Land capability:			
Land suitability for road construction	Flood plain location, not difficult to build on, but hydrology could require drainage works	Major cutting and filling would be needed in the Wolli Creek Valley, with a new channel for the creek in two places	No new construction on unsuitable land except near Muddy Creek (Harrow Road)
Construction costs attributable to the landscape	$18.5 mil	$23.8 mil	$4.1 mil (Harrow Road) $3.6 mil (Bestic Street)
Ecological effects:	Minimal	Major impact on remnant of natural vegetation and wildlife habitat, displacing 23 ha between Undercliffe and Bexley North	Minimal
Visual effects:			
New construction through relatively attractive areas	9.0 km	8.5 km	0.4 km
Houses with views			
(a) obscured	20	60	32 (Harrow Road) 36 (Bestic Street)

(b) extended	66 (minimum property effect) 80 (maximum open space)	65	5 (Harrow Road) 47 (Bestic Street)
Houses with landscape views affected	4200	2430	145 (Harrow Road) 225 (Bestic Street)
Length over which travellers' affected	1.5 km of Illawarra line 1.0 km of East Hills line 1.0 km of Princes Highway	1.5 km of Illawarra line 7.0 km of East Hills line 1.0 km of Princes Highway	None
Views from adjacent open space	Not yet assessed	Not yet assessed	Not yet assessed
Air quality changes:	Not yet assessed	Not yet assessed	Not yet assessed
Noise intrusion:	Not yet assessed	Not yet assessed	Not yet assessed

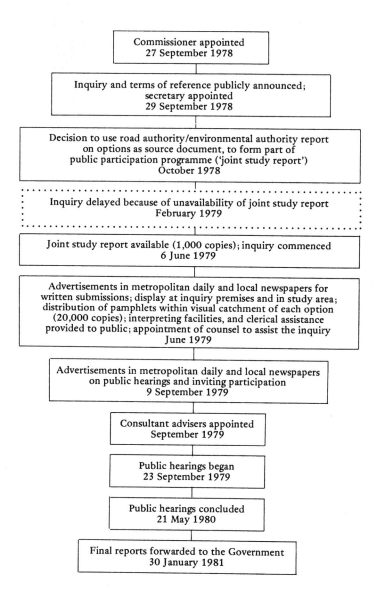

Figure 5.1   The inquiry sequence and timing

The commissioner was appointed in September 1978 and reports were completed in January 1981, a total of 28 months. The sequence of inquiry activities is shown above. A total of 1,429 written submissions were received and 3,000 signatures to various petitions; public hearings were conducted from September 1979 to May 1980. In the public hearings, 180 appearances were made.

conclusions of the analysis to the research workers responsible, which might have produced modifications to calculations for the four options. Nor were new options submitted to parallel analysis. The inquiry process did throw up new options, and new data became relevant during its months of hearings. These had to be dealt with *ad hoc*. Cost—benefit analysis was, then, a base from which discussions started. Its role in the inquiry was to discover, rather than to be a means of settling, the claims of conflicting interests.

The chapter first examines the background to the study, including a brief resumé of the initial set of road options. Sources of information are outlined and an assessment is made of the contribution of cost—benefit analysis in the inquiry process. The final part presents some lessons learnt and defines some benefits of the inquiry.

Background

The inquiry was motivated by an earlier decision to establish two large container terminals and a bulk liquids terminal at Port Botany (see figure 5.2). It was expected to add greatly to the traffic problems of the area as trucks in particular moved between the port and the inland container depots. The provision of a major road became an election issue in 1978. The real issues of the inquiry became the separation of through traffic from local traffic and truck routing.

The issues were addressed as five questions:

1   What are the transport needs of the study area?

2   What are the means available to satisfy these needs?

3   What social and environmental consequences attend their satisfaction?

4   Are the proposals capable of modification so that the community and the environment are spared, even whilst the transport needs are satisfied?

5   What, on balance, should be done?

In answering the final question the inquiry was guided by three further questions:

1   Is the environment (whether natural or manmade) which is being sacrificed to construct the road, such a precious part of our natural heritage that the option should be excluded from further consideration?

2   If the environmental sacrifice is considerable, has it been demonstrated that there is no prudent or feasible alternative?

117

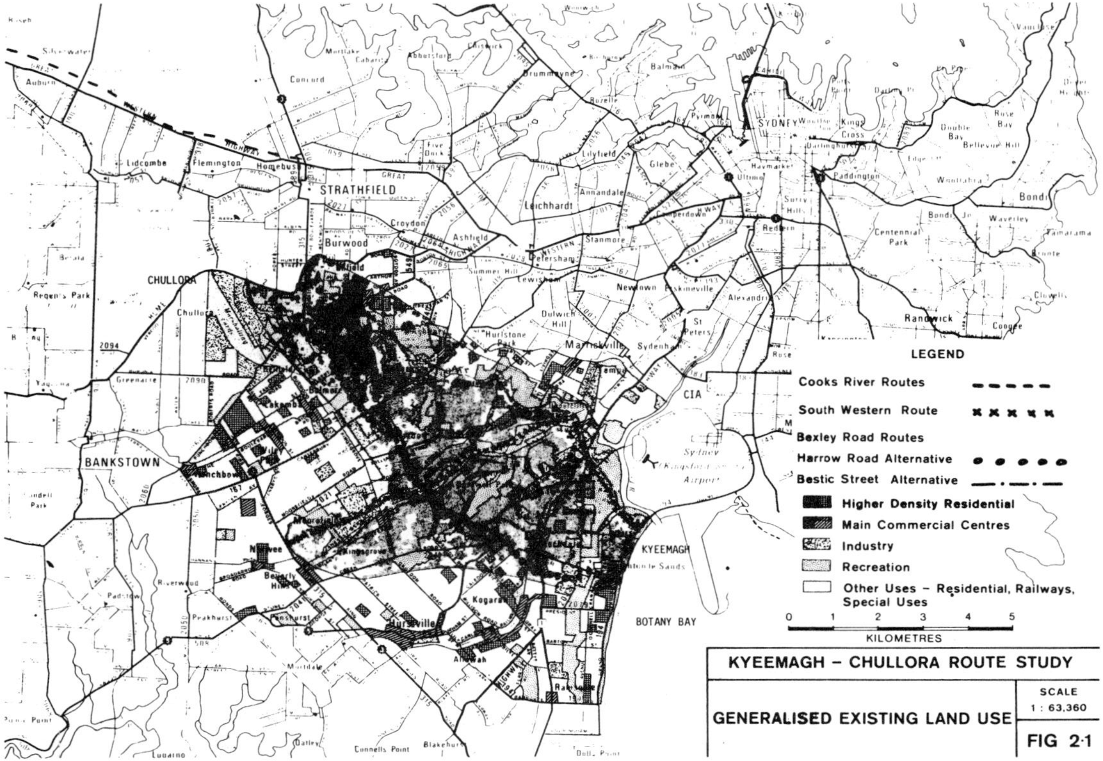

LEGEND
Cooks River Routes
South Western Route
Bexley Road Routes
Harrow Road Alternative
Bestic Street Alternative
Higher Density Residential
Main Commercial Centres
Industry
Recreation
Other Uses – Residential, Railways, Special Uses
0 1 2 3 4 5
KILOMETRES
KYEEMAGH – CHULLORA ROUTE STUDY
GENERALISED EXISTING LAND USE
SCALE
1 : 63,360
FIG 2·1
SYDNEY
STRATHFIELD
CHULLORA
BANKSTOWN
KYEEMAGH
BOTANY BAY
Burwood
Leichhardt
Lidcombe
Flemington
Homebush
Concord
Ashfield
Croydon
Stanmore
Newtown
Glebe
Annandale
Lilyfield
Marrickville
Dulwich Hill
Hurlstone Park
Summer Hill
Petersham
Lewisham
Sydenham
St Peters
Alexandria
Redfern
Paddington
Kings Cross
Randwick
Coogee
Bondi
Waverley
Centennial Park
Rose Bay
Double Bay
Drummoyne
Balmain
Pyrmont
Ultimo
Haymarket
Surry Hills
Chullora
Greenacre
Regent's Park
Auburn
Riverwood
Padstow
Peakhurst
Kogarah
Hurstville
Mortdale
Oatley
Connells Point
CIA

Figure 5.2 The principal road options studied

3   Where there is no prudent or feasible alternative, and where, despite the best efforts of engineering design, schemes will still have a damaging effect upon the community or upon the environment, do they demonstrate high economic rates of return?

At the time the inquiry was appointed, a study was already under way, arising from a directive from the NSW Government to the road building authority (RBA) and the environmental authority. This required an evaluation of alternative proposals for a major road to link the Botany Bay/central industrial area with the western and south-western parts of Sydney. The study was used as the main background document to the inquiry (referred to as the 'joint study report'). The options proposed at the start of the inquiry are known as: (a) the Cooks River option (CRO); (b) the south-western option (SWO); (c) the Bexley Road Harrow Street) option (BRO(H)), and (d) the Bexley Road (Bestic Street) option (BRO(B)). The routes are shown in figure 5.2, together with other relevant spatial information. The specification of each option is briefly summarised as follows:

CRO: A new 13 km arterial road with signal controlled intersections at major cross streets; 50 per cent would be six lanes with a median strip, 50 per cent four lanes with no median. The alignment was established in 1951 as a road corridor. Two sub-options were evaluated, a 'minimum property effect' and a 'maximum open space' alternative; each differing in the breadth of the band of open space between the route and the Cooks River. It absorbs a number of important parks adjacent to a river. Estimated capital cost of $50 million.

SWO: A new 16.7 km arterial road; about one-third identical to the CRO alignment. The remainder is one carriageway of a planned freeway, two lanes of traffic each way and no median. Grade-separated at major cross roads. Median not considered for cost reasons only ($4 million). Passes through the only remnant of natural vegetation in this area of Sydney and absorbs 36 hectares of important open space. Estimated capital cost of $56 million.

BRO(H) and BRO(B):   Upgrading and connecting of existing roads to form a continuous four-lane route with no median and appropriate bypasses at ends where major suburban shopping centres are located. This is the low cost option (approximately half of CRO). It is characterised by a series of steep hills and shallow valleys; with curves of radii as low as 60m and grades up to 8 per

119

cent. It is not sufficiently wide to permit a median strip. Land use on both sides is residential with a heavy sprinkling of schools (mainly infant and primary). Estimated capital cost of $17 million.

The inquiry process was complicated by the presence of two related issues, the plans for a second Sydney airport and the future role of the central industrial area (CIA). The existing airport and the CIA are in close proximity to the eastern end of the road options (see figure 5.2). An early task of the inquiry was to establish the relationship between the road options and the traffic implications of the airport and the CIA. This turned out to be a secondary matter.[2] The proposed options would carry some airport traffic but it was forecast to represent only a minor proportion of total traffic flow; most airport traffic, predominantly cars, did not come from the west/south west. The inquiry concluded that the airport could not justify any of the options.

The central industrial area is undergoing change[3] with the resident population remaining stable or slowly declining. The number of jobs is declining with the manufacturing industry being replaced by warehousing and freight forwarding. Car traffic was expected to decline (1 per cent) and truck traffic marginally to increase (3 per cent). New council ordinances requiring significant amounts of open space would reduce the floor space per hectare for redeveloped old manufacturing establishments, further restricting the growth of traffic. The average trip length for commercial traffic was relatively short. The inquiry concluded that the proposed road options would cater for the smaller commercial traffic volumes generated by the CIA.

The western and south-western regions of Sydney, potential beneficiaries of the proposals, are major growth regions. The western region is 44 per cent of the physical area of the Sydney metropolitan area, with in 1976, 25 per cent of Sydney's population. As outer areas, the population forecasts are necessarily more speculative for outer than for inner areas. Assumptions were initially over-optimistic, reflected in 1991 traffic growth forecasts — as high as 32 per cent.

2 Forecasts of airport traffic were made as part of the CIA study (prior to the Major Airport Needs aviation forecasts) and by the Bureau of Transport Economics (as part of the Major Airport Needs study). The CIA study forecast 79,000 vehicle trips per day to and from the airport in 1985, and 83,000 in 1990. These forecasts were criticised during the study as high, failing to accommodate higher fares due to scarcer aviation fuel and less disposable income. The Bureau of Transport Economics initially forecast a 275 per cent increase up to year 2000, over the 1976 level of passenger movements, using a medium forecast with unconstrained growth. Since the initial forecasts, revisions (down) of population growth have led to support for the low estimates; 60,000 vehicle trips per day in 1985, and 10,200 am peak vehicle trips to the airport.
3 Manufacturing jobs have declined by 31 per cent between 1969 and 1977; and the resident labour force declined between 6 and 17 per cent between 1971 and 1976.

Sources of information

Four sources of information were used in the inquiry: the cost–benefit analysis (including demand forecasting), formal submissions, public hearing transcripts, and traffic data. The major debates centred around the traffic forecast model and output, and its relationship to the issue of 'getting container trucks out of residential streets'. Forecasts of the traffic used two techniques: extrapolation of traffic growth (based on daily monitoring of vehicles at counting stations) and a four-step aggregate transport planning model (Stopher and Meyburg, 1975). The study area was (correctly) viewed as part of the Sydney area and the trip assigment model calibrated by the State Transport Study Group (STSG) on 11,000 links, using 1976 data and applied areawide. A 1991 trip table was developed for the 500 traffic zones, given assumptions on population, employment, other activities and car ownership. The 1991 forecasts were restricted to the am peak vehicle trips (passenger only) using a single (low) population projection and a single set of assumptions:

(a) workforce participation ratio of 0.42 (equal to the 1976 estimates);

(b) employment distribution based on continuation of present trends;

(c) car ownership levels increasing from 0.364 vehicles per person in 1976 to 0.426 vehicles per person in 1991;

(d) use of vehicles in the peak not being constrained by either availability or price of fuel;

(e) public transport fares on government services being 50 per cent of 1976 levels (in real terms), and equal to the 1976 levels on private services;

(f) petrol prices (in real terms) double 1976 levels;

(g) parking charges double 1976 levels (in real terms), with central business district level charges being more widely applied;

(h) congestion on the road system, regionwide, not changing substantially.

Expansion factors (5.5 for cars, 8.5 for other) were subsequently applied to obtain daily benefits. The 1991 base case ('do nothing' situation) included roadworks already programmed for completion before 1991. A complication of major concern arose in the modelling because two trip tables (C and D) were used at various stages, table D

121

correcting for some major omissions in C (notably the omission of a major population jurisdiction in the south-west). Unfortunately no re-analyses of forecasts put into the economic evaluation were undertaken. The joint study report results were based on trip table C whereas a subsequent report by the road authority was based on trip table D. It became evident later that the relativities between options are absolutely consistent irrespective of which trip table was employed. However, the worth of all options, compared to that of other road investment, did become an issue, and one on which little light could be shed.

The contribution of cost—benefit analysis

The contribution of a cost—benefit analysis depends on (a) how it handles option definition; (b) how it generates options for analysis; (c) the quality of the underlying information, and (d) how the items of cost and benefit are treated. All these raise questions about how results are presented. The quality of these determines what use, if any, an inquiry has for CBA.

The main problem on *option definition* arose because the 'do-nothing' alternative was left implicit. The committed programme and implications of varying the staging of commitments, which affected measured rates of return on the other options, were mentioned but not explicitly evaluated. This became an important concern when the road authority redefined the base from which calculations were originally made. The 'extended base' included further works on the south-western corridor beyond the SWO which, in combination, increased the benefit—cost ratio of the SWO to 4.9 (from 1.7).[4] But it was feasible to separate the study area part of the SWO, relevant for the inquiry. The calculations concerning this were termed the 'marginal' calculations, presented as being different in kind from others. They produced considerably less impressive positive results than the SWO plus its extended base viewed as a joint project. It was not appreciated by the RBA that *all* relevant calculations are marginal in the sense of proceeding from a given base. Moreover, it became clear that in general healthier B/C ratios were associated with projects outside the study area.

This raised the question of the complementarity of options. The inquiry's terms of reference viewed them as pure substitutes. The joint study report had the effect of directing the inquiry along the line of option competitiveness, that is, alternative ways of performing a similar

---

4   The extended base in isolation from SWO has a B/C ratio of 9.6.

122

service. The submissions revealed a partial complementarity, that is that sections of each option were interdependent. The truth now seems to be that the projects serve substantially different populations. However, no tests were undertaken of running the original options in combinations against a common base.

The calculations which were undertaken gave the following results. The initial B/C ratio for the SWO (joint study report) was 1.16. It was modified to remove a minor error in accident 'benefits', giving 1.14. Subsequently the inquiry identified an underestimation of the construction costs of 20 per cent (further reducing the B/C ratio to 0.95); the need for downward revision of SW and W population forecasts, and an expansion factor (for am peak to 24-hour benefits conversion). When the trip table was corrected for the initial deletion of a major population jurisdiction in the south-west the 0.95 became 1.5.

For the Bexley Road options (BRO), the initial B/C ratios (using trip table C) were 1.78 for BRO(H), 1.83 for BRO(B), contrasting with 1.39 for CRO and 1.14 for SWO. After adjusting for a 20 per cent increase in construction costs the B/C ratios were respectively 1.51, 1.54, 1.16 and 0.95. No account of the trip table D correction was taken. The quantified social concerns, e.g. dwellings displaced, properties partially acquired, effects on historic or notable features, jobs displaced, ecological effects and visual effects, with one relatively minor exception (number of homes partly affected), had lower negative impacts on BRO than the other options.

This made the BROs the most attractive of the formally evaluated alternatives, results contrasting markedly with the submission and transcript documentation. The C/B ratios were not reported in the joint study report; as a result the submissions had no opportunity to assess the strength, on face value, of the BRO. The nature of the BRO, namely a modification of an existing series of roads, tended to bring out a great deal of local discontent with the existing roads, something less evident for new alignments.

Throughout the inquiry arguments were put for higher marginal B/C ratios in other parts of the Sydney area. The Bureau of Transport Economics had indicated a 2.0 level nationwide for urban arterials, at 10 per cent discount rate; on this basis the SWO (in study area) and CRO would each be doubtful investments, in CBA terms, when measured correctly as additions to investment further west.

With rare exception (e.g. third London Airport study, second Sydney Airport study), *generation of alternatives* is not given adequate consideration. The inquiry was given a set of options selected without the terms of reference in mind. They preconditioned much of the debate in the inquiry. Negative criticism of documented evidence is always an easier course of debate than substantiation of alternatives based on qualitative judgement, and was duly pursued. But new options were introduced during the inquiry. They might have been picked up by including option selection in the early stages of the inquiry. While this might have necessitated distinguishing levels of evaluation to eliminate options, it would at least have ensured that the relevant set of options for prime consideration were subjected to equal levels of analysis. As it was, the options raised in submissions (a rail alternative, a route north of the airport and various transport systems management alternatives to accommodate truck rerouteing) were not given any cost–benefit analysis at all. Scepticism about CBA was directed to the original, not fresh, options further imbalancing evaluation.

The inclusion of a 'small-scale' option with the large-scale options highlighted difficulties in the quality of underlying information. Apart from the fundamental issue of comparing like with like, the network underlying the traffic forecasting model was too coarse to produce results capable of debate about expected flows on particular links of the network. A disproportionate amount of inquiry time was spent establishing why differences do exist between screenline counts, actual road counts and the model's network link estimates. It was a clear example of the failure of the technicians to present their work simply to the public and the uninformed bureaucrat.

The traffic forecasts for the BRO were more likely to underestimate traffic on the BRO links than the CRO and SWO links, because the relative advantage of the BRO in the set of corridor links was less. But they overestimated traffic on all links. A more appropriate course of action, while maintaining the basic aggregate model, would have been to 'window' the inquiry area, treating the rest of Sydney at the current level of aggregation, but conducting a more fine modelling exercise within the study area. Information was poor because the inquiry was bound to the data inputs and outputs of a modelling process not designed for the purposes of detailed sub-area comparisons of very specific options.

The results which were presented could be criticised for the way in which *items for evaluation* were themselves handled. With respect to the BRO, for example:

1   Costs of construction were underestimated; the costs of re-location and loss of profits are both relevant costs in a forced resumption of properties, and were ignored.

2   The value of properties taken was determined by reference to 'comparable' sales. However the principle was not followed in BRO's case. The value was calculated by reference to the value of properties in the CRO corridor, which were dissimilar. Since the cost estimates were made, the NSW

Government has introduced the Environmental Planning and Assessment Act 1980. Section 116 adds a new element to the principle of compensation: when a person's place of residence is resumed a 'solatium' is payable. This is designed to cushion the blow of having to relocate. The amount suggested, but not yet approved by the court, is 20—25 per cent of the purchase price.

3　The opportunity cost of losing open space was not recognised.

4　Cost estimates did not allow for widening the Hume Highway (part of a major link between Sydney and Melbourne), and demolition of some shops.

5　The expansion factors were viewed as too high.

While the joint study report suggests that all options were better than the base case, further analysis by the STSG for the RBA suggests the contrary (for all options):

CRO　　＝　- $91,000 per annum
SWO　　＝　- $160,000 per annum
BRO(H)　＝　- $63,000 per annum
BRO(B)　＝　- $99,000 per annum

The BRO figures are viewed as low, given the simplified assumptions of the traffic model and topography of the BRO (i.e. the losses might in fact be expected to be even greater). The overall conclusion for the BRO is that safety of road users and adjoining residents should not be traded off against increased capital costs of other alternatives.

Some lessons from the inquiry

An inquiry of the magnitude of the Kyeemagh-Chullora Road Inquiry will always be somewhere on a learning curve. However some fundamental lessons have been learnt as important guidelines for future inquiries. This section outlines these lessons under four headings: objectives, sequence and conduct, technical input and personnel.

Objectives

While the terms of reference were well defined, the supporting documents made available to those making formal submissions distorted the full intent of the inquiry, concentrating a disproportionate amount of effort away from the container traffic issue towards commuter travel demand. The initial concern with freight movements and the environmental impacts in residential streets became confounded with technical detail on peak passenger movements. It is the responsibility of an inquiry to ensure that support documentation is not in itself used to direct the debate to elements of the full objectives that suit the interests of a third party. The inquiry failed in ensuring representative support material. The source documents also gave no balanced consideration to public transport alternatives, a particularly deficient element in the light of a comment in a formal submission by one of the joint authors of the source document:

> Whilst the south-western may be serving a corridor with possibly greater long-term demand, much of this can be satisfied by public transport which runs parallel to it. Construction of a road would tend to accelerate the decline in patronage of existing rail services (Submission 947, Attachment A, Appendix 7, 2−3).

In ensuring adequate linking of objectives and source material, a necessary, but not sufficient, condition is that at least a road authority, a public transport authority and a land-use authority should prepare a joint contribution. The public transport authority displayed disinterest in preparing, during the inquiry, a comparative source document. In evidence it was stated:

> The Commission did not see that it had a need to respond in detail to the Inquiry. In the past all roads have been constructed without a great deal of input from the Public Transport Commission, and it was only recently that we saw there was a need for more detailed input into the Inquiry (Transcript ATC, 2).

As a consequence any arguments for, and against, public transport were highly generalised. The same concern is expressed about the insufficient attention given to the possibility of strengthening the existing road system; a notable omission was that no account was taken of SCAT (Sydney Coordinated Adaptive Traffic System) in formulating the base case. SCAT is assumed to increase the capacity of the road network by as much as 10 per cent, making 1991 traffic conditions similar to current levels except where very high growth is predicted. If SCAT has such potential benefits, then intersection improvements may be a preferred investment rather than major road options, or in conjunction with major road options.

Sequence and conduct

The inquiry illustrated the problems that arise when major modifications are made to the source documents after the submissions are complete. It made a mockery of the process. A further source document from the road authority not only confused the non-technical parties, it also exposed their attitude to the original set of options. The additional report was prepared by consultants who, in closer liaison with another government authority, were able to prepare a document (in the name of the road authority) without scrutiny for consistency and for statements of great implication. This document was designed to promote the south-west option, by viewing it as part of a commitment beyond the study area. Indeed it became clear that the road authority viewed all the initial options as low priority; using the inquiry as some kind of holding operation which does not necessitate a detailed justification of highly specific routes. The 1,429 submissions were supplied with route specific assessments. While one of the inquiry's roles might be viewed as that of identifying such positions, it appears highly questionable that such a role should be predominant. Its predominance in this inquiry has not added positively to the reputation of the inquiry process. Future inquiries should seek out this position early in the sequence, preferably while the source documents are being prepared.

Although the error in the trip tables did not affect the relativities amongst the options, it had a disenfranchising effect on a large segment of the community which believed it made its submissions upon a false premise. Many lacked the energy to redo their submissions.

The inquiry demonstrated the benefits of informality in public participations. Parties were given the right to respond to the submissions or evidence of any other party before the inquiry. The only legal concept used in the inquiry was 'onus'. If someone maintained that something should be done, it is up to the person to make a case for change.

Technical input

There was a great deal of modelling input. Standard procedures were applied using existing techniques and data; if the technique was unsuitable no alternative was available, if the data was inappropriate no new data was obtained. The result was that the needs of the inquiry had to fit into the technical specifications traditionally used by authorities — this conditional relationship hampered the resolution of many technical issues, many of which could have been answered if the inquiry process included technical specification, data and estimation. The dialogue was two-way but the technical input was one-way, and very much predetermined. The phrase 'inquiry *process*' is questionable in this inquiry.

The traffic model was stretched beyond its capacity. Very specific increases and decreases were suggested for individual links. The networks were developed to illuminate investment at a higher level such as priorities in major corridors. However, the need to have any information about the proposed options overcame methodological good sense. There was as a consequence the absurd spectacle of debates about expected flows on *particular* links of the network and how they *individually* are expected to grow.

There was a conflict between the need to identify levels of traffic passing through certain shopping centres, traffic filtering through residential areas, and a traffic model which reproduced flows on a network which was not sufficiently detailed to assess traffic on local streets. The model was calibrated on traffic flows during a period outside the period of major use of the shopping centres. The network used was not a reliable basis to draw inferences on traffic away from residential areas.

Cost—benefit analysis (CBA), in the sense of both values and underlying models, became an active issue, but the groundwork for economic understanding had not been laid. CBA forces greater precision of thinking about the definition of projects and the comparisons to be made, and treats options in a consistent way. However, no sense of the uses and limits of CBA could be conveyed because their uses and limits had not been decided internally in the road authority. This undermined the cohesion and consistency of the presentation of source documents.

It was pointed out in the introduction that CBA's essential contribution to the inquiry was to reveal, not settle, conflicts of interest. Might it however have been more influential in the conclusions made had the analytical shortcomings been avoided?

Doubtless, the techniques and data could and should have been made more directly relevant. An outside standard or standards for payoffs to road investment, in comparable CBA terms, would have greatly helped. We have noticed several other drawbacks in the analysis. But it would have been extremely difficult to have produced CBA studies to have coped with all the options eventually deemed relevant by the parties concerned. They were simply too diverse and numerous, a consequence of an exceptionally open mode of inquiry. Partly also, the diversity arose because the measured options were not simply alternative routes; they served quite dissimilar sets of interests. Moreover equal treatment, via CBA methods, for all options (even if treated widely) would have greatly extended the inquiry period; and since options were being formulated practically all through, any cutoff would have appeared particularly attractive in allocative or efficiency terms; each had low priority in the Department of Main Roads' plans for road development. The issues confronting the inquiry were overwhelmingly distributive. Certain interests clearly bore more of existing costs than others and were likely to do in any solution. There could have been more attention, in measurement terms, to distributive issues. For example, no measure, simple or complex, of the populations at risk to different types of hazard was even attempted. Here again, however, proliferation of options would have proved a handicap had the attempt been made.

The conclusion for analysts and others contemplating the future for CBA analysis on inquiries must be that it may well pay to adapt measurement procedures to the facts of inquiry processes, rather than to attempt to impose a standard, conventional CBA as a means of settling upon the preferred option. Added sophistication *would* have clarified issues in this case; but it could hardly have provided a convincing solution to the problems facing the inquiry. If CBA is to adapt to the needs of inquiries a premium must be placed on speedy production of relevant information about the many options which appear during the inquiry process. In this particular inquiry, committed to wide participation, there was a special need for direct access by parties to formulate their objections and suggestions on CBA terms.

The general public must have some basis for assessing the technical content, so that a clear distinction can be made between the concern about the method and the concern about an option *per se*. If the strengths and weaknesses of CBA are made explicit, then the inquiry process can concentrate efforts on useful debate. While its role as a medium for educating the interested parties should not be played down, nevertheless education requires complete exposure of the pros and cons of all approaches to problem solving, something markedly lacking in this inquiry. One reason for this is the suitability of personnel.

Personnel

The full-time inquiry professional personnel all had a legal background; the government authorities were represented by a well qualified team of engineers, planners and one economist. At a somewhat late date in the inquiry (twelve months after it began), consultant advisers were appointed who had backgrounds in economics, transport planning and town planning. The advisers were very much part-time. The bureaucratic dispersal of technical expertise made it exceedingly difficult for the inquiry to pursue lines of further inquiry both because of the division of labour and the special position of confidence held by the major 'modelling' authority. The lack of in-house specialists in the road authority on economic and transport demand matters, together with the lack of in-house expertise in the inquiry team between them explain much of the reason for the poor source documentation. An 'inquiry process' must be effective in lines of communication, which requires both in-house technical expertise to have a dialogue with the sources of technical detail, and in-house communication expertise to ensure that all contributors to the inquiry understand the matters of detail.

Conclusion — some benefits of the inquiry

> There was a time when people were satisfied to express their views upon the action of Governments at an election every three years. That time has passed. People demand a say in matters which intimately affect them. And so they ought. The Government and Inquiries are likely to make better decisions if they are made aware of the community's view (Inquiry, IV, 5)

The inquiry process should provide a dispassionate and rational balancing of the interests of the community and a number of Government departments, including the departments responsible for public transport, for roads, and the environment. Each department has its own empire. Each has its own perspective. Each is less well placed than an outsider, therefore, to see the broad canvas. An outsider inevitably brings his or her own prejudices. But the decision is less vulnerable to attack than one made by the nominee of only one department, or even a committee comprising representatives of all departments.

The inquiry process is one of assembling the evidence. The inquiry is also called upon to make recommendations. Its recommendations, however, are not the final word. The matter is then open to debate. Hopefully the debate will be better informed by the inquiry having traversed the ground beforehand. The ultimate decision must be made by the elected representatives of the community. That is entirely appropriate.

There are benefits in periodically calling upon the bureaucracy to justify its actions. There was one dramatic illustration in the inquiry. The RBA in presenting the south-western option chose an alignment on one side of the valley. The inquiry explored the possibility of placing the road on the other side. The result was startling. The revised alignment had the following advantages:

It was $6 million cheaper ($A50 million compared to $A56 million).

Fifty fewer homes would be demolished, which was approximately one-third of the total.

Ten hectares of open space would be preserved (26 ha compared to 36 ha).

Significant environmental features, including certain large sandstone cliffs, would remain intact.

Given the clear advantages, financially and environmentally, of the revised alignment, why was the original alignment chosen? The answer was extraordinary. The inquiry report quotes from the transcript of the RBA:

> From the point of view of ease of constructing the second carriageway in the future, it is easier now to build the western carriageway because it must be accepted that when we need to build a second carriageway, and if we have to construct through environmentally significant features, that in the future this is going to be harder than at present. (Inquiry, IV, 238)

Later the following was said:

> . . . It is possibly better to grasp the nettle and build the carriageway which has the most significant environmental impact first so that the job in the future is made easier, bearing in mind that there appears to be [a] continuing increase in reaction of people to large public works programmes. (Ibid)

The approach seemed to the inquiry to be odd. The second carriageway may never be needed. The following exchange took place:

> COMMISSIONER: I am just trying to [understand] what seems to me [to be] something of a paradox. It is one thing if you know you are definitely going to need something in the future. I can well understand in that situation why one may perhaps grasp the nettle now; but in a situation where the future is very much unknown, it becomes a little less easy to understand [why the western carriageway was chosen]. Where the environmental impacts of the two alternatives are different, the cost of the two is different, and the amount of disruption in terms of people being displaced is different, and the difference in each case favours the route which was not selected by the Department, that prima facie seems to be odd.

> RBA: Much of what you have just described has only become known subsequent to participation in the inquiry. (Inquiry, IV, 239)

The shortcomings of the alignment chosen by the RBA were a matter of embarrassment to them. The mere presence of the inquiry process, and the possibility of its decisions being closely scrutinised, is likely to improve the decisions which are made. An occasional inquiry has a deterrent effect far beyond the matter examined.

Departments which hitherto had confined themselves either to matters of public transport, or to the building of roads, or the environment, were forced to consider all three. Their sharp focus may have been upon their particular speciality but their field of vision, when making a presentation before the inquiry, had to encompass each of the other disciplines. There can be little doubt the inquiry process has made the bureaucracy far more sensitive to the environmental and social consequences of its actions than it was before it was called upon to defend its point of view.

References

Commission of Inquiry into the Kyeemagh-Chullora Road (Inquiry), *Kyeemagh-Chullora Road Inquiry*, vols I–IV, New South Wales Government Printer, Sydney, 1981.

Department of Transport, *Report of the Advisory Committee on Trunk Road Assessment*, HMSO, London, 1978.

Stanley, J.K. and Nash, C.A., 'The evaluation of urban transport improvements' in D.A. Hensher (ed.) *Urban Transport Economics*, Cambridge University Press, Cambridge, 1977.

Stopher, P.R. and Meyburg, A.H., *Urban Transportation Modelling and Planning*, Lexington Books, Lexington, 1975.

Wachs, M., 'Transportation policy in the eighties' in *Transportation*, 1977, vol.6, pp. 103–20.

6 The assessment of transport technology

N. J. Ashford and J. M. Clark

Introduction

Any transport plan or strategy, however defined and with whatever objectives, is eventually implemented by innovations in, modifications to or extensions of transport technology. Personal rapid transit systems and high-speed moving pavements may be regarded as genuinely innovatory approaches to the solution of transport problems; dial-a-ride systems, segregated bus lanes and even the introduction of novel pricing policies represent modifications to the operation of existing technology; urban motorway schemes and new railway or tramway lines are examples of extensions of the use of well established technologies. In every case, whether innovatory or conventional technology is applied and whether the scheme involves a large or small commitment of resources, there exists in principle a need to assess the various implications of the scheme in order to establish the extent of the benefits, or disbenefits, which are likely to accrue to the community as a whole.

This chapter is a critical review of the methods currently used in transport technology assessment. It is based upon a reappraisal of the work and experience of the authors themselves, an extensive search of both published and unpublished literature and a large number of interviews with transport practitioners in Western Europe, North America

1 An earlier version of this chapter appeared in *Transportation Planning and Technology*, 1975, vol.3, pp. 31—43. This is a revised and updated version of that paper.

and Japan. One is led to believe that there are serious deficiencies in the available framework of assessment and consequent critical shortcomings in the manner in which technological development is being assessed. A gulf appears to exist between the assumptions inherent in the complex and extensive analytical assessment studies which are presently being carried out and the major issues as perceived in the real world by the decision maker. It is the intention therefore to identify some of the logical weaknesses in assessment methodology and to indicate the areas in which a more applicable and comprehensive framework should be sought.

One can begin by establishing the role of transport technology assessment studies and identifying the major components in any system assessment exercise. The manner in which these components are currently handled can then be described, indicating the factors considered and the weightings commonly placed upon them. This enables the isolation of six areas of assessment criteria with comment on the extent to which they are taken into account in current assessment programmes. Finally, recommendations can be made regarding the establishment of a more realistic and applicable framework for assessment, and suggestions for some of the key areas of research which will assist in developing such an approach.

Role and structure of transport technology assessment

Technology assessment is by no means a new activity and has been widely used in a variety of areas, perhaps most extensively in the defence and weapons fields. Its application to transport is logical, and special problems arise only in so far as modern transport offers a particularly wide range of potential technology options, a very disparate set of implications and the requirement of very high levels of resource allocation. Resource allocation is in fact the key to transport technology assessment. Transport development involves the investment of a wide range of resources including money, time, manpower, materials, energy, environment and many others. Each of these resources is of course finite, but equally they are in principle interchangeable and substitutable. The intention of technology assessment is to ensure that the allocation of these various resources be made in an acceptable fashion, where the notion of acceptability is defined by a set of social, political and economic attitudes which are usually changing, often from year to year. The various impacts of any given technology change must be evaluated in the light of these transitory attitudes and, since many such changes (especially the more innovatory ones) involve long development lead times, there exists a need to forecast the changes in such attitudes.

However, the technology changes themselves are by comparison well defined and predictable, and assessment techniques can in principle lend themselves to the application of sensitivity analysis for the investigation of the more complex variations in social, political and economic attitudes. For this reason, although keenly aware of the many problems of quantification, forecasting and evaluation, technology assessment can be regarded as one of the most coherent and immediately useful approaches to transport planning.

Despite its long history in a variety of investment fields, technology assessment has generally been applied in an *ad hoc* fashion, oriented directly towards the particular problem or situation under study. For most purposes it is important to establish the general principles involved in current transport assessment exercises. One of the present authors has outlined a framework (Clark, 1972) which has proved useful both for describing previous studies and developing new ones. A fuller description may be found in that paper, but it will be useful to reiterate the main stages of the process here.

Any technology change will be experienced in different ways by different categories of person. The operator of a transport system is concerned with: the total operating costs; the revenue he can gain; and the flexibility of the technology to cope with varying demands and attitudes. The user, whether a traveller or customer of a freight transport undertaking, is concerned with such factors as: money cost (usually fare); journey time (from real origin to real destination); safety and security; comfort; and convenience.

The precise definition of the above factors is not important to our present considerations, since most relevant user impacts can conveniently be considered under one of these headings. In addition to these directly involved parties, there remain a large number of people who, while neither travelling themselves nor causing goods or people to move, are affected by the means of movement. These non-users of a transport facility are affected by such factors as: air pollution; noise, visual intrusion; safety; economic effects (sometimes beneficial, sometimes not), and land-use changes.

A successful change in the provision of transport facilities will be one for which the community as a whole benefits from the effects of this change by whatever criteria current obtain (recognising, of course, that almost every change brings benefit to some individuals and disadvantage to others).

In order to evaluate the effects of the change, it is essential to establish the demand for the new system. This is generally done by setting the system in some suitable geographical situation (or preferably a range of such situations), considering the social and economic characteristics of these scenarios, and developing some technique for forecasting the demand for the new system (and importantly for the other systems it will complement).

If such forecasts can successfully be made, it will be possible to know the number of people (or the amount of goods) who will be using the system, the costs and potential revenue for the operator and the number of non-users whose life style will be affected by the change. All that remains is to weight the effects by their social, economic and political importance (however defined) as well as by the number of people involved and establish the extent of benefit or otherwise to the community as a whole; this is no small task.

The foregoing discussion has been necessarily brief, but it indicates the basic stages of any assessment process, namely:

the description of the effects of the change;

the forecasting of the demand for the use of the new system, and

the evaluation of the total benefits of the change.

The following sections discuss the way in which the techniques used in current studies handle these stages and also consider how far these techniques appear to meet the intention of optimal resource allocation to which technology assessment is meant to be applied.

Specification of transport technology impacts

The previous section indicated the types of impact which any technology change and *ipso facto* any transport plan was likely to have on the community at large. Some of these impacts can already be described in a quantified manner. All of the economic and time effects exist by definition in that form. Others, such as noise, air pollution, safety, etc. are readily amenable to measurement at least in terms of their physical effects (decibels, weight of noxious material and numbers of incidents respectively). Most of the other impacts almost appear to defy the concept of quantification. In such cases one can only hope to establish a measure of the perception of the nuisance or advantage involved.

In this context, however, 'only' is clearly a quite inappropriate word. Even in the cases where some element of physical measurement is possible, the numbers so obtained are frequently less relevant than the perception which individuals or groups of people have of the impact involved. Thus, for example, the money cost of operating a private car can be definitively quantified in the range 6–10p per mile (at 1974 prices), depending on the type of vehicle and the extent of usage. The driver's perception of this cost is often substantially less — possibly as low as 1–2p per mile (see Harrison and Quarmby, 1969). Similarly, the measurement of traffic noise adjacent to a busy urban street may indicate very high noise levels. It does not follow that the inhabitants of the houses in that street are significantly disturbed by that noise, and their perception of its importance is a much more meaningful measure for most evaluation purposes.

In most current assessment studies, only the immediately quantifiable variables are treated explicitly. As will be argued later, this frequently leads to a very unbalanced and in some cases irrelevant analysis. There is a clear need to use the techniques of market research and attitudinal surveys to establish quantitative or semi-quantitative measures of people's perceptions of all factors relevant to the decision-making process. In doing so the possibility must not be ignored that the readily quantified variables may not in fact immediately exist in the form in which they are actually perceived.

The establishment of numerical statements concerning the impacts of a technology change provides a specification of that change. This is the fundamental starting point of any assessment exercise. In order that the assessment shall be capable of general application, it is important that the specification should incorporate some understanding of how the factors will vary in different geographical scenarios and over different time periods.

Forecasting travel demand

The next component in the assessment process is travel demand forecasting. Models developed for this purpose are frequently used in two quite different ways:

to provide estimates of the number of travellers who will use the set of modes available to them at some future time;

to infer from travellers' existing behaviour the values they appear to place on various properties of the transport modes.

These are two distinct objectives and the extent to which the models may be regarded as successful depends critically on which of these objectives is the one for which the model is being used. In a sense there have been almost as many forecasting techniques as there have been transport studies, and it is not the intention here to attempt a comprehensive review (see Jones 1977 for a fuller discussion). Instead, comment shall be on the general principles on which most of the existing techniques are based.

Most models are developed in a number of consecutive stages, the first of which is to estimate the total demand for travel within the study area (trip generation). This forecast is almost invariably based solely on a set of socio-economic characteristics. In an urban area typical factors considered include income, car-ownership and number of employed persons. The quality of the transport facilities offered is rarely considered at this stage, and there is thus no mechanism for estimating whether an innovation or development will have the effect of generating new journeys which were not previously made — the so-called latent demand. It is sometimes argued that this is a usefully pessimistic assumption, since if a new system can attract a sufficient proportion of the existing demand to be viable, any additional traffic it generates is a happy bonus. However, this type of uncertainty cannot be regarded as either satisfactory or acceptable.

The next stages are to estimate in more detail how the total demand is distributed in space (trip distribution), and what proportion of this demand will be carried by each of the available modes (modal split). These estimations are generally made by introducing a function, often called generalised cost (for a critique, see Grey 1978), which is intended to describe the properties of the available modes. This function is usually some combination of the money cost and travel time associated with the journey.

Finally, the trip matrix associated with the particular system under study is assigned in detail (trip assignment) to the system network to test its capacity and capability of satisfying the demand. At this stage it is sometimes found that it is impossible to supply enough of the facility to satisfy the total demand and this point is recognised by suppressing a part of the total trip matrix. This represents a sort of negative latent demand effect. Some rudimentary techniques have been developed to simulate it, but few of them appear to describe adequately the spatial, modal and temporal redistribution of trips which occurs in consequence.

It has frequently been suggested that this four stage prediction process (generation, distribution, modal split and assignment) although convenient to apply in practice does not in fact reflect the decisions which potential travellers are taking. Intuitively it seems probable that decisions as to whether or not to travel, where to travel to and which mode to use are highly interdependent, and therefore they should be modelled simultaneously. Accordingly, a variety of models have been proposed which attempt to do this, and they are frequently referred to as integrated models, abstract mode models or utility models. These are both conceptually more satisfying and are in principle capable of taking account of a larger number of relevant factors. However, the specification

138

of the utility function is a major source of difficulty and many attempts to use the approach merely define a simple example function which does little more than reproduce in more elegant terms the conventional modelling strategy.

Despite these drawbacks, integrated models are pointing the way to advances in forecasting procedures. For example, considerable success has been achieved in the interurban context with an abstract mode model developed by British Rail (Tyler and Hassard 1973), which appears to forecast adequately patronage of rudimentary specifications of the properties of competing modes. The argument is that rail type travellers make rail type trips for rail type purposes and the element of complete choice which conventional models tend to assume is largely illusory. Similar arguments can be advanced in the urban context where limitations in mode availability for specific trip purposes and types of traveller considerably restrict the range of choice actually available. Furthermore, the developing use of attitudinal and market research techniques to establish in quantitative form and at a disaggregated level the factors which influence traveller behaviour, promise to offer a much more explicit understanding of choice phenomena if they can be successfully incorporated in mathematical models.

However, at present it largely remains the case that demand models are basically crude and take account only of simple ideas about the effects of economic and industrial activity and of the money costs and travel times associated with making journeys. In consequence, these models lack the robustness which would give them credibility and enable them to be applied without extensive recalibration in different geographical scenarios and over different time periods. This point is particularly relevant where attempts are made to infer values placed on mode attributes from such models. At present the values inferred are no more than curve-fitting parameters which may be quite useful for forecasting purposes in a limited and carefully chosen number of situations, but attempts to use these values for evaluation purposes are frequently very suspect.

This discussion of demand forecasting techniques has been intentionally brief. It is generally accepted that the issues influencing the demand for travel must depend upon:

the purpose for which the trip is to be made (which encompasses the activities being pursued at both ends of the trip);

the properties of the modes of travel available (and particularly the perception the intending traveller has of these properties);

the nature and attitudes of the person or persons intending to make the trip.

The extent to which existing models fail to deal adequately with these issues is sufficiently demonstrated by the points made so far. The authors are aware of, and indeed are involved with, several studies which aim to extend the models so as to take these issues explicitly into account. However, before embarking on a comprehensive critique of such approaches, it is important to establish the criteria and methods by which transport technology developments should be evaluated. The remainder of this chapter concentrates on this aspect, and attempts to provide a framework both within which such evaluations can be undertaken more successfully and which provide a basis for a coherent discussion of system impact and demand modelling to be pursued.

Evaluation techniques

Cost—benefit analysis

In a great many countries, cost—benefit analysis or more restrictive approaches such as cost-effectiveness studies are the preferred (in some cases statutory) methods of evaluation. In basic terms, the discounted stream of money costs is compared with the discounted stream of benefits converted into monetary terms. Where benefit—cost ratios in excess of unity are obtained, the project or plan is considered worthwhile. Where alternatives are to be evaluated, that with the highest benefit—cost ratio or the highest marginal benefit—cost ratio is selected (Pearce and Nash, 1981). These methods frequently lead to calculations of great complexity but the value of these calculations can never be better than the accuracy with which the multiplicity of factors influencing the decision can be described and quantified. Since so very few of these factors are currently described even in detail (whether or not with accuracy), it is scarcely surprising that the results of cost—benefit analysis have in the recent past appeared to become less relevant to the actual decision making. A case in point is the selection of the Foulness site for the third London Airport in the face of strong cost—benefit arguments in favour of all the other evaluated sites. The work of the Roskill Commission Study team must rank as one of the most extensive cost—benefit analyses ever carried out (Commission on the Third London Airport, 1971). The rejection of the majority findings of the Commission by the British Government is perhaps a classic example of the result of the application of an evaluation technique to a problem too complex for the technique itself. This is not to criticise the methods, which are in principle very much more powerful than their present application and appreciation by decision makers would imply. There is a serious danger, however, in using powerful and sophisticated techniques in an incomplete fashion, particularly since the complex and detailed technical arguments sometimes appear to suggest a spurious accuracy. The credibility of assessment studies is done a great disservice each time the recommendations of a study are seen by intelligent laymen to be 'obviously wrong'. Often this is due to the fact that in cost—benefit analysis, quantification in money terms is essential for inclusion; the exclusion of unquantifiable amenity considerations may render the exercise unreliable.

The application of cost—benefit analysis to the development of transport technology raises serious fundamental questions. First, the treatment of externalities as additional monetary costs and benefits to be added into the direct cash flow stream is a source of constant disagreement among planners themselves; a situation which inspires the political decision maker with little confidence in the final evaluation result. For example, there appears to be little general community agreement on the true value of noise disturbance, which can be related to either the amount an individual is willing to pay to avoid noise or to the amount he is willing to receive as compensation for enduring it (Ollerhead, 1973).

There is similar disagreement both on the true value of travel time savings and the question of whether very small time savings have any value at all. Often called 'notional values', such indirect costs and benefits account for a large proportion of the total costs and benefits in the more sophisticated analyses. The stability of such notional values over the very long periods of time which must be considered in the evaluation of new technology is highly questionable at a time when such writers as Kahn and Wiener (1967) indicate that values will undergo substantial change as the developed nations enter the post-industrial phase.

The question of the discount rate itself poses severe philosophical questions when examined in the context of long-term technological planning. In many countries, for example the USA and UK, it has been required for years that public investment should bring rates of return that reflect to some degree return on capital invested in the private sector (e.g. see Cmnd.7131, 1978 for a summary of UK policy). Under current conditions, the use of high discount rates might therefore appear rational in the evaluation of technological development. High discount rates tend, however, to militate against the long term in favour of the short term. Economic planners use the discount rate to reflect future uncertainty. High discount rates in conjunction with very long-term planning periods effectively nullify consideration of long-term impacts. Thus discounting, by its very nature, tends to favour the short term in an evaluation procedure which may well attempt to analyse long-term impacts. If a government is seen to be the custodian of the nation's future interests in addition to its current needs, it would seem irrational to act on decisions made primarily on economic justifications where the future is heavily discounted by the application of current discount rates applied largely to notional values determined under current conditions.

In as much as the philosophy of cost—benefit analysis has been well documented (Mishan, 1972) it is sufficient to summarise these comments by indicating that the technique offers severe problems when applied to very long-term planning. Numerous other evaluation procedures appear in the literature offering alternatives to cost—benefit analysis. Some planning techniques are so complex in conception and application that it is fair comment to state that they relate more to the satisfaction of the intellectual demands of the technocrat than providing a realistic basis for policy making by a decision maker. Experience of statewide transport planning in Massachusetts, urban transport planning in Nottingham, the planning of the third London Airport and motorway planning in Toronto, clearly indicate that unless decision makers are satisfied that assessment procedures are comprehensive and logical, the planner faces the prospect of summary rejection of his proposals. Such rejections, often deprecated as 'political' in fact reflect the politicians' need for a comprehensive evaluation of all factors that impinge on the investment decision. Too often, this comprehensive view is clearly lacking in evaluation procedures which strive for mathematical rather than philosophical rigour.

Planning balance sheet

A modification of the cost—benefit evaluation technique which seriously attempts to deal with the overall implications of a planned change is the planning balance sheet (Lichfield, 1960, 1964, 1970). Its application in the past has been principally in the area of urban and regional planning, although there is no theoretical reason why this could not be applied to the evaluation of long-term transport planning. Essentially, this technique recognises that whereas a definite evaluation of a proposal from the viewpoint of all affected individuals is impossible, it should be feasible to divide the community into affected groups. Having defined these groups or 'actors', their accrued costs and benefits as a result of the alternative proposals are compiled and compared. Non-monetary considerations, for example disruption and time impacts, are quantified and immeasurable factors are taken into account.

Thus the balance sheet cannot, and does not, aim to provide a conclusion in terms of rate of return or net profit measured by money values as is the case in some typical cost benefit studies.

Its value lies in exposing the implications of each set of proposals to the whole community, and in indicating how the alternatives might be improved to produce a better result. (Lichfield, 1969)

Lichfield's approach substantially broadens the evaluation procedure. Planning balance sheet has been used in the evaluation of transport and the Leitch Committee (Department of Transport, 1978) favours the adoption of a modified form, the project impact matrix, in road investment appraisal. This particular application of the methodology was a highly quantitative approach to non-quantifiable variables using rank scores and implicit factor weights. A less quantitative approach would better correspond to the uncertainties of long-term technology development, yet still accord with the general theory of the planning balance sheet. The strength of the method lies in the identification of the principal actor groups affected by plans and the inclusion of non-quantifiable impacts.

Goals achievement matrices

Goals achievement matrices have been developed in an effort to measure the combined effect of financial, quantitative and qualitative impacts of plans (Hill, 1967, 1968). Earlier work had recommended similar procedures for evaluating transport plans specifically (Jessiman et al., 1964). The procedure hinges on the ability of the analyst to specify a definitive number of goals to be achieved by a plan and to apply weights to individual criteria within the goal areas. Plans are scored by the degree to which the criteria are met. Discussions with the Japanese National Railway, for example, indicate that the selection of mag-lev technology has proceeded from an evaluation of how well the system could meet the following criteria:

(a) approximate speed of 500 km/hr;
(b) ability to carry large numbers of passengers and freight;
(c) safety and comfort;
(d) dependability;
(e) minimum pollutants;
(f) convenience, and
(g) economic self sufficiency at reasonable prices.

Because of the apparent ability to include a variety of heterogeneous considerations while reducing the evaluation output to a single quantitative score, this evaluation procedure has proved popular in evaluating new technology (Columbia Transit Program, 1970). The goals achievement matrix in its purest form suffers from the failure to take note of the social justice of the solution which has been reached via the goal of maximising an implicit objective function without setting minimum levels of achievement in critical areas.

Rational models

This problem is to some degree overcome by an evaluation procedure suggested some time ago and which has been used in adaptation in various areas since. Threshold analysis selects and defines the criteria by which a plan or technology is to be evaluated. In each of the criterial areas, minimum acceptable levels of achievement are defined. Systems which fail to reach these minimum levels are rejected or redesigned in such a way that they can meet the prescribed threshold levels. Selection between systems meeting the necessary entrance requirements is carried out by a single dimensional analysis technique such as cost—benefit or the optimisation of some objective function. Threshold analysis and goals achievement matrices can be regarded as special cases of the rational model of conventional systems analysis (Schoeffler, 1954; Baumol, 1965; Ackoff, 1962) which seeks to:

define system objectives and construct from these objectives a system utility function;

enumerate all possible alternate courses of action;

identify the consequence of each alternate course of action;

compute the system consequences in terms of effect on the utility function, and

select the system which produces the best utility function.

It has been found that socio-political decisions such as transport are not amenable to such a simplistic approach for various reasons. System objectives are not clear and unidimensional; it is not possible to define all feasible alternate courses of action; nor is it possible to estimate system consequences to the degree of precision that this sort of analysis requires. Finally, should it be possible to construct some form of utility function it could clearly not be unidimensional, and in the absence of known trade-offs between various factors, system selection is not possible.

Factor profiles

It is fairly clear that a number of the evaluation procedures in current use rely on procedures which weight various factors entering into consideration. Often these weightings are applied to a mixture of quantitative and qualitative factors in an effort to make comparisons between plans with differing end products, impacts and externalities. In most cases, the subjective selection of factor weights hides the implicit assumption of trade-offs between factors. The evaluation procedure thereby acquires a degree of complexity of an order different from the reliability of the input information in the case of very long-range forecasting.

Since weighting, with its implicit assumptions of known trade-off coefficients, appears unjustifiable, what type of judgement is the technological planner in a position to supply? Oglesby et al., faced this problem squarely in their approach to community decision making by modifying cost–benefit analysis to reflect community opinion by the use of factor profiles (Oglesby et al., 1970). After the argued rejection of weighting procedures, it is recommended that, in evaluating alternative road plans, beneficial changes in the factor profile should be compared with incremental cost–benefit relationships on a systematic basis. A somewhat similar procedure was used at one stage of selection of the third London Airport (Llewelyn Davies and Associates, 1970). This would imply that the planner, while unable to quantify the trade-offs between factors is able on the basis of professional experience and judgement to advise on the relative importance of factors and therefore implicitly to be able to apply rankings with some degree of certainty. Oglesby's system, which appears rational for the purpose designed, presents some problems in application directly to long-term technological planning. Financial forecasts are much more tenuous and the construction of factor profiles for future impacts would be largely conjectural and essentially non-quantitative.

Problem-solving process model

The generation and testing of an array of different transport options by conventional systems analysis has been recognised for some time as having underlying conceptual problems (Manheim, 1966). This form of analysis is therefore seen to be an arid approach. Predicting the possible shifts in demand, related as they are to the structure of social and economic activity, the nature and patterns of land use and population, present the planner with identifiable difficulties. There is an underlying requirement not only for an understanding of the basic structure of the economic and social system, but also for a knowledge of both the workings of policy making and the specific role that transport can take in the modification of growth patterns and of the social and economic structure itself. Manheim (1969) points out that the framework of analysis of transport systems relates to:

the generation of a limited, feasible set of options each comprising a meaningful system worth testing with complex models;

the determination of the equilibrium relationship between the supply of facilities and the generated demand, and

the specification and evaluation of impacts and the choice between alternative actions.

Transportation choices have been described as essentially socio-political choices where the differing interests of the various groups are considered and balanced. It has been suggested that, where transport is viewed in context with a number of supplementary programmes, concerted strategies can be evolved which ensure that no single group is unduly penalised (Manheim et al., 1967).

In an effort to organise and process the large amounts of data available, planners have put forward the problem-solving process (PSP) model which utilises computer techniques to provide the planner with the ranking of alternative solutions (Manheim, 1967; Manheim et al., 1968). This procedure is based on an iterative procedure which:

formulates goal statements;

carries out search procedures which produce solutions which relate to the stated goals;

selects among the alternative solutions to provide a ranking relative to goal structure;

based on determined solutions, adjusts the goal statements where necessary.

This approach appears to represent a clear advance over the rational model in its abandonment of the search for that single dimensional transform of multidimensional goals, the utility or objective function. Manheim (1969) further indicates a clear insight into the true complexities of quantifying decisions which are truly political and social by stating:

The analyst uses predictive models and search techniques to stimulate his perception and understanding of the problem. Neither the predictive model system nor the 'kit' of search techniques will specify the solution to a transport systems problem. The systematic analysis of alternatives and the results of search procedures serve to build up the analyst's image of the issues of a problem. This understanding, conscious and unconscious, provides an experience base from which he will create intuitively that synthesis of technical and political elements with which he will try to solve a transportation problem. The solution comes from the analyst's understanding and imagination, not the models; but the models are an important aid.

While the PSP approach to system or technology selection would appear to represent a more satisfactory approach than other available methods, it appears to lack adequate sensitivity to the involvement of the decision makers themselves in the formulation and reformulation of goals. Decision makers can be interactively involved only when the complexity of the approach is such that the general rationale of the analysis procedures are comprehensible to those responsible for policy. One distinct advantage of the simplistic approach of cost—benefit analysis is that the concept is simple and the underlying substitution of monetary costs for outcomes is understandable. Manheim (1969) appears to be aware of the necessity of operating the PSP model at several levels of analysis, indicating that at gross level the accuracy of the detailed analysis is lost by aggregation. Since failure to involve and carry the decision maker along in the analytical procedure will ultimately lead to arbitrary decision making and, by implication, failure of the assessment process, the PSP model would be strengthened if the model could detail procedures whereby the interaction between analyst and decision maker was effected. To do this it is necessary to define the analytical outputs in a form which enables the decision maker to comprehend fully the implications of the interim decisions being carried out. This would appear to be crucial to the successful implementation of the model and the procedures which are developed must ensure successful interaction. Equally important is the scale of data manipulation in the very complex systems which makes the process of analysis incomprehensible to all except the analyst; the decision maker is effectively isolated by computer technology from the parameters of decision making. Why, one might ask, is the decision maker able to accept the computer calculations of the engineering technologist relating to a vehicle or guideway, yet unable to accept sophisticated computerised techniques in evaluation techniques? The answer must lie, surely, in the fact that whereas the former provides the basis for decision making the latter removes from him the process of decision making itself, presenting him with a *de facto* decision for approval. Successful complex evaluations are therefore possible only when the decision maker works closely with the analyst throughout the period of evaluation analysis to avoid situations such as have recently occurred in such diverse areas as the Spadina Expressway abandonment in Toronto, the rejection of highway development plans in Nottingham, the selection of the Maplin site for the third London Airport and the political failure of bond issues for public transport plans in areas such as Atlanta and New York State.

Six areas of criteria for evaluation

It is clear from our investigations that assessment techniques take into consideration a number of general areas of evaluation criteria. The better techniques appear to attempt to consider a broad range of areas, while more narrowly conceived evaluations clearly ignore several of these criteria.

From a survey of both the theoretical literature and discussions with a wide selection of officials engaged in the evaluation of transport supply, the authors have identified six general areas of evaluation criteria (Clark and Ashford, 1973). Experience would further indicate that where any or all of these criteria are considered they are generally weighted in the following stated order of importance:

1 The availability of the technology or its potential for development.

2 Estimation of demand for travel at a fairly rudimentary level of consideration, taking cognisance of such variables as money cost, travel time and a limited number of socio-economic factors including comfort and convenience.

3 The optimality of financial resource allocation using available techniques. In the evaluation of some modes, time savings are invariably converted into financial benefits using the concept of generalised cost.

4 Some limited, largely qualitative considerations of environmental effects in the areas of:

(a) amenity;
(b) noise pollution;
(c) air pollution;
(d) safety;
(e) water pollution, and
(f) solid waste pollution.

Where physical environmental damage is treated in a quantitative rather than a qualitative manner, the ability to integrate successfully this analysis with stages 2 and 3 above has been questionable and frequently debated at length.

5 Socio-political impacts on the various levels of the national and local community.

6 Constraints on solutions imposed by the limited availability of natural resources.

It would appear from our research that while the above criteria should be considered in the assessment of systems, there is in fact at the level of decision making for system selection and implementation, seldom any consideration of criteria of ranking lower than 4(c) at the technological planning stage. Our findings indicate that the environmental considerations of safety, water and solid waste pollution and the socio-political impacts are areas which receive only minor consideration well after plan formulation, and that the limited availability of natural resources has to all intents and purposes been largely ignored.

These six areas of criteria used in the assessment of transport will in all likelihood remain permanently pertinent to the evaluation of systems. It is however not inconceivable that their relative importance in the assessment procedure will change, resulting in a radical modification in the implicit weighting given to factors. For example, the probability of exhaustion of economically extractable fossil fuels within the next fifty years is widely predicted. Because of the exponential growth of demand, even the doubling of known reserves has only a small effect on the final exhaustion date in terms of one or two decades. All 'long-term' transport plans ignore warnings that either oil resources may be exhausted in the next thirty years or that the demand and supply relationship will be so modified that fuel will be greatly more expensive. Demand models calibrated under current cost conditions are insensitive to the massive cost changes which are associated with the possible depletion of petroleum. Nor has sufficient work been carried out to make projections of future fuel costs better than highly conjectural. The problems associated with forecasting travel demand for new systems even under relatively stable cost conditions are reported to be extremely difficult (Tomazinis, 1972).

Planning for the introduction of long-term technological developments requires careful evaluation of the effect of the increased importance of such areas as resource availability, the environment and social impact. For example, limitation of available fuel resources is likely to lead to greatly increased energy costs. Consequently there would be incentives over the long term to develop low energy modes of transport phasing out, where possible, 'high energy' modes. Under the classification of relatively low energy technology we could expect to find interest for example in rail systems, travellators, shared dial-a-bus, airbus and jumbo jets. Technology which has relatively high energy demands would include VTOL, STOL, supersonic transport, the motor car and, under certain design parameters, PRT systems. Equally important, should the problems of fuel resource availability surpass the environment as a major consideration in technological development, the planner is led to the conclusion that the solution to exhaust pollution should not be sought by the use of inherently low efficiency engines such as external combustion engines or gas turbines at low power outputs.

Similarly, investments in transport infrastructure requiring high energy inputs should be considered with first priority, since long-term deferral of these investments is likely to make them much more expensive, e.g. the extensive use of aluminium could become increasingly costly as energy costs rise dramatically. Under conditions of dwindling fossil fuels and high energy costs, the planner must inevitably speculate on the consequent effect on travel demand of the induced changes in urban form which could follow from such a radically changed energy situation. The high energy city of the late twentieth century with a dense multi-storey central office core and low density outer suburbs could, under the conditions of changed pricing and taxing associated with fuel scarcity, gradually modify to a lower energy urban form similar to cities of the Victorian age. The structure of the urban fabric will respond strongly to the introduction of low energy buildings and re-emphasised public investment in the type of fixed track public transport systems now being re-examined with great interest by transport engineers.

Of equal interest are the implications of increased emphasis on the assessment criteria relating to pollution. Systems and technology with high levels of noxious emissions and deleterious environmental impact will be increasingly unacceptable. This clearly leads to the conclusion that the conventional automobile engine is either to be modified or avoided as a general means of transport propulsion. It is however clear that certain technological developments are being pursued which could lead to insatiable demands on some metals (lead and platinum for example) and severe problems of solid waste disposal (sulphur) unless recycling processes are planned at an acceptable level. Other similar conflicts of objectives can arise where an incomplete procedure is employed in the assessment of technological development.

Manpower resources are considered important in the developed countries. In Japan, for example, automation is expected to ease the problems of manpower shortage in transport. The computer-controlled vehicle system, a PRT system now under testing, is similar to systems in concept or development in the West. In the evaluation of these future systems however it will be necessary to predict the levels of future trade-offs of labour and energy resources under an environment which can only be described as highly uncertain when viewed from current conditions.

150

Conclusions

The previous discussion has highlighted a number of inadequacies in the analytic techniques currently used to assist in the assessment of transport technology developments. As a consequence of these inadequacies, it is frequently the case that many complex, expert and extensive studies are apparently ignored at the actual point of decision taking. It has been suggested that there are a number of ways in which the analyst can improve the quality and relevance of his techniques, and such advances must form an essential part of future assessment research. However, such advances will not of themselves lead to the establishment of a successful assessment framework.

Figure 6.1 indicates the following major stages in the assessment of any technology development:

1   The identification of a project for assessment. This is both a trivial and a crucial starting point for any assessment exercise. Such identification is presently done in an *ad hoc* and not always necessarily rational manner.

2   The identification of the major actors affected by the introduction of the technology. All major groups and organisations should be included in the manner recommended by Nash in work related to the assessment of the Boston Inner Loop (Nash, 1968) and by Lichfield (1968) in early planning work.

3   The identification of the scale of impact on the major actors within the six areas of criteria previously defined.

4   The establishment of threshold values for the various impacts so identified.

5   The estimation of cash flow impacts, other quantifiable impacts and non-quantifiable effects. How far it proves possible to carry out estimation of these three types in a consistent and comparable manner represents one of the key research issues.

6   The establishment of a consensus ranking of all these various impacts. Many attempts are presently being made to introduce public participation at this stage.

7   Selection (or rejection) of the technology for implementation.

At present the decision maker is directly involved only with project identification and technology selection (as indicated by the solid horizonal lines in figure 6.1).

By contrast the assessment analysis team works in great detail on all

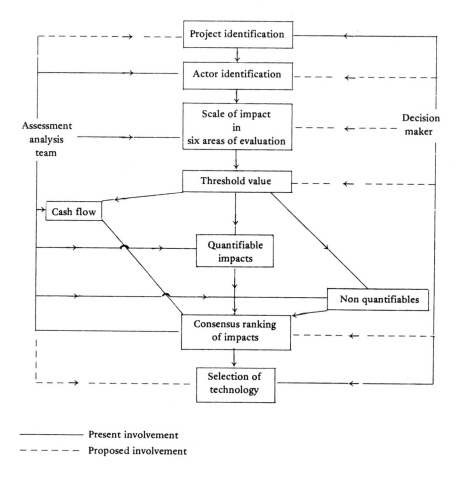

Figure 6.1   Major stages in technology assessment and the role of the
analyst and the decision maker

of the other stages with the exception of project identification and
technology selection. It is suggested that this segmentation is even more
responsible for the gulf between analysis and decision making than is
the inadequacy of existing techniques. Certainly the analyst should be
involved with project identification and it is possible to argue the case
for him playing some explicit role in system selection. More important
however is the need for the decision maker to take an active part in
actor identification, in establishment of impact scales and threshold
values, and in consensus ranking of impacts. By active involvement it is
not suggested that the analyst's role should be usurped, but rather that

it can be enriched and made more relevant by the explicit participation of the decision maker in the analytic processes.

It is believed that if analytic techniques can be improved as suggested earlier in the chapter and if the decision-making and analytic functions can be more closely integrated as suggested in this section, then the relevance of assessment studies will be confirmed and the choice of projects for study can be established in a coherent and rational way.

References

Ackoff, R.L., *Scientific Method*, John Wiley, New York, 1962.

Baumol, W.J., *Economic Theory and Operations Analysis*, 2nd edition, Prentice Hall, Englewood Cliffs, New Jersey, 1962.

Clark, J.M., 'The Objectives and Methodology of Transport Assessment' in A.G. Wilson (ed.) *Patterns and Processes in Urban and Regional Systems*, Pion, London, 1972.

Clark, J.M. and Ashford, N.J., 'An Assessment of the Status and Development of Transport Technology' in *Proceedings of the International Conference on Transportation Research*, Bruges, R.B. Cross, Oxford, Indiana, 1973.

Cmnd 7131, *The Nationalised Industries*, HMSO, London, 1978.

Columbia Transit Program, *Phase 1 Final Report — Concept Formulation*, prepared by Bendix Corporation, Ann Arbor, Michigan for Columbia Park and Recreation Association, 1970.

Commission on the Third London Airport, *Report*, HMSO, London, 1971.

Department of Transport, *Report of the Advisory Committee on Trunk Road Assessment*, HMSO, London, 1978.

Grey, A., 'The Generalised Cost Dilemma' in *Transportation*, 1978, vol.7, pp. 261–80.

Harrison, A.J. and Quarmby, D.A., 'The Value of Time in Transport Planning: a Review' in *Report of the Sixth Round Table on Transport Economics*, European Conference of Ministers of Transport, 1969.

Hill, M., 'A Method for the Evaluation of Transportation Plans' in *Highway Research Record*, 1967, no.180, pp. 21–34.

Hill, M., 'A Goals-Achievement Matrix in Evaluation of Alternative Plans' in *Journal of the American Institute of Planners*, 1968, vol.34, pp. 19–29.

Jessimann, W., Brand, D., Tumminia, A. and Brussee, R., 'A Rational Decision-Making Technique for Transportation Planning' in *Highway Research Record*, 1967, no.180, pp. 71–80.

Jones, I.S., *Urban Transport Appraisal*, Macmillan, London, 1977.

Kahn, H. and Wiener, A.S., *The Year 2000: A Framework For Specu-lation on the Next Thirty-Three Years*, Macmillan, London, 1967.

Lichfield, N., 'Cost—Benefit Analysis in City Planning' in *Journal of the American Institute of Planners*, 1960, vol.26, pp. 273—9.

Lichfield, N., 'Cost—Benefit Analysis in Plan Evaluation' in *Town Plan-ning Review*, 1964, vol.35, pp. 160—9.

Lichfield, N., 'Cost—Benefit Analysis in Urban Expansion: A Case Study — Peterborough' in *Regional Studies*, 1969, vol.3, pp. 123—55.

Lichfield, N., 'Evaluation Methodology of Urban and Regional Plans: a Review' in *Regional Studies*, 1970, vol.4, pp. 151—65.

Llewelyn-Davies, Weeks, Forestier-Walker and Bor and Sharkland, Cox and Associate, *Airport City: Urbanisation Studies for the Third London Airport*, HMSO, London, 1970.

Manheim, M.L., 'Transportation Problem Solving and the Effective Use of Computers' in *Highway Research Record*, 1966, no.148, pp. 49—58.

Manheim, M.L., 'Problem Solving Processes in Planning and Design', *Professional Paper P67—3*, Department of Civil Engineering, MIT, 1967.

Manheim, M.L., 'Search and Choice in Transport Systems Analysis' in *Highway Research Record*, 1969, no.293, pp. 54—81.

Manheim, M.L. et al., *The Impacts of Highways upon Environmental Values*, Urban Systems Laboratory, MIT, 1967.

Manheim, M.L., Follansbee, K.G. and Walton, R.E., 'Modelling the Evolutionary Nature of Problem Solving', *Research Report R68—43*, Department of Civil Engineering, MIT, 1968.

Mishan, E.J., *The Elements of Cost—Benefit Analysis*, Allen and Unwin, London, 1972.

Nash, W.W., *Disaggregative Impact Studies — Their Potential Use in Transport Decisions*, Transportation in Service, New York Academy of Sciences, 1968.

Oglesby, H.C., Bishop, B. and Willeke, G.W., 'A Method for Decisions among Freeway Location Alternatives Based on Use and Community Consequences' in *Highway Research Record*, 1970, no.305, pp. 1—14.

Ollerhead, J.B., 'A Pilot Survey of Some Effects of Aircraft Noise in Residential Communities near London Heathrow Airport', *Depart-ment of Transport Technology TTT303*, Loughborough, 1973.

Pearce, D.W. and Nash, C.A., *The Social Appraisal of Projects — A Text in Cost—Benefit Analysis*, Macmillan, London, 1981.

Schoeffler, S., 'Towards a General Theory of Rational Action', *Kyklos*, 1954, vol.7, pp. 245—71.

Tomazinis, A.R., 'Forecasting Travel Demand for New Urban Transportation Systems' in *Highway Research Record*, 1972, no.392, pp. 26—35.

Tyler, J. and Hassard, R., 'Gravity/Elasticity Models for the Planning of the Inter-Urban Rail Passenger Business' in *Proceedings of the PTRC Summer Meeting*, PTRC, London, 1973.

7 Risk and uncertainty in road investment appraisal

A. D. Pearman

Introduction

Many road investment projects have, by their very nature, long gestation periods and high capital costs. The infrastructure provided is immobile and it is frequently difficult to modify its capacity significantly in the light of fluctuations in demand once construction is completed. Moreover, it is rarely feasible to achieve adjustments in demand levels through the price mechanism, either because demand is relatively inelastic, or because technical and political constraints forbid it. Particularly because transport is a derived demand, the environment in which such investments will have to function is conditioned by social, political and economic events which, collectively, are highly unpredictable. Infrastructure investments can also be very pervasive, influencing as well as being influenced by, the circumstances in which they operate in ways which are far from straightforward. All these characteristics suggest that road schemes are likely to require careful long-term planning and appraisal, properly taking into account the wide range of uncertainty about the possible future circumstances in which any chosen scheme may have to operate.

Yet if road investment policy so clearly requires long-term planning, and so clearly has to accommodate a highly uncertain future, why is it that it is only within the last few years that formal consideration of the effects of uncertainty has been written into official trunk road appraisal procedures in England? Why is it that in most other countries too it seems to have been accorded iittle importance? Four factors, at least, are relevant. Firstly, until the 1970s, the body of theoretical knowledge concerned with decision making in an uncertain environment was relatively underdeveloped, and mostly unfamiliar to those involved in transport investment appraisal. This is no longer so much the case. A considerable volume of work has now been undertaken in economics, management science and psychology, both on the question of forma- lising decision makers' views of an uncertain future and concerned with optimal decision making in uncertain conditions. A significant amount of applied work exists, although little of it is in the transport sector.

The second factor is computation. Many of the techniques for eliciting consistent judgements about the probabilities of future events, and then using them for appraisal purposes, require computational assistance which, until recently, was only available on large main-frame computers. The advent of the cheap microcomputer has gone a long way towards removing this constraint.

The third factor also has computational elements to it, but relates primarily to the history of the development of formal transport model- ling. Transport planning, based on formal quantitative models, although it has been through a period of very rapid growth, is scarcely past its infancy. Moreover, its individual components — trip generation, attrac- tion, distribution, mode choice, assignment etc. — each are concerned with highly complex processes, and there are further complicated feed- backs between the components. It is not surprising, therefore, that in the first instance, the concentration in developing modelling procedures, should have been on forecasting single best-estimate figures for all relevant quantities. The question of how sure an analyst could be about the accuracy or reliability of such forecasts was bound to be treated as secondary. Nor should it be unexpected that in the wake of development of complex and often elegant modelling procedures, a certain false confidence might develop. Only when the forecasts arising from a number of major early transport studies proved to be seriously in error could it be expected that a more circumspect approach would be adopted. Although a great deal of development is still required, it is arguable that the individual components of the conventional four-stage transport planning process have now reached a position where it is at least as important to recognise the uncertainty inherent in their specifi- cation and estimation and in their use as forecasting tools as it is to complicate further their fundamental behavioural structure.

The final factor is essentially psychological. A natural reaction to misplaced confidence in long-range quantitative planning is disappoint- ment and rejection. In the later 1970s, growing feelings of this kind, coupled with severe restrictions on investment funds for transport, encouraged planners in the use of short-term, low cost strategies to contain transport problems as they developed. Such actions clearly have their place, but short-term policies can have decidedly long-term consequences, and doubts about long-range planning should really have been directed at the techniques employed, rather than the concept itself. However, recently society has grown very sensitive to the speed of change of events, to how rapidly changes in one area can be transmitted to another and to how profound the effects of planning decisions in one sector can be for developments elsewhere. It is conscious too of increasing uncertainty about the pattern of the future, consequent on rapid changes and strong interdependence. The effects of the oil crises of the 1970s have contributed to a growing awareness of the vulnerability of western industrialised countries, and their transport sectors. A general social environment of this kind is likely to be conducive to what, from a technical point of view, has been required all along — a mode of appraisal which seeks properly to take into account the long-term nature of road investment and, at the same time, the uncertain future in which investments of this type will operate.

Not only is this development desirable, it is also attainable. Putting it into practice, it must be admitted, may well call into question on occasions the basis upon which the evaluation of projects takes place, hence causing some change of emphasis in the types of project which are planned in the first place. However, such a reorientation does not demand the development of radically new techniques. For the most part, appropriate tools already exist. What are required are strenuous efforts to come to terms with the problems of applying, as a matter of practice, existing techniques in a field where, as yet, their application has been rather limited.

Investment appraisal undertaken from this point of view is likely to encourage the development of adaptive strategies, not just the creation of one 'optimal' plan focused on a single target year. Pressures for the development of more flexible long-range transport planning techniques have been reflected recently in the work of a number of transport analysts. A growing number of studies are now seeking to encourage the formal recognition of uncertainty in appraisal procedures. In the UK, the Leitch Committee Report on Trunk Road Assessment (Department of Transport, 1978) accorded major importance to a reorientation of evaluation techniques which, among other things, required a much fuller and more systematic recognition of the implications of uncertainty for project appraisal. A recent report for the Inland Transport Committee of the United Nations Economic Commission for Europe (Timar, 1980) has also emphasised the importance of taking proper account of uncertainty.

Thus from the point of view not only of theoretical desirability but, just as importantly, from that of social acceptability and technical feasibility, it seems that a reorientation of road investment appraisal procedures is timely. The intention of this chapter is to set out what has been done already, and to indicate likely future developments. It will draw mostly on British experience, starting with a brief account of the development of the present Department of Transport COBA computer-based appraisal technique for trunk road investments. Then a more general view is taken, with an emphasis on techniques, followed by a consideration of the special requirements of long-range strategic planning for the road sector as a whole. The final section of the chapter summarises the arguments put forward previously and offers some concluding comments.

The appraisal of trunk roads in England

This section is concerned with the procedures followed in England for assessing the value of improvements to the network of major inter-urban (trunk) roads. It does not deal with local decisions about changes to the road system within towns, nor with the occasional instances of very wide-ranging proposals, such as the Greater London Development Plan. In both these cases the administrative structure and decision-making processes are different.

In England there are about 250,000 km of public roads, of which about 10,000 km are designated as trunk roads. Although they are a small proportion of the total, they carry about 25 per cent of all vehicle traffic, and the responsibility for the development of the system lies with the central government. The programme of trunk road development is guided at two levels. Firstly, its general shape and emphasis is determined by statements of government policy about the road system. Secondly, there are carefully structured procedures laid down for assessing individual schemes which are put forward in the light of the general framework. An important element of the assessment of individual schemes is an economic appraisal, based on cost—benefit principles. It is this element of the assessment procedures as a whole which will be the focus of attention, and especially the way in which amendments have begun to be made to it in an attempt to take into account uncertainty. For a more wide-ranging view of the trunk road assessment procedure as it was in the mid-1970s a good source of reference is the Leitch Committee Report (Department of Transport, 1978). For developments since then, the best references are the Department's own *Traffic Appraisal Manual* (Department of Transport, 1981a) and *COBA-9 Manual* (Department of Transport, 1981b).

Systematic economic appraisal, in one form or another, has been required for trunk road schemes in England since 1967. The structure of the appraisal process is common to all schemes and is laid down by the Department of Transport. Thus its view as to what is the correct way to carry out an appraisal is of considerable practical importance. Since 1973 the majority of important interurban trunk road schemes have been subject to economic appraisal using a specified set of instructions incorporated in a computer programme, COBA (cost–benefit analysis).

The Department has taken the attitude that the only user consequences of road building which can be measured and evaluated with sufficient precision to be considered in a formal cost–benefit analysis are time savings, vehicle operating cost savings and accident cost savings. Other user effects are considered, but outside the strict cost–benefit calculation. Furthermore, COBA works on the assumption that the number of trips between each pair of origins and destinations is unaffected by the proposed improvement to the network which is under consideration. Reassigned flows cause no problem, but redistributed trips and generated traffic cannot be handled. Within this limited frame of reference, COBA performs an incremental cost–benefit analysis over a base 'do-minimum' set of forecasts, taking into account construction costs (land costs, civil engineering costs, compensation costs and an allowance for delays to traffic during construction), changes in maintenance costs, and the categories of user effect described earlier.

Using a time horizon of thirty years after a scheme's opening, COBA calculates its net present value (NPV), employing a discount rate (currently 7 per cent) regarded as appropriate for investment appraisal in the non-trading public sector. If, as is common, a number of alternative schemes are under consideration for any particular location, choice between alternatives is based on an incremental analysis between options, such that the option with the maximum NPV is located, and not just the first option to secure a positive NPV, nor that with the highest capital cost. The NPV to net present value of cost ratio is sometimes used, if there is an explicit budget constraint. Usually this is at the national level, when there are more positive NPV schemes proposed than can currently be funded, rather than at the local level of appraisal.

In addition, if it is appropriate, other factors may be taken into account. Schemes with significant elements of diverted or generated traffic are subject to more sophisticated traffic modelling, although the basic principles of evaluation remain the same. If a significant proportion of the traffic affected by a scheme is recreational (e.g. holiday traffic), special procedures are used. Finally, the overall evaluation of a scheme, to which the COBA calculations are just part of the input, requires that a large number of environmental consequences must be assessed — areas of land taken, noise, vibration, air pollution, visual effects, severance and, in addition to their economic evaluation in COBA, accidents. A particularly good, or bad, set of environmental consequences can cause the economic ranking to be overturned.

Until 1978, there was no formal element in COBA requiring the recognition that any of the traffic forecasts or other building blocks for the economic appraisal process might be subject to error or uncertainty. However, in that year, the recommendations of the Leitch Committee were published, including:

(a) that instead of a single set of traffic forecasts, COBA and related evaluation procedures should acknowledge the high degree of uncertainty in such projections by working with a range of figures. The consequences of selecting different values within the range should be demonstrated.

(b) that evaluation of each scheme should be presented within a multiple criteria framework, essentially an impact matrix presenting alongside each other both the economic and other impacts attributable to each alternative under consideration.

From the latter point of view the general principles used in COBA were regarded as acceptable, but the intention was to give more importance to the non-economic factors which previously tended to be afforded low priority. Some form of multiple criteria assessment based on pairwise comparison of alternatives was suggested, although it was recognised that there were limits to how far purely mechanistic techniques could be employed.

Of these two areas of recommendation, the one to which the Department of Transport has so far given the greater attention is the first. Its response has been in two main directions. Firstly, it has revised COBA in such a way that, instead of a single set of projections, 'high' and 'low' forecasts of traffic are available and are taken into account in evaluation. Secondly, it has commissioned studies into the sensitivity of traffic models, including economic evaluation, to uncertainties about data inputs. In providing only 'high' and 'low' forecasts with no intermediate figures and, importantly, no probability assessments, the Department's response to the first recommendation has arguably been less far-reaching than was suggested. With the modelling capability presently at its disposal, it does not feel able to suggest a range of possible traffic levels, spanning the next thirty years or more, with probability assessments attached to different parts of the range. The two alternative sets of projections, while they have some foundation in formal modelling, are not the result of the application of any explicit, quantitative procedure. They are not maximum and minimum levels derived from imposing certain assumptions about the future on a single model, nor do they correspond to 95 per cent confidence intervals or anything of that type. Rather they are subjective judgements, made by Department officials, of what would be appropriate traffic levels for design and evaluation purposes under what might be regarded as optimistic and pessimistic views of future traffic levels.

From a theoretical point of view, the Department's response is a long way short of ideal. The question which is relevant however is a more practical one. Given the current state of knowledge about modelling and forecasting traffic flows, could more coherent and detailed forecasts have been constructed? And, if so, to what extent would the COBA appraisal exercise be a more reliable guide to policy making? To adjudge this issue, some discussion of the theory of decision making in an uncertain environment is required.

Decision making in an uncertain environment

Error and uncertainty about the accuracy of the output of conventional transport planning exercises can result from one or more of three basic causes:

1 *Measurement error.* The mathematical models on which much transport planning is based depend usually for the values of their parameters on fitting a model form to a set of survey or similar observations. Apart from random sampling error, such data is bound also to contain distortions as a consequence of accidental or deliberate misreporting. To the extent which it does, completely accurate calibration of the models is impossible.

2 *Specification error.* There are few if any areas of transport systems analysis where understanding of the processes at work is complete. If important variables are omitted from the formal specification of the models, specification error results. Even with data conceptually free of measurement error, an incorrectly specified model cannot be relied upon to yield accurate outputs when used as a forecasting tool.

3 *Forecasting error.* The transport sector, and its individual elements, especially because it services a derived demand, is strongly influenced by variables such as population size, GDP levels, fuel prices etc. If, as is inevitable, such exogenous variables are forecast inaccurately, the predictions of transport models which depend on them are likely in turn to be inaccurate.

While steps can be taken to attempt to diminish the difficulties which these sources jointly create for the choice between road investment options, there is bound to be a considerable residual uncertainty about the realised values of any indicators of performance of alternative schemes. A sufficiently wide range of plausible values is likely to remain to ensure that decidedly different choices of investment policy would be appropriate, depending upon which future set of circumstances happened to develop.

The presence of such uncertainty can be handled in one of two, not necessarily mutually exclusive, ways. One response is merely to present to the decision maker a summary of the possible values which analysis suggests may occur for the indicator of relevance (e.g. NPV). At the simplest level, this is the effect of undertaking calculations based on high and low traffic forecasts in the recent versions of COBA. More sophisticated analysis may provide a probability distribution of outcomes, usually termed a risk analysis. In either case, no guidance is provided to the decision maker about how to choose between alternatives on the basis of the information presented. The second possible response is to assume that the decision maker has or should work to some rules for decision making in such circumstances and to present to him only what is required for the application of those rules, say the mean NPV and the standard deviation of NPVs for each scheme. Although this second approach generally assumes more than the former, they share many of the same problems. Both will be discussed in the course of this chapter.

Before it came to be accepted that the proper assessment of investments in the face of uncertainty requires their evaluation across the whole range of anticipated possible futures, it is not true to say that uncertainty was ignored altogether. Although this was a frequent response, it was also not uncommon for the inputs to an evaluation, or the evaluation process itself to be manipulated, more or less consciously, in an endeavour to respond to the existence of uncertainty, while still presenting only a single evaluation of each investment. The induced response in such cases is one of conservatism. It is intended to reflect the frequently adopted view that decision makers, especially in the public sector, are risk averse. But the reflection is not undistorted in one important respect. The bias is applied in just one direction; there is no counterbalancing opportunity for the optimistic view, which a rational decision maker, even a risk averse one, should certainly allow. The conservative approach can manifest itself in a number of ways. One possibility is merely to make pessimistic assumptions about costs, planning delays, potential benefits etc. It is particularly commonly applied to the cost side of appraisals in the form of contingency allowances. Alternatively, or even additionally, more stringent criteria may be applied to uncertain prospects at the final valuation stage. One possibility is to restrict the number of years for which the scheme under appraisal is held to yield benefits below its true economic life. Another is to add a risk premium to the discount rate.

All adjustments of this kind are arbitrary and militate against an economically rational assessment of alternatives. They are also biased in their treatment of different types of project. For example, either shortening the economic life of a project or imposing a risk premium will favour short-term, inflexible schemes by ignoring or diminishing the effects of their inappropriateness in the long term. Also, such techniques do not take proper account of uncertainty in the short- and mid-term future, which is by no means insignificant.

If a rational approach to appraisal in the presence of uncertainty is desired, it must identify explicitly the existence of different possible futures and their associated probabilities. No form of *ad hoc* adjustment will suffice. Indeed the key to what form of appraisal will be possible lies in assessing what form of statement the decision-making body is prepared to accept about the future. This is a contentious question at the best of times, even in relation to a single individual undertaking a private decision. In the public sector, where a collective view of the future is necessitated and where political constraints may inhibit an honest declaration of views, matters are doubly complex. There is little value in developing an elegant decision-making framework depending, say, on attaching firm probabilities to different rates of growth of GDP, if the government is not prepared to sanction such a statement. In what follows it will be important to distinguish what can from what should be done.

In the theoretical treatment of decision making under uncertainty, three main alternative sets of assumptions are considered about the form in which the decision maker is prepared to express his/her view of the future. Depending upon the one chosen, different ways of presenting the performance of schemes are possible, and different rules to guide investment choice are available. Most assume that it is possible to specify an m x n payoff matrix, $[X_{ij}]$, where X_{ij} ($i=1....m; j=1....n$) is the NPV (say) of the ith project should the jth state of nature (i.e. possible future set of circumstances) occur. The three possible sets of assumptions are then:

1   *Decision making under uncertainty*. Here it is assumed that although n mutually exclusive and collectively exhaustive possible states of nature can be identified and corresponding payoffs computed, no knowledge is possessed of the P_j ($j=1.....n$) (the probabilities that the states of nature will occur).

2 *Decision making under risk.* In this case, the opposite extreme to the first one, it is assumed that the P_j can be specified precisely.

3 *Decision making with incomplete knowledge.* Here the assumption is that some information is available about the P_j (say in the form of inequality constraints), but that precise values cannot be assessed.

A variation on the above possibilities is that individual states of nature cannot be identified, but that a matrix of outcomes $[O_{ij}]$ can be specified where, in general, an outcome (here an NPV value) could be associated with more than one possible future state of nature. Alternatively, rather than a vector of outcome values being associated with each project, it may be that a probability distribution of outcomes can be specified. All these departures from the basic model, however, can be assessed within the context of discussing the characteristics of the three sets of assumptions in terms of the payoff matrix $[X_{ij}]$.

Decision making under uncertainty assumes that the decision maker is unwilling to make any judgement about the probabilities of future states of nature. This may be regarded as rather unrealistic, given that the decision maker is assumed capable of specifying a complete set of possible sets of nature and calculating corresponding X_{ij}, but it is an important point of reference as a limiting assumption in the direction of zero knowledge of probabilities. It is also not without some practical relevance in road investment appraisal. The output of COBA is suitable only for this type of decision method, in this case there being just $j=2$ states of nature.

Given that little information is available about the probabilities of the states of nature, it is not surprising that the available rules to guide decision makers faced with this form of uncertainty are rather crude. They tend to caricature attitudes to risk in a way which parallels the extreme assumption of complete ignorance about the P_j. Typically five 'complete ignorance' rules are discussed in the literature. Three (maximin, minimax regret and Bayes-Laplace) will be discussed here. Maximax and the Hurwicz criterion are less relevant and will be omitted (see, for example, Kmietowicz and Pearman, 1981, pp. 7–8 for a description of these other rules).

Consider the following numerical example, where the entries in the body of the matrix represent NPVs in £million:

States of Nature

	1	2	3	4	5
Investment schemes A	14	-4	35	-9	-21*
B	35	25	15	-21*	-14
C	12	10	-12*	14	17

The maximin rule states that the scheme selected should be that with the maximum minimum payoff. The row minima are the elements starred in the above matrix and the chosen strategy will be C. Minimax regret is an opportunity cost criterion. First a regret matrix $[R_{ij}]$ is constructed, by subtracting each element of the payoff matrix from the maximum element in its column. Thus R_{ij} represents the loss recorded when state of nature j occurs by selecting scheme i rather than the best possible scheme available for this state of nature. Here, $[R_{ij}]$ is

States of Nature

	1	2	3	4	5
Investment schemes A	21	29	0	23	38*
B	0	0	20	35*	31
C	23	15	47*	0	0

and the optimal strategy choice by the minimax regret criterion is B. The Bayes-Laplace rule derives from the point of view that, if no judgement can be made about which among a set of states of nature is the more likely, then each should be treated as equally likely. Thus, in the above example, each state of nature is regarded as having a probability, P_j, of 0.20 and the scheme with maximum expected value, $\sum_j P_j X_{ij}$, is chosen — here, scheme C.

Of these three decision rules, Bayes-Laplace stands apart from the rest. It represents a neutral 'rational' response to the uncertain situation, taking into account all possible outcomes and effectively turning the problem into one of decision making under risk. The other two rules both superimpose a risk averse attitude on to the decision maker's choice by concentrating on avoiding poor outcomes. Selection is based on the value of just one X_{ij} for each scheme, ignoring the valuations for each state of nature except the one least favourable for the strategy concerned. While it is perfectly possible that the decision maker has this attitude to strategy choice, it is a highly pessimistic one which it is hard to regard as being common.

Nevertheless, if no information, explicit or implicit, is held to be available about the P_j, then there seems to be little alternative to the adoption of one of the five complete ignorance rules if a formal choice rule is to be used at all. *COBA-9* contains no advice about the adoption of formal decision rules if one scheme is favoured under the high traffic forecasts and another under the low ones. However *COBA-8*, which incorporated the Department of Transport's first attempts to appraise projects with two alternative sets of traffic forecasts, did adopt an approach somewhat of this kind. The basis of the choice mechanism was that if the economic ranking of schemes was the same under both high and low traffic forecasts, then choice should be based on the maximin criterion. In the event that the rankings proved to be different under the two sets of traffic forecasts a maximin criterion was again applied, but with the supplementary requirement, that should the maximum regret of the scheme with the highest NPV on the low forecasts (i.e. in normal circumstances the one selected by the maximin rule) be more than twice the maximum regret of some other scheme, then the choice should be referred to the Department's headquarters for a decision. This was because the normal regret criterion was regarded as too conservative in such circumstances. For example, suppose scheme *B* in the following matrix of NPVs (in £m) relates to a bypass which would yield significant benefits if the high traffic forecasts materialised.

	High	Low
Scheme *A*	7	6
Scheme *B*	20	5

The maximin rule here would select scheme *A*. However, the maximum regret for this scheme (£13m) is thirteen times the maximum regret of scheme *B* and so reference for a central decision would be required. In this example the case for scheme *B* looks strong, because the maximin judgement in favour of *A* is a very marginal one. In less clear cut circumstances what would have to be assessed is how persistently *B* outranked *A* for levels of traffic lower than the planning extreme represented by the high forecasts.

In *COBA-9* the type of approach just described is abandoned. Instead, the use of informed judgement is emphasised, including the possibility that schemes' performances may need to be assessed using intermediate traffic growth forecasts. There is also a more or less official suggestion that a 60:40 weighting in favour of the low traffic forecasts can be used in the event of different schemes proving optimal under the two different projections and it is stated that research is being carried out on the possibility of attaching probability assessments to different levels of traffic growth. All this suggests that the complete ignorance decision rules have not proved to be practicable tools in the road appraisal context.

At the other extreme from decision making under uncertainty is decision making under risk, that is, where exact probabilities can be attached to each of the identified future states of nature. At first sight, the availability of complete information about the P_j makes logically defensible decision making much more straightforward. Each investment has an expected value, $EV_i = \sum_{j=1}^{n} P_j X_{ij}$, which takes into account all, not just extreme, payoffs and which balances the likelihoods of the different payoffs actually being achieved. Selecting for implementation the investment with the highest EV_i seems both straightforward and sensible.

On closer inspection, however, a number of problems present themselves. Firstly, there is the question of specifying the precise values of the P_j. Objective evaluations are clearly impossible for the kind of decision under consideration here. For individual decisions there is a well-established line of argument in support of defining the P_js subjectively, as the best estimate the decision maker can arrive at of the probabilities of the different states of nature. For collective, public decisions, however, the position is less clear. The P_j would have to reflect the balanced view of a group, rather than the single view of an individual. Also it is not entirely clear which the group should be. If it is the government, in some sense, then there is a clear danger of bias in the estimates, and also of decisions being artificially hastened or retarded if a change of government seems imminent. If it is the Department of Transport's collective expert view, there is a problem of consistency with other Departments of State. If it is a civil service non-government view, the question of political acceptability, raised earlier, looms large.

In addition to this problem, two others should be borne in mind. The first, which is relevant to all three approaches to decision making outlined earlier, is the question of whether expected utility rather than expected payoff should be the choice criterion. In principle, because of the diminishing marginal utility of money, and because a loss of a given monetary value may well weigh much more heavily in a decision maker's thinking than a gain of equivalent monetary size, conversion of the payoff matrix $[X_{ij}]$ to a utility matrix $[U_{ij}]$ followed by expected utility maximisation would seem desirable. Again, however, there is the question of whose utilities should they be for a public decision, and how should the relationship mapping X_{ij} values to U_{ij} values be elicited.

The second problem, which overlaps with the first, is what attitude should be taken to dispersion of payoffs if, for example, two investments have the same expected value but different overall distributions? Empirical evidence suggests that an investment with a small dispersion will be preferred to one with an equivalent mean value but a larger dispersion, on grounds of risk aversion. If this is the case, then a trade-off between mean payoff and, say, standard deviation of payoff exists which, if it is taken into account, undermines the attractive simplicity so far regarded as a feature of decision making under risk. Specifying what the trade-off is, or should be, is another hurdle to be overcome. It can also be argued that the same problem arises when working on the basis of maximising expected utility. One school of thought, however, argues that if the U_{ij} are calculated as Von Neumann-Morgenstern cardinal utilities (see, for example, Schoemaker, 1980), then, since the calculation of the U_{ij} subsumes both the intrinsic value of the payoffs and the attitude to risk of the decision maker whose U_{ij}s are being calculated, no account need be taken of dispersion. Ranking on the basis of $E(U_{ij})$ is all that is required. The use of Von Neumann-Morgenstern utilities is not without its critics, however. Kahneman and Tversky (1979) cast a number of doubts on it. The paper by Allais (1953) is a well known criticism, and has recently been subsumed in Allais and Hagen (1979). In addition, it should be noted that the cardinality of the Von Neumann-Morgenstern utility index does not extend across individuals in the way in which the utility of neoclassical economic theory was held to do. A collective, public Von Neumann-Morgenstern utility hence presents problems.

For all these reasons, treating road investment appraisal as a problem of decision making under risk is not as attractive as it might at first appear. A risk analysis approach to individual schemes can provide useful insights, as will be described shortly, but the underlying assumptions may be too severe to make it workable as a decision-making tool for investment choices undertaken through the public inquiry system. The possibility of informing decision makers through estimates of probabilities which are less specific than those required for decision making under risk appears worth considering.

Attempts to derive rules for decision making when information about the probability of states of nature exists, but is incomplete, can be traced back to the work of Fishburn (1964). This pioneering work, although it did not lead directly to any practicable decision-making techniques is at the root of recent developments which seem more promising from the point of view of application to real problems, such as road investment appraisal. Fishburn considered the situation where the decision maker was presumed to have enough confidence about his beliefs concerning future states of nature that he could rank them in subjective likelihood, $P_1 \geq P_2 \geq \ldots \geq P_n$. Starting from this ranking, Kmietowicz and Pearman (1981) show how, for each investment under consideration, it is possible to calculate in a very straightforward fashion the maximum and minimum attainable expected values consistent with the ranking. If the payoffs of each investment are ordered in the same way as the probabilities are ranked, all that is required is to compute the n 'partial averages', $1/k \sum_{j=1}^{k} X_{ij}$, $(k=1 \ldots n)$ for the investment. The maximum partial average gives the maximum expected value, and similarly for the minimum. Choice between investments can then be made on the basis of one of the complete ignorance criteria, but applied to extreme *expected* values, rather than to the extreme values themselves. Such an approach takes account of all the information which the decision maker is prepared to specify about his view of the future. It can easily be shown (Kmietowicz and Pearman, 1981, pp. 21–3) that consistently using extreme expected values in this way over a series of decisions leads to better investment choice than the complete ignorance criteria discussed earlier.

If the decision maker does not wish to be committed to the risk aversion implied by choice on the basis of, say, maximin expected value or minimax expected regret, then the Bayes-Laplace criterion is readily applicable under ranking restrictions. Agunwamba (1980) and Rietveld (1982) have shown that the mean point of a uniform distribution over the convex feasible probability space determined by the ranking constraints can easily be computed as the unweighted average of the n extreme points. In this way the single point 'most representative' of the probabilities of states of nature can be found, and strategies compared in terms of their expected value and other parameters for that set of P_j.

An important extension of this approach to decision making with incomplete knowledge is to specify different types of restrictions on the P_j. Kmietowicz and Pearman (1982) consider a strict ranking of probabilities, $P_j \geq P_{j+1} + k_j$ $(j=1 \ldots n)$ where the k_j are positive constants. This enables stronger statements about relative probabilities to be made, thus more tightly constraining the range of expected values

170

which each available strategy can take. This type of approach is also developed by Kofler and Menges (1976) in terms of decision making with 'linear partial information' (LPI), which embraces all possible sets of linear constraints on the P_j. In particular, interval restrictions of the form $\alpha \leq P_j \leq \beta$ and constraints of the form $P_j \geq k_{j+1} P_{j+1}$ can be used, both of which reflect the way that decision makers often think about probability statements in real life. Although the calculations required for the application of LPI are likely to require computer assistance in all but the simplest cases, they are nevertheless straightforward, and the extra complexity is a small price to pay for the greater flexibility gained.

Given the existence of three different formal approaches to decision making in an uncertain environment, what can be said in answer to the question posed at the end of the section 'The appraisal of trunk roads in England', about the increased value of COBA if uncertainty were to be taken formally into account? From a general point of view, there is a fair consensus that application of the elementary complete ignorance rules for decision making under uncertainty is not a satisfactory approach. There will almost always be some type of subjective view which can be teased out about the probabilities of states of nature, and not to use what is available can only be to the detriment of good decision making.

The choice between decision making under risk and decision making with incomplete knowledge or LPI is much less clear cut. In a theoretical environment, axiomatic rigour and decisiveness would tilt the balance of choice towards decision making under risk, preferably in terms of utilities, U_{ij}. In practice the alternative approach is arguably the more attractive one. Even though there remains an element of imprecision in many of the procedures, they do achieve the important aim of removing optimistic bias and making explicit the costs of uncertainty (Gilbert and Jessop, 1977). At the same time, their very imprecision has a value. Most decision makers are well aware of the inaccuracy of much of the data and many of the forecasts with which they are dealing. They are unwilling, therefore, to commit themselves to a 'black box' which makes investment choice recommendations. The preference is for a succinct summary of the possible outcomes, taking into account views of the probabilities of different futures.

One approach which comes close to this, albeit initially on the presumption that probabilities of different input values could be stated precisely, is the risk analysis, pioneered in a transport context by the World Bank (Pouliquen, 1970; Reutlinger, 1970). Similar sensitivity analysis has been applied recently to COBA. Some sensitivity testing of the COBA programme was initially undertaken by the Leitch Committee (Department of Transport, 1978), and this was later extended in some Monte Carlo simulation work commissioned by the Department (Ashley, 1980; Copley, 1981; Martin and Voorhees, 1980).

To do this, a Monte Carlo simulation exercise has been applied to a case study. Each of the major sources of error and uncertainty was considered — uncertainty about planning data, income and fuel costs, model growth factors, trip distribution and trip assignment. With each was associated an appropriate probability distribution designed to reflect reasonable ranges of variation in the relevant parameters. Using a simplified version of the COBA programme, the case study project was then evaluated repeatedly, with randomly chosen combinations of values of the uncertain parameters (likely correlations between parameter values were taken into account in order to ensure consistency within the 'futures' generated in each occasion). The output of the simulation was a series of probability distributions, one for the project's NPV and others relating to various traffic flows. In the case study chosen, undertaking the simulation exercise enabled a risk analysis to be performed which was found to be helpful in both economic and operational appraisal of the scheme. In particular, the risk analysis gave valuable information about pavement and junction engineering design, both of which are potentially very sensitive, in terms of their economic implications, to variations in forecast traffic levels.

As a result of this exercise it was recommended (Martin and Voorhees, 1980, p.54) that steps be taken to implement some form of risk analysis as part of standard appraisal procedures. It was recognised, however, that the computational requirements of the Monte Carlo procedure were too great to permit its use on a regular basis. Research is now under way (see Copley, 1981) to try to develop a simpler, more mechanistic method, concentrating on the major areas of uncertainty and identifying especially those where extra survey or similar work might significantly reduce the effects of such uncertainty. A movement away from random simulation towards a more systematic testing of effects is also being sought.

Whether this alone will prove satisfactory is not clear. One of the complicating and difficult features of risk analysis is that it is important to take proper account of correlations between uncertain variables. If this is not done, considerable distortions in the distribution of possible outcomes can arise. Also, decision makers may prefer the approach of identifying just a small number of explicitly specified futures, assessing their probabilities individually and consciously, perhaps through a Delphi exercise (see Carruthers, 1980). In this way planning is seen to be oriented towards likely states of the world and not to be based on random combinations of a series of possible influences, where the likelihood of any particular combination of circumstances has not been explicitly assessed. If this latter line of thought predominates, decision making with incomplete knowledge and LPI are the more applicable tools, although what is achieved is broadly the same as in the original conception of risk analysis — an indication of the likely range of values which a project may have. In either case, however, the answer to the question of whether COBA might be a more valuable tool if uncertainty is formally taken into account is the same. Either approach is, with certain qualifications, practicable. Both have the potential for making considerably more useful information available to all those interested in decisions about road improvements.

Long-range strategic planning

So far in this chapter, discussion has concentrated on the availability and value of formal techniques for taking into account uncertainty when appraising individual investment proposals. Not a great deal has been said about longer-term, strategic planning.

In practice, the extent to which the techniques described in the previous section can help throw light on the broader question of long-term developments in transport is limited. In this section, therefore, some other methods of specifying and analysing uncertain futures are briefly outlined. In developing and selecting appraisal techniques, it is most important to bear in mind their scale of application, in both time and money terms. It is unlikely that the use of any single universal methodology will prove effective (see Gilbert and Jessop, 1977, pp. 126–7). The development of an internally consistent hierarchy of techniques seems more promising. At the highest level, a scenario-based method looks likely to be the most helpful, as will shortly be described. With overall strategies selected on this basis, decisions about the implementation and timing of individual components of the strategy could be based on risk analysis, or some generalisation of the 'complete ignorance' rules for decision making under uncertainty, with the probability ranges associated with the inputs and parameters of the modelling process determined by the higher level scenarios. At the lowest level, uncertainty and attitudes to risk aversion might simply be incorporated through the use of engineering standards, specification of particular sets of traffic forecasts or simple rules of thumb.

The value or otherwise of adopting scenario-based techniques for strategic transport planning involves many considerations, of which the treatment of uncertainty is but one. The volume of modelling work required is potentially considerable but, providing the cost of implementing such approaches can be contained by advances in strategic transport modelling (redefining its function, developing more efficient models etc) — and it probably can — then there is, *prima facie*, reason to believe that scenario-based techniques may produce important advances in methodology, which will permit (although not ensure) equivalent advances in the quality of decision making.

A concomitant to the application of such techniques is a re-examination of the framework for evaluation, and in particular the replacement of the concept of optimisation against a single scenario by a broader view, incorporating additionally robustness and flexibility in the face of several explicit scenarios.

The appropriateness of a scenario approach in the transport field has been argued by a number of analysts (e.g. Gilbert and Jessop, 1977; Stopher, 1980) and, indeed, it differs from risk analysis more in emphasis than in fundamentals. Here, a scenario-based approach will be taken to be one where a (relatively small) set of broad futures is identified, either by discussion among experts, or by reference to work undertaken by other bodies (e.g. the use of the OECD Interfutures scenarios; OECD, 1979). Initially, it is assumed that very little, if any, information is available about the relative likelihood of the scenarios. In contrast to risk analysis where each simulation effectively creates a scenario, the scenario approach is less automated. The scenarios are not created by a random sampling process across a whole set of more or less independent inputs and parameters. Instead they represent a more aggregate and considered view of a range of possible futures, subject so far as possible to the disciplines of internal consistency and quantification. As argued in the previous section, this type of approach may be more politically acceptable than one based on risk analysis in its basic form, partly because it is more explicit and comprehensible and partly because no actual probabilities are associated with different types of future.

The validity of the approach rests on a number of conditions which must be met. The range of scenarios as a whole must be comprehensive (encompassing the reasonable range of possible futures); they must be internally consistent (for which macroeconomic models and other checks may typically be used); and they must be defined in terms of all the exogenous variables having a significant impact on the transport sector, now or in the future. This is clearly a formidable task.

The process of transport strategy selection reflects the nature of strategies themselves — it is necessarily complex, and for good reason. Rarely is one seeking to identify one of a number of tested strategies, but to formulate a preferred strategy incorporating elements of the tested strategies. Again, evaluation criteria are likely to be wide ranging, reflecting the nature of strategic impacts, as well as lack of clarity in objectives. Finally there may be problems of making decisions due to the number and views of the decision makers. For all these reasons the process of strategy selection (development would be a better word) is not automated to anything like the extent which is a feature of risk analysis. This is not a deficiency but a strength in that it provides a much clearer insight into the trade-offs involved in evaluation, and allows decisions to be linked much more clearly to conditions in the future.

In view of the increased complexity of the outputs on which decisions may be based, it is desirable, and with recent advances in computing, probably possible to develop improved techniques both for presenting information concisely, and demonstrating in 'real time' the effect of variations in inputs on outputs.

In the discussion so far of the scenario approach it has been assumed there is little or no knowledge of the probability of individual scenarios. It may be that decision makers have views which would require this condition to be relaxed. If for example scenarios could be ranked in order of probability $(P_1 \geqslant P_2 \geqslant \ldots \geqslant P_n)$ then a number of interesting methods for informing decision makers about the implications of their views of the future exist which can considerably increase the value of the outputs of the planning exercise (see 'Decision making in an uncertain environment'). If, beyond this, scenario probabilities can actually be estimated, rather than just ranked, then further improvements may be feasible — the cross-impact method (Godet, 1976; 1979) is one possible approach to estimating scenario probabilities.

A second topic, relating to choice criteria, which arises through consideration of a scenario-based approach to strategy evaluation is the treatment of dynamically staged decision making. This question exists independently of the precise form in which uncertainty is taken into account. Even though the majority of important transport strategy decisions are implemented stage by stage over time, and are therefore susceptible to amendment in the light of changing views about the future, little explicit account is taken of this in standard appraisal procedures.

In the operations research literature, the special characteristics of dynamic decision making in an uncertain environment have been analysed using the concepts of 'flexibility' and 'robustness' (see Gupta and Rosenhead, 1968; Rosenhead et al., 1972; Rosenhead 1980a, 1980b). This recognises that strategies vary in the extent to which they enforce a rapid commitment to a particular general long-term course of action. Some schemes will remain flexible for longer in that they leave open a wider range of acceptable alternatives before the commitment of funds to expenditure which would only be justified if the future unfolded in a particular way. Although there has been some discussion and use of robustness as a criterion in transport planning applications and in theory (Maltby et al., 1976; O'Sullivan et al., 1979) wider

175

empirical testing is required. The trade-off between robustness and conventional evaluation measures needs more thorough investigation, as do the implications of valuing robustness for changing the way in which projects might be designed. Also needed in the transport context is experience of the way in which decision makers in practice form their judgement about acceptable and unacceptable outcomes of sequences of decisions. Is there a clear threshold, as the straightforward view of robustness implies, or is some more subtle measure required that recognises gradations of acceptability?

Indeed, the consideration of alternative criteria for decision making in transport planning, raises two questions which are important both for long-term strategic planning and for shorter-term decisions. The first of those questions is quite simply, what is the criterion (or criteria) which should guide decisions? The explicit recognition of uncertainty in a dynamic framework leads to the discussion of robustness, but there is also outstanding the recommendation of the Leitch Committee that some move towards formal multiple-criteria decision making with respect to non-monetary impacts of road schemes should be implemented. Although some initial exploration work has been undertaken (Pearman, 1978), at present it seems that the Department of Transport is unwilling to commit itself in this direction.

A second fundamentally important point with both long- and short-term implications is the question of what attitude public decision makers should take to risk. Is it appropriate that they follow the apparently common trend of private individuals to be risk averse, or not? Certainly the procedures and general commentary in COBA-9 all point to a risk averse attitude, but this is not something which is universally accepted. Arrow and Lind (1970) have argued that, in certain circumstances, public decisions should be risk neutral. However, this view has been questioned by Foldes and Rees (1977). Additional complications arise when an investment project has irreversible consequences, see Pearce and Nash (1981), who have also pointed out that risk neutrality to the monetary consequences of an investment does not necessarily imply that the same attitude is appropriate to other non-monetary impacts, such as pollution, the effects of which are generally more localised.

What is clear is that, in a world where there is considerable uncertainty about even the broad pattern of long-term developments, strategic thinking about the general guidelines for transport investment must recognise such uncertainty. No matter how effectively uncertainty is taken into account in day-to-day decisions about individual projects, if the overall guidelines are too strongly linked to a single narrow view of the future, there is a strong likelihood of the wrong pattern of investment being undertaken.

176

Summary and conclusions

The purpose of this chapter has been to argue the case for a fuller and more formal recognition of the consequences of uncertainty in medium- and long-term transport planning. It has done so by recognising the very considerable range of uncertainty which exists; by reviewing the imperfect state of current practice for incorporating uncertainty in transport planning procedures; and by suggesting how, by utilising existing methods, amendments to present practice are likely to be cost effective in realising significant advances in techniques — providing a sounder basis for decision making.

The evidence suggests that the case for such amendments is a strong one; transport planning involves major commitments of funds frequently to inflexible investments, just where the potential influence of uncertainty is at its greatest. The aim in seeking a more comprehensive treatment of uncertainty is essentially two-fold:

(a)   achieving better knowledge of uncertainty through improved identification and measurement, and

(b)   properly taking its effects into account in appraisal to inform decision making.

The type of techniques described can, suitably applied, go a long way towards achieving this aim; and in addition there are likely to be valuable side-effects from applying such methods — better use of survey resources to concentrate information gain on those areas where the effects of uncertainty are most costly, identification and design of projects which are less affected by uncertainty and the critical appraisal of assumptions about the values of inputs and model parameters for example. Principally, however, the gain is in the encouragement of an explicit and rational evaluation and decision process which discourages public decision making through the balancing of advocacy of extremes (Howard, 1975) and also disassociates as much as possible the creational and informational aspects of policy questions from the preferential aspect.

Fortunately, not only does the balance of opinion within the transportation planning community appear to favour moves in this direction, but the extent to which new *techniques* are required appears limited. A good deal of progress can be made by making fuller use of developments in risk analysis and decision theory culled from other areas of application and by encouraging the development of scenario-based techniques. The major need now is for a series of *applications* to real projects, rather than for new theoretical work.

References

Agunwamba, C.C., 'Decision theory and expected probability distribution' in *Operations Research Verfahren*, 1980, vol.40, pp. 253–6.

Allais, M., 'Le comportement de l'homme rationel devant le risque: critique des postulats et axiomes de l'école Américaine' in *Econometrica*, 1953, vol.21, pp. 503–46.

Allais, M. and Hagen, O., *Expected Utility Hypotheses and the Allais Paradox: Contemporary Discussions of Decisions under Uncertainty with Allais' rejoinder*, Reidel, Dordrecht, 1979.

Arrow, K.J. and Lind, R.C., 'Uncertainty and valuation of public investment decisions' in *American Economic Review*, 1970, vol.60, pp. 364–78.

Ashley, D.J., 'Uncertainty in the context of highway appraisal' in *Transportation*, 1980, vol.9, pp. 249–67.

Carruthers, R., 'Evaluation under extreme uncertainty' in *Transport Economics*, Proceedings of the 1980 PTRC Summer Annual Meeting, Seminar L, PTRC, London, 1980.

Copley, G., 'The quantification of uncertainties in traffic forecasts' in *Highway Planning and Design*, Proceedings of the 1981 PTRC Summer Annual Meeting, Seminar P, PTRC, London, 1981.

Department of Transport, *Report of the Advisory Committee on Trunk Road Assessment*, HMSO, London, 1978.

Department of Transport, *TAM User Manual*, Department of Transport, London 1981a.

Department of Transport, *COBA-9 User Manual*, Department of Transport, London, 1981b.

Fishburn, P.C., *Decision and Value Theory*, J. Wiley, New York, 1964.

Foldes, L.P. and Rees, R., 'A note on the Arrow–Lind theorem' in *American Economic Review*, 1977, vol.67, pp. 188–93.

Gilbert, D. and Jessop, A., 'Error and uncertainty in transport models' in *Transportation Models*, Proceedings of the 1977 PTRC Summer Annual Meeting, PTRC, London, 1977.

Godet, M., 'Scenarios of air transport development to 1990 by SMIC 74 – a new cross-impact method' in *Technological Forecasting and Social Change*, 1976, vol.9, pp. 279–88.

Godet, M., *The Crisis in Forecasting and the Emergence of the 'Prospective' Approach*, Pergamon Press, Oxford, 1979.

Gupta, S.K. and Rosenhead, J.V., 'Robustness in sequential investment decisions' in *Management Science*, 1968, vol.15, pp. 18–29.

Howard, R.A., 'Social decision analysis' in *Proceedings of the IEEE*, 1975, vol.63, pp. 359–71.

Kahneman, D. and Tversky, A., 'Prospect theory: an analysis of decision under risk' in *Econometrica*, 1979, vol.47, pp. 263–91.

Kmietowicz, Z.W. and Pearman, A.D., *Decision Theory and Incomplete Knowledge*, Gower, Aldershot, 1981.

Kmietowicz, Z.W. and Pearman, A.D., 'Decision theory and strict ranking of probabilities' in *European Journal of Operational Research*, 1982, vol.9, pp. 397—404.

Kofler, E. and Menges, G., *Entscheidungen bei unvollständiger Information*, Springer-Verlag, Heidelberg, 1976.

Maltby, D., Monteath, I.G. and Lawler, K.A., *Urban Transport Planning and Energy: Techniques for Long Term Appraisal*, Working Paper, Department of Civil Engineering, University of Salford, 1976.

Martin and Voorhees, *Highway Appraisal Under Uncertainty*, Martin and Voorhees Associates, London, 1980.

OECD, *Interfutures — Facing the Future, Mastering the Probable and Managing the Unpredictable*, OECD, Paris, 1979.

O'Sullivan, P., Holtzclaw, G.D. and Barber, G., *Transport Network Planning*, Croom Helm, London, 1979.

Pearce, D.W. and Nash, C.A., *The Social Appraisal of Projects*, MacMillan, London, 1981.

Pearman, A.D., *An Assessment of Multiple Criteria Decision Making Methods and the Potential Use in Comparability Studies between Trunk Road and Rail Investment*, Report prepared for the British Railways Board, 1978.

Pouliquen, L.Y., *Risk Analysis in Project Appraisal*, World Bank Staff Occasional Paper No.11, John Hopkins University Press, Baltimore, 1970.

Reutlinger, S., *Techniques for Project Appraisal Under Uncertainty*, World Bank Staff Occasional Paper No.10, John Hopkins University Press, Baltimore, 1970.

Rietveld, P., *Using Ordinal Information in Decision-Making under Uncertainty*, Research Memorandum, Department of Economics, Vrije University, Amsterdam, 1982.

Rosenhead, J.V., 'Planning under uncertainty: I The inflexibility of methodologies' in *Journal of the Operational Research Society*, 1980a, vol.31, pp. 209—16.

Rosenhead, J.V., 'Planning under uncertainty: II A methodology for robustness analysis' in *Journal of the Operational Research Society*, 1980b, vol.31, pp. 331—41.

Rosenhead, J.V., Elton, M. and Gupta, S.K., 'Robustness and optimality as criteria for strategic decisions' in *Operational Research Quarterly*, 1972, vol.23, pp. 413—31.

Schoemaker, P.J.H., *Experiments on Decisions Under Risk: the Expected Utility Hypothesis*, Martinus Nijhoff, Boston, 1980.

Stopher, P.R., 'Transferring urban transport planning methods to developing countries' in *The Highway Engineer*, 1980, vol.27, pp. 8–14.

Timar, A., *Assessment of Uncertainty in Evaluating Investments in Transport Infrastructure*, Report prepared for the Inland Transport Committee, Economic Commission for Europe, UNESCO, 1980.

8 Time in transport investment
C. H. Sharp

Introduction

Although there are some people for whom the process of being transported has intrinsic value transport is normally only a means to an end. Sports car owners, walking enthusiasts or steam train fanatics may travel, not in order to arrive, but because they enjoy travelling itself. Most people, however, travel in order to reach another point on this globe. If their bodies could be conveyed instantly to the desired destination by one of the more attractive devices of science fiction then they would gladly use this facility. Goods transport is a part of the process of production and distribution and there will normally be advantages, other things being equal, in making transit as quick as possible. The main benefit resulting from most transport investment, except in the special case where there were previously no transport facilities at all, will therefore be to produce time savings. According to the 1976 government 'Consultation Document' (Department of the Environment, 1976, para.5(13)) the value of time savings amounted to 80 per cent of the total benefit from an average trunk road improvement scheme. In the Roskill Commission report on the third London Airport the major factor determining that Cublington should be recommended as the approved site was the time costs of travel between the different proposed airports and London.

Although time may be regarded as a scarce resource in economic analysis it has some peculiar characteristics. Time cannot be saved in the sense that chocolate or iron ore can be saved, nor can the total stock of time possessed by an individual be increased, except in so far as his lifespan can be extended. But time can be transferred to alternative uses and could perhaps be regarded as the most versatile of all 'raw materials'. The value of transport time savings is thus derived from the benefit that individuals or society gain from the ability to use the time saved from travelling for some different purpose. A five-minute reduction in the time needed to get to work may be used to enjoy a more leisurely breakfast. Raw materials that are delivered more quickly may be used in the process of manufacture during the time that they would have been resting in a lorry or railway wagon.

If all time savings were sold on the market then the reasons why people attach value to them, although interesting, would be of no special concern to the economist. Some important time savings are evaluated by the normal mechanism of the market. The higher charges imposed for travelling by Concorde, or on inter-city trains instead of coaches partly reflect the time savings advantages of these forms of transport. But all roads in Britain, and most of those in other countries, are provided without any direct charge to consumers so that evaluating time savings has become an important part of road investment appraisal. Some proposed transport investments, such as the building of a Channel Tunnel, even if the services they provide are subsequently allocated to consumers through the pricing mechanism, also require estimates to be made of the value likely to be placed on the expected time savings.

The theory of time-saving evaluation

The philosophy underlying the British Department of Transport's time-saving evaluation method is, perhaps, best described in an ECMT study on time-saving (Harrison and Quarmby, 1969). This study makes some reference to underlying theory, although the main concern is with practical research and efforts to find actual money values for transport time savings. The authors argue that there are two reasons for valuing time savings. These are that 'time savings allow further activities to be engaged in' and because 'for most occasions travel can be assumed to have positive disutility'. These are not, however, logically distinct reasons. Travellers will value the ability to use travel time for some alternative use which will give them greater utility. This will be the case whether the utility yielded by travel is negative, or just lower than that provided by the preferred alternative use. It is not very clear what meaning should be attached to the 'positive disutility' of travel time unless this means that travellers would, if they could, choose to have the time annihilated. For those travelling in working time the main benefit from shortening journey times will accrue to employers who could make use of the time saved. Ideally the preferences of work-time travellers themselves should also be taken into consideration. Some might prefer travelling to spending extra time at work, but others might gain utility by transferring time from travel to a work activity.

A study by Bruzelius contains a detailed theoretical discussion of the problems of measuring the benefit from a time-saving transport investment (Bruzelius, 1979). He assumes public sector investment and bases his analysis on the theories of welfare economics. He argues that there is market failure in the provision of transport services and that transport investment should be judged by the Pareto ranking or according to the accepted social welfare function. Thus he would measure the benefit from building a new road (for an individual consumer) as the area between the compensated demand curves for the old and new road and above the price line.

For the purposes of this study income distribution problems may be temporarily ignored, and it is assumed that the amount people are willing to pay to enjoy a speed increase represents the benefit that it is desired to measure. The position with known demand curves for an existing and improved road (or a new alternative road) is illustrated in figure 8.1. (It must also be assumed that 'units of traffic' are homogeneous and that any increased traffic flow does not offset the speed improvement.)

The demand, or flow of homogeneous units of traffic is measured on the horizontal axis and price, or 'willingness to pay' on the vertical axis. The original demand curve for the unimproved road is $P_1 D_1$. It is assumed that the 'price' charged is what people would be prepared to pay for the use of the existing road apart from any payments already made in the form of fuel or other running costs. Thus, given an existing level of running costs, including fuel tax, $P_1 D_1$ represents the total payments that could be extracted as a toll on the road by a monopolist who could practise perfect discrimination between all consumers. It is also assumed that the amount that would be paid in toll covers all the private benefits that use of the road would provide. This means, for example, that it includes the contributions made by employers towards the cost of carrying their employees during the course of the working day. $P_2 D_2$ represents the new demand curve that would exist if the road was improved. It is assumed that some new demand $D_1 D_2$ is generated when the road is improved, though this assumption is not essential. The new demand curve $(P_2 D_2)$ has been drawn parallel with $P_1 D_1$ which suggests that all the existing road users $(O D_1)$ put the same value $(P_2 P_1)$ on the road improvement. The argument is not affected if this assumption is changed. The total gross gain from the speed im-

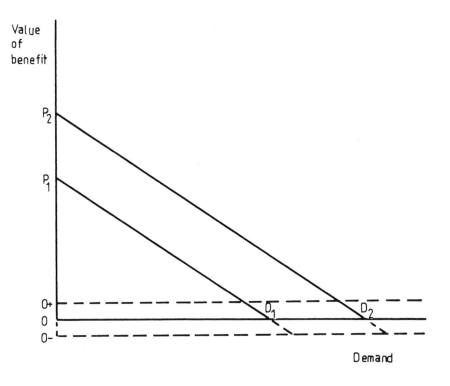

Figure 8.1   Value of benefits v demand for road space per time period

provement is therefore represented by the area $P_2 D_2 D_1 P_1$. This represents the gain that would represent the actual gross value of a time saving resulting from a transport investment given the simplifying assumptions. This model can be used to examine the problems that are encountered when actual time-saving values have to be used in real-world investment appraisal. The main problems are:

(a)   income distribution considerations;

(b)   the effect of changes in vehicle operating costs;

(c)   the relationship of resource costs to perceived costs, and

(d)   the choice of indicators to represent willingness-to-pay values.

The income distribution issue is a familiar problem of welfare theory and cost—benefit analysis. If income is not distributed optimally then

184

'willingness to pay' may be an unreliable guide to economic welfare. Public bodies making transport investment decisions may wish to provide some transport facilities even to those who could not afford the full average cost price and they may not be willing to accept an unadjusted willingness-to-pay measurement as their only guide when allocating investment.

The 'zero price' position in figure 8.1 measures the situation when no specific charge is made for the use of the road (or other transport facility) but, as already explained, is assumed to measure demand given an existing level of vehicle operating costs. The value of the time saving on the improved road, $P_2 D_2 D_1 P_1$, therefore depends on the further assumption that these costs do not change when journey times are shortened. But this is not realistic. Vehicle operating costs may be reduced with less stopping, braking, and gear-changing, or they may increase because of higher fuel consumption and greater tyre wear. The new 'zero price' positions on figure 8.1 are shown at 0+ and 0−. Changes in operating costs cannot be treated easily (in the same way as changes in accident costs or noise costs) as another distinct factor that can be added to the overall investment appraisal. This is because it is necessary to know whether willingness-to-pay measurements have taken account of the perceived cost, or benefit, resulting from changes in vehicle operating costs. An associated problem is that of relating perceived changes in vehicle operating costs to variations in actual resource costs. Taxes such as vehicle excise duty and fuel tax may cause perceived costs to differ from resource costs, and tax changes could cause apparent changes in the measurement of the value of time savings.

The last problem will be the main concern of most of the rest of this chapter. The demand curves of figure 8.1 are unknown and some kind of real-world measurements must be made from which estimates of willingness-to-pay figures can be developed. It is obvious that it is impracticable to try to measure the preferences of innumerable individual consumers and the figures used in practice are all based on very broad average values.

Time-saving evaluation in practice

In current British practice 'personal' time-savings values and vehicle operating costs are treated separately. Time values are divided into two major categories covering 'working' and 'non-working' time savings. For working time the Department of Transport have estimated time-savings values for nine classes of traveller. The 1980 figures (in 1979 prices) are shown in table 8.1.

Table 8.1
Values of time savings — working time

Class of traveller	Value pence per hour (average 1979 prices)
Car driver	411.2
Car passenger	328.8
Bus passenger	272.9
Rail passenger	440.4
Underground passenger	400.0
Bus driver	276.8
Bus conductor	270.6
Heavy goods vehicle occupant	300.0
Light goods vehicle occupant	258.4

Source: Department of Transport, 1980.

These values are based on average earnings plus employers' national insurance and pension contributions. The assumption behind this practice is that earnings represent the value of the extra output which those travelling during working time could produce if their journey times were reduced. It has been argued that earnings may not reflect the marginal value of output accurately but, while this is often true, it is difficult to think of any more satisfactory indicator.

If the average earnings of each group of travellers represented the willingness-to-pay value accurately, then this measurement would be equivalent to that described in our model and illustrated in figure 8.1. There would be a different average saving value for each of the relevant classes of traveller but these would aggregate to the same total. In figure 8.1 the total value of the time saving would be the same whether it is calculated as the area of $O\,P_2D_2 - O\,P_1D_1$ or the product of the average value of using the road after the improvement and the traffic flow minus the equivalent pre-improvement figure. In both cases the value of the benefit is equal to $0.5\,OD_2\,(OP_2) - 0.5\,OD_1\,(OP_1)$, but this only applies, however, for a specific transport investment project. The use of national average figures for road investment means that the averages may not apply very closely to any particular road. Where investment is allocated on a regional basis, as with road investment, this means that relatively low wage-level areas will be treated in the same way as areas with higher earnings levels and some adjustments are made to the willingness-to-pay criterion. (This only applies in so far as time-saving values influence road investment. In practice other factors may be decisive.)

The use of earnings figures to evaluate time-saving values means that work-time travellers' own preferences are ignored. This is an area in which more research needs to be completed, but it is probable that this omission is not of crucial importance. Some of those travelling during the course of their workday might prefer being at work to travelling, while others might take the opposite point of view. The low average positive time-savings values of the former group could be approximately equal to the negative average value of the second group, so that the net value placed on time savings by work travellers may be very low and leaving it out of the calculations is unlikely to have any decisive effect on investment decisions.

A more important problem is that of deciding when travellers really are 'at work' in the sense that any travel time savings could be translated into increased output. The position may depend upon the nature of the work task. It may be possible to carry out some work at any time but undertaking jobs which require the co-operation of other workers or the use of capital equipment may only be feasible inside the framework of normal working hours. In some situations a work journey-time reduction may lead to a fall in earnings rather than an increase in productivity. Suppose that a worker's wage is based on the assumption that he will spend one hour of an eight-hour 'working day' travelling. If a transport investment makes it possible for him to travel for only 0.5 hours then the employer might be able to reduce the wages paid by a factor of 15/16 instead of demanding an extra 30 minutes of output. The employer's money gain would be offset by the worker's loss and the net gain to society would be the value of the employee's increase in leisure time.

There has been a considerable debate about whether small-time savings should be valued at the same rate per minute as larger savings. Tipping (1968) and Mishan (1970) for example, have both argued that time savings of only a few minutes cannot be used productively. The counter argument put forward by the Department of Transport and supported in the Leitch Committee report (Department of Transport, 1978b) is that transport investments lead to a large number of small time savings and that these can be aggregated to make one 'useable' increment of time. This argument may be justified for travellers making long journeys, but it seems doubtful whether it can be applied to routes used mainly by commuter traffic where the opportunity to add small time savings is very limited (Heggie, 1976).

The Department of Transport recognises only one class of 'in-vehicle' non-working time. The values chosen are based on empirical evidence suggesting that the appropriate figure is 25 per cent of average earnings. Separate behavioural and resource values are estimated, the difference between these being equivalent to the average rate of indirect taxation in the economy. The 1980 figures were:

Behavioural = 65.3 pence per hr
Resource   = 55.4 pence per hr

187

Although this is not specifically stated it must be assumed that the willingness-to-pay data reflects consumers' behaviour when they know what other price or benefit they will receive from changes in vehicle operating costs. As with work-time, changes in vehicle operating costs are added to personal time-saving values.

Theoretical considerations suggest that non-work time-saving values will be below marginal wage rates because the utility of work may be lower than the utility of travel and because the amount that people are willing to pay to 'buy' additional leisure time will be less than the sum that they will require as compensation for 'selling' further leisure time to their employers. It is apparent that the values of non-work time will vary very widely for different travellers. As is assumed by the Department of Transport a direct relationship with income levels is to be expected, and is suggested by some empirical evidence. Average values are also likely to vary between different classes of non-work traveller. People making trips for pleasure on a Sunday afternoon may have very low or even negative time-saving values, whereas those hurrying to an urgent appointment may have very high values. The Department of Transport single value is based on the equity principle that the leisure time of all travellers is of equal value to society whether they are rich or poor. The Leitch Committee disagreed with the adoption of the equity principle for non-work time savings, arguing that this is 'inconsistent with the general philosophy of cost—benefit analysis' (Department of Transport, 1978b). The 1978 Department of Transport *Highway Economics Note* gave a single value for non-working time, but contained the statement that 'the Department no longer adheres to the principle of equity value of non-working time. Where local income distribution differs from the national average, and where sufficiently reliable data about the incomes of travellers exist, appropriate values may be adopted'. (Department of Transport, 1978a). The 1980 Note, however, argued that 'the single value of "in-vehicle" non-working time reflects the Department's continued adherence to the equity principle'. The issue depends on a value judgement rather than theoretical analysis. Whatever the philosophy of cost—benefit analysis it does not remove the government's right to decide that the leisure time savings of all their citizens are of equal value.

Although a good case can be made for treating non-work travellers in different income groups equally, it is less easy to justify the practice of ignoring all other differences as well. Different classes of travellers with the same levels of income may put very different values on time savings. If these groups can be identified, and constitute a significant proportion of average traffic flows then there seems to be no good reason, apart from administrative convenience, for imputing a single average time-saving value to them. The one class of traveller that is both distinct and important is that of commuters making the journey to or from work. In the 1975/76 National Travel Survey sample 23 per cent of all mileage undertaken by travellers was on journeys to or from work (Department of Transport, 1979). In an international survey of time-budgets average commuter journeys ranged from 38 to 89 minutes (Szalai, 1972). Both theoretical considerations and empirical evidence suggest that the average time-saving value of commuters may be higher than that for other leisure travellers. Journeys to work that are repeated every day, perhaps for years, become monotonous and uninteresting so that the utility gained from the ability to transfer some commuter travelling time to another use may be high. The marginal utility of leisure time is also likely to be higher on weekdays than at weekends. Time savings cannot be saved and leisure time on a Saturday cannot be transferred to a weekday. Workers may have about five hours' freely allocable leisure time on a weekday, but as much as thirteen hours on Saturdays or Sundays. This argument would also apply to non-commuting travel time savings on weekdays, but these are much more difficult to identify than the large blocks of commuting travel.

In the Leitch Committee report it is argued that the valuation of commuter time savings would be expected to be closely related to hourly wage rates and that 'this has consistently been shown to be the case in empirical work'. The committee recommended that separate values should be attached to commuter and 'pure leisure' travel time savings. If this recommendation was adopted there would be some interesting consequences. If commuter travel time savings were valued at 75 per cent of average earnings then, according to some calculations (Sharp, 1981) it would be necessary to give a negative value to pure leisure time savings if the average return from transport investment was not to be increased. In so far as the rate of return on transport investment is compared with that in other industries, this could mean increased investment in transport. It could also lead to more road rather than rail investment since the Department of Transport time evaluation techniques are generally used only for appraising road investment. (This point is further developed later in this chapter.) Of more practical importance would be the effect on the ranking of alternative road investment projects. The use of higher commuting values would obviously increase the net present value to cost ratios for roads leading into the central business districts of large towns and conurbations. These would tend to attract investment rather than holiday or other largely rural routes. Since the increased values would apply mainly to those travelling in cars and buses, the rate of return on roads carrying heavy flows of this type of traffic would increase relative to that on roads carrying a high percentage of goods vehicles.

The effects of journey time changes on vehicle operating costs are measured by the Department of Transport through the application of a formula:

$$\text{operating cost (pence per vehicle km)} = a + \frac{b}{v} + cv^2$$

where a, b, and c are parameters estimated separately for cars, light goods vehicles, 'other' (or heavy) goods vehicles and buses. The parameter b covers depreciation and those parts of fuel and maintenance costs which are believed to fall with speed increases while c measures fuel and maintenance costs that increase with speed. Fuel costs may fall for speed increases over some ranges (when running in low gears can be avoided, for example) but will increase over higher speed ranges. If v is the average speed (in km per hour) before a road improvement and v_1 is the speed after an investment has led to a reduction in journey times, then the net change in vehicle operating costs will be:

$$\frac{b}{v} - \frac{b}{v_1} + cv^2 - cv_1^2$$

Since the constituents of the a parameter are not influenced by speed changes they do not affect the comparison. For an average motorway or trunk road investment the net change in vehicle operating costs works out at zero.

The figures in table 8.2 show the effect of some speed changes on the resource operating costs of cars and heavy lorries, according to the formulae given in the Department of Transport's 1980 Note (Department of Transport, 1980).

In each case the second figure shows the maximum possible reduction in vehicle operating costs. This occurs, of course, where the marginal cost resulting from increasing speed changes from being negative to positive which will be the minimum vehicle operating cost position. If these points are found by treating the formulae as differentiable functions then they occur at 60.33 kph (or 37.49 mph) for cars, and 56.59 kph (or 35.16 mph) for medium and heavy lorries. Any increases in speed beyond 60 kph for cars and 57 kph for lorries will therefore increase vehicle operating costs and the only gains, according to the Department of Transport formulae, will come from personal time savings. The third figure of speed increase given for each initial speed in table 8.2 represents the point at which there would first be a net increase in vehicle operating costs.

The main doubt about the vehicle operating cost calculations is whether these measure adequately those benefits of reducing lorry journey times that are not covered by the personal time-savings values. Increasing the speed with which lorries can complete their journeys might be expected to bring two forms of benefit. Loads will be

Table 8.2
Journey time changes and vehicle operating costs

Initial speed kph	Speed after improvement kph	Cost decrease (−) or increase (+) pence per km
Cars		
30	31	−0.075
	60	−0.434
	107	+0.001
40	41	−0.017
	60	−0.156
	87	+0.003
50	51	−0.007
	60	−0.034
	73	+0.006
60	61	+0.001
Lorries		
15	16	−0.336
	57	−3.354
	149	+0.057
30	31	−0.075
	57	−0.766
	91	+0.003
40	41	−0.032
	57	−0.239
	78	−0.016
50	51	−0.009
	57	−0.032
	60	+0.002
60	61	+0.005

delivered more quickly and more work can be obtained from each vehicle. The load delivery factor is ignored in the Department's calculations, so that the benefits from reducing the journey times of an empty lorry are held to be the same as those that would accrue from a lorry carrying 20 tons of high value goods. The resource value of time for 'other' goods vehicles according to the Department of Transport (1980 figures, 1979 prices) at 360p per hour was only slightly higher than the value for light goods vehicles of 335.9p per hour as the higher wages paid to drivers of the heavier vehicles were partly offset by the higher occupancy rate of light vehicles. The resource value of buses was 1170.4p because allowance is made for the time savings of each member of the 'load' of passengers. The reasons for ignoring the value of speeding up deliveries, according to the evidence given by the Department to the Leitch Committee are that 'the evidence on appropriate average values is insufficient to yield a reliable estimate and that, on average, any allowance would be insignificant compared to the other items included in the calculations'. While the first part of this statement may be true, the second argument seems to be questionable. Studies of the allocation of goods traffic have shown that firms consigning goods are generally prepared to pay higher rates in order to obtain speedy deliveries. The interest savings on a consignment valued at £10,000 could amount to as much as 17p per hour.

Probably more important than the load issue, however, is the question of how far the Department's formula can be said to measure the benefits from better vehicle utilisation. The Leitch Committee report, while expressing some doubts about the methods of valuing the time savings of goods vehicles, did not consider the matter to be important, as sensitivity tests carried out for them showed that even if the capital saving element in the Department's formula was multiplied by 10 the average NPV to cost ratio for sample improvement schemes would only be increased by 0.02 from 0.38 to 0.40. This is an area which requires further research. If the capital cost element in the Department's formula is increased to $822.6/v$ then a speed increase from 15 to 30 kph would reduce operating costs by 27.27p per km, which means that a vehicle averaging 500 miles per week on the improved road would save £219.4 which does not seem to be insignificant. Since the hours that a goods vehicle can be driven by one driver are now legally restricted to eight per day (with some detailed modifications) and as it is difficult to produce replacement drivers, the use of each lorry may be restricted to the same hours as that of its driver. An hour's time saving could therefore mean an hour's extra production from the lorry. Some calculations based on the net value of one hour's use of lorries suggests that for a 14-ton gross weight vehicle running 500 miles a week the value of an hour's extra output would be 958p while if its weekly mileage was 1000 miles the gain would be worth 1102p. These compare with estimated Department of Transport time-saving values of 440p and 413p respectively (given certain assumptions about the initial speeds). For 32-ton vehicles the 'increased output' values would be 1430p (500 miles per week) and 1645p (1000 miles), while the Department's values would remain unchanged at 440p and 413p per vehicle. It is interesting to note that the COBA sensitivity tests commissioned for the Leitch Committee showed that doubling the time values of goods vehicle occupants had a considerable increase on NPV to cost ratios, increasing the average ratio on the sample schemes from 0.38 to 0.67.

The application of time-saving values to the ranking of actual road investment projects will be influenced by the nature of the traffic flow figures used. In the 'travel and accident loss' method of road investment appraisal that preceded the development of the COBA appraisal technique standard traffic mix figures were used for all roads. The measured traffic flow, in vehicles per hour, was assumed to conform to the national average mix of cars, buses, and heavy and light goods vehicles. This meant that the relative time-saving values of different classes of traffic could not affect the ranking of projects, which was determined solely by the size of the total traffic flow and the costs of the scheme. COBA assumes that local traffic flow figures will be used, but it is not clear how far accurate local figures are employed in practice. National average figures can be fed into the COBA computer programme evaluation. The results of using crude traffic flow figures and national traffic-mix proportions would probably be to favour roads with large flows of non-work private cars, since these make up a large part of the flow on most roads but would receive a relatively low 'time-saving value' weighting if the actual local traffic mix figures were used. Where national traffic mix figures are used all vehicles, in effect, are treated as being of equal importance in contributing to the value of the total time-saving benefit. Even where the local traffic flow mix is used, however, the proportion of working and non-working travellers in cars and buses is assumed to conform to the national average. The authors of the Leitch Committee report argued that the fixed proportion assumed (17 per cent working cars and 83 per cent non-working) will vary widely in practice and that many road investment projects would be ranked differently if actual local proportions were observed. The use of actual working and non-working proportions would have a similar effect to the adoption of higher time values for commuters and tend to rank roads used for the journey to work more highly relative to holiday and leisure routes.

The use of willingness-to-pay criteria for measuring time-saving values usually means that the influence of income predominates over other factors. If the influence of income was removed the relative utilities of different forms of travel would result in a changed ranking of these classes of transport. The Department's time-saving values rank working rail travellers, car travellers and bus travellers in descending order of time-saving values. But the 'disutility' ranking with the influence of income removed would be bus, rail, car in descending order of time-saving value (Tanner et al., 1973).

A final problem could arise in relating time-saving values to real-world investment appraisal if a direct comparison was made between road and other transport investment projects where a direct charge is made for the service provided. If a rail investment resulted in a reduction in journey time, British Rail might measure the value of the gross benefit as the extra revenue earned from additional passengers with prices constant, or from raising prices (presumably with a smaller growth in the number of passengers). In either case the total benefit would be smaller than the full consumer surplus gain that the Department of Transport's techniques seek to measure (unless the demand curve was perfectly elastic with all consumers having the same willingness to pay values). If the position was similar to that shown in figure 8.1 with parallel straight line demand functions and if the railway charged revenue maximising prices before and after the improvement, then the total value of the time savings would be only half that indicated by the consumer surplus measurement. Road and rail (or other transport mode) investment projects are not, however, normally compared in Britain and the rail method of appraisal differs in other important ways from that used for road projects (Department of Transport, 1978) so that this problem is not of immediate significance.

Summary and conclusions

The main points made in this chapter can be summarised as follows:

1 The objective of 'official' measurements of the values of time savings in Britain is to estimate the total amount that consumers would be willing to pay to enjoy the reduction in journey time resulting from a transport investment project. These estimates are mainly used for evaluating road investment projects.

2 The Department of Transport bases its estimates of the value of time savings for people travelling during the course of their work on adjusted average earnings and those for all other 'non-work' travellers as 25 per cent of earnings.

3 The averaging process adopted, with national average figures for each main category of traveller, means that actual willingness to pay on individual roads is not reflected.

4 Roads with a high proportion of people travelling during the course of work do not show a high value for time savings in practice, because a standard mix of 'working' and 'non-working' cars is assumed for all roads.

5 A single 'equity' value is used for all non-work travellers so that investment is not directed towards wealthy areas where actual willingness to pay values would be high.

6 There is a good case for believing that the average time-saving values of commuters are significantly higher than those of other non-work travellers.

7 The authors of the Leitch Committee report argued that the equity principle should be abandoned.

194

8   The formulae used for evaluating changes in vehicle operating cost resulting from reductions in journey times ensure that this factor has little affect on investment decisions.

9   No allowance is made for any benefits resulting from speeding the delivery of goods and alternative methods of measuring the benefits that might accrue when lorries can complete more work each day give higher values for goods vehicles than those obtained by using the Department of Transport's techniques.

10   The zero pricing willingness-to-pay or consumer surplus measurement is not comparable with measurements of the value of time savings based on increases in revenue.

References

Bruzelius, N., *The Value of Travel Time*, Croom Helm, London, 1979.

Department of the Environment, *Transport Policy: a Consultation Document*, vols 1 and 2, HMSO, London, 1976.

Department of Transport, *Highway Economics Note No.2*, Department of Transport, London, 1978a.

Department of Transport, *Report of the Advisory Committee on Trunk Road Assessment*, HMSO, London, 1978b.

Department of Transport, *National Travel Survey 1975/6*, HMSO, London, 1979.

Department of Transport, *Highway Economics Note No.2* (Revision), Department of Transport, London, 1980.

Harrison, A.J. and Quarmby, D.A., 'Theoretical and practical research on an estimation of time-saving' in *Report on the Sixth Round Table on Transport Economics*, European Conference of Ministers of Transport, 1969.

Heggie, I.G. (ed.) *Modal Choice and the Value of Travel Time*, Oxford University Press, Oxford, 1976.

Mishan, E.J., 'What is wrong with Roskill?' in *Journal of Transport Economics and Policy*, 1970, vol.4, pp. 221–34.

Sharp, C.H., *The Economics of Time*, Martin Robertson, Oxford, 1981.

Szalai, A. (ed.) *The Use of Time*, Mouton, 1972.

Tanner, J.C., Gyenes, L., Lynam, D.A., Magee, S.V. and Tulpule, A.H., *Development and Calibration of the CRISTAL Transport Planning Model*, TRRL Report LR 574, Crowthorne, 1973.

Tipping, D., 'Time Savings in Transport Studies' in *Economic Journal*, 1968, vol.78, pp. 843–54.

9 The practical problems of traffic forecasting — the prediction of car ownership

K. J. Button

Introduction

Traffic forecasts play a central role in any transport investment appraisal or planning exercise. The forecasts provide predictions of the physical changes which will take place in travel patterns as a result of a change in the transport system and are also an important intermediate step in the estimation of the costs and benefits, in the widest sense, associated with alternative schemes. The high cost and relative inflexibility of most transport infrastructure combined with its durability makes it important to forecast accurately the longer-term demands for such facilities. Equally, the complex interactions between both alternative routes and alternative modes make it essential that the full implications of any investment or management proposal can be traced through the entire transport system.

While the need for traffic forecasts has long been accepted, the actual approaches to forecasting and the methods employed have changed considerably over the past few decades. In part this is due to the changing emphasis in transport policy, with a movement away from high cost, capital-intensive investment programmes to rather more specific, piecemeal traffic management policies, but it is also due to advances in our understanding of forecasting techniques and changes in the way that transport appraisals are conducted. The advances in computing technology have reduced the computational costs of forecasting and have permitted the introduction of more sophisticated forecasting models. (Computational constraints were serious limitations on the types of approach which were practicable in the immediate postwar period.) In general, therefore, there has been a gradual shift over time in the type of traffic forecasting models employed and, indeed, in the types of predictions which are ultimately produced. This chapter looks at these changes but, rather than offering a detailed review or critique, it is primarily concerned with some of the more practical problems of producing useful forecasts. Its main focus is on the difficulties encountered in devising useful, robust techniques which permit the generation of the types of traffic forecast required to appraise successfully a transport project or plan.

There is no such thing as a 'perfect' forecast in transport, the levels of uncertainty are too great, the potential outcomes too large and 'ideal' procedures too costly. As one commentator said following the presentation of a paper by J.C. Tanner (1978) on traffic forecasting to the Royal Statistical Society:

> For he who would forecast traffic up to 30 years ahead has an impossible task. On the one hand, the numbers of vehicles and their journeys are outcomes of demographic, social, political and economic factors, of international trade and travel, and none of these permits reliable forecasts. On the other hand, the available data are poor in predictive information and hard to get; simple statistical models are impossible to formulate validly; and consequently reliable statistical methods hardly exist. Any choice of approach and method must be a flagrant compromise, and identifiable weaknesses are inevitable.

Despite these problems forecasts must be made and are made. The central issue is to determine the best practical compromise possible.

Traffic forecasting is an extremely wide-ranging and complex topic and in order to reduce the discussion to manageable proportions the main focus of the chapter will be on the practical problems associated with forecasting for the evaluation of road investments and in particular with car ownership forecasting. While car ownership forecasting is only one sub-model in a series of stages which together provide the basis for the overall road traffic forecasts, e.g. it is central to both trip generation and modal split forecasting, the development of the forecasting methodology has closely paralleled the development of traffic forecasting in general while the practical problems encountered are common to most forms of forecasting employed in the transport sector. The chapter proceeds by, firstly, considering the particular qualities one is seeking from a traffic forecast; strangely a completely accurate prediction is not always the primary concern, especially if it does not relate to the specific problems under review, e.g. the sensitivity of future traffic flows to various transport policy options. Some discussion of the main methods of car ownership forecasting then follows with attention directed almost exclusively at the practical usefulness of various forecasting methodologies rather than at their intellectual elegance. Clearly, theory and practice are often closely related but conceptual strength may need to be sacrificed on occasions to permit useful application. This discussion is couched in somewhat historical terms to reflect the backgrounds against which the alternative methods evolved, but it should not be seen as a simple narrative. The intention is to offer a critique not a story. Finally, some comment is made about the ways in which car ownership forecasting may be improved and some indications given of the ways in which it may usefully develop in the future.

In at least one major respect this chapter differs from the majority of other contributions that have appeared in recent years dealing with traffic forecasting, including the voluminous theoretical and applied literature on car ownership forecasting: it is, in the main, non-technical. Rather than pursuing mathematical rigour it offers discussion of some of the more fundamental, underlying problems of forecasting together with suggestions for ways in which they might be tackled. It is hoped that the lack of mathematical rigour is not seen as a major shortcoming. A more detailed and technical survey of car ownership forecasting is contained in Button, Pearman and Fowkes (1981).

A further restriction is that most of the argument is couched in terms of the British experience, although this limitation is more apparent than real since the general conclusions are of universal applicability. Indeed, because of the considerable official interest which has arisen in traffic forecasting over recent years in Great Britain, partly as a result of revisions to overall transport policy and partly due to public disquiet over previously established forecasting philosophy, developments in transport demand forecasting, and car ownership modelling in particular, have been extensive.

The qualities sought in traffic forecasts

Any traffic forecasting involves a series of stages. Firstly, one has to decide exactly what it is that is to be predicted. Secondly, there is the need to collect data and information on the existing situation prior to constructing some form of forecasting model. Finally, from this model one produces projections by feeding in further information about anticipated trends in key exogenous variables. In many cases, therefore, it may prove more important to meet certain, specific criteria in relation to that *particular* stage in the sequence rather than to obtain

198

the most accurate result possible. For example, financial budgets may necessitate relatively small samples being used, while lack of computing capacity or data-handling facilities may require the use of rather simple modelling and simulation techniques. Consequently the quality one is looking for in a forecasting methodology is not always exclusively accuracy although this will, obviously, be of considerable importance. Other important qualities may include, for example, economy, flexibility, policy sensitivity, speed, theoretical respectability etc. In many cases the choice of forecasting method is determined by a process more akin to satisficing (see Simon, 1977) than maximising; the approach which is preferred is accepted because it meets certain minimum, satisfactory levels for each of a set of low-level but clearly definable criteria.

One of the major problems in traffic forecasting is that the qualities sought by the forecaster may not coincide with those preferred by those responsible for the actual appraisal. National car ownership forecasts employed in trunk road appraisal have, since the mid-1970s, for example, been given within a maximum and minimum band, while those responsible for road construction tend to base their decisions on a single, expected future level of car ownership (and, *ipso facto*, traffic flow) at some target date. (Usually the traffic flow anticipated fifteen years after opening determines the engineering standard of a road while economic assessment involves traffic flows throughout an assumed thirty-year life.) Clearly this raises problems at the interface between forecasting and appraisal, the result of which has been some modifications to the latter. The decision, for example, whether to use the upper or lower limit of the range affects the relevant levels of expenditure and impact on the environment. Variations may be considerable and alternative forecast could well support options ranging from improvement of an existing route to the construction of an entirely new alignment. The choice to be made has become less mechanical as choice has increased. Such problems will be discussed in more detail below.

Given the fact that the adoption of a forecasting methodology is rather more complex than is often supposed, what exactly determines the approach finally employed? The most frequently sought qualities in a traffic forecasting framework may usefully be considered under the following general headings.

Accuracy

Accuracy is not quite the simple concept it is often thought to be. There is clearly the obvious distinction between short-term and long-term accuracy, whereby a forecasting methodology may yield

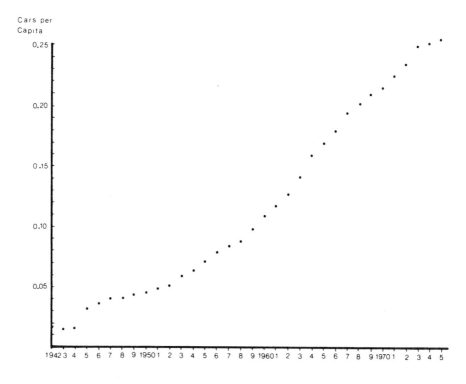

Figure 9.1   Per capita car ownership in Great Britain, 1942–1975

extremely good predictions of traffic volumes over a period of perhaps two or three years but thereafter cease to yield useful results. Alternatively long-term forecasting models may be extremely unreliable in the short term. If we look at figure 9.1, for example, which traces the growth in car ownership per capita in Great Britain between 1942 and 1975, it is clear that while a straight-line extrapolation from, say, 1942 to 1952 would produce reasonable forecasts for several years, by the end of the period serious under-predictions would result. Possibly of more importance, but subject to considerable neglect, are the short-term inaccuracies which often accompany long-term forecasts. In many cases, provided the long-term projections are reasonable, short-term fluctuations around the projected trend are of little consequence. In some instances, indeed, the important point is the rather simple one of whether car ownership is going to grow *at all*.

The use of extrapolative forecasts of car ownership in interurban road investment appraisal illustrates the importance of the long- and short-term distinction. The benefits of road investments accumulate as a consequence of road use, which is assessed over the forecast period. Because of the discounting procedure within cost–benefit analysis, inaccuracies towards the end of the forecast period are of relatively little importance, so that slightly incorrect projections will not greatly affect assessed benefits. The same is not so clearly true with regard to costs, as road designs are based, in the first instance, on expected traffic levels fifteen years after the *opening* of the new road, say about twenty-five years from when initial planning commences. If traffic forecasts are so grossly inaccurate as to recommend a quite inappropriate scale of provision, say a three-lane motorway instead of two-lane, this will have a major effect because most costs are incurred at the start of a project's life and are not greatly diminished by discounting. For forecasting at the local, urban level of aggregation such arguments hold less weight because the types of policy under assessment, e.g. public transport subsidies, traffic management schemes etc., frequently have much shorter-term consequences. Consequently, accuracy must be defined in the context of the use to which forecasts are to be put rather than in terms of pure predictive power *per se*.

Accuracy has a second dimension involving the confidence with which the predictions may be viewed. Normally, and almost by convention, single figure projections are given of, for example, the expected number of cars or volume of traffic over a specific route for a specified target date with some indication of the path followed over the intervening period. Such forecasts clearly involve making a number of assumptions concerning the expected values of varous influential variables. Each of these will, however, in fact have associated with it a distribution of possible outcomes. Thus, if these distributions are known it is possible to subject the forecasts to various sensitivity tests and to obtain a range for the *probable* outcome. The users of forecasts, however, are often not altogether indifferent as to which of the two sides of the distribution around the expected value actual traffic flows fall. In the case of a road appraisal, for example, if the actual outcome falls within the lower range of the traffic forecast then reliance on a more central prediction could result in excess capacity being provided and resources wasted. Alternatively, if the outcome is higher than the designer had assumed there are likely to be heavy congestion costs and incremental adjustments to expand capacity are likely to be expensive. On balance the Department of Transport (1980) seems to feel the latter situation the most undesirable:

> The penalty of providing inadequate capacity at junctions, or of building a carriageway with inadequate strength to withstand the

demand on it from heavy vehicle traffic can be higher in relation to initial cost, than the penalties of under developing roads in other respects. The cost of remedying such faults when the road is in use and near its capacity can be very considerable.

Consequently, one of the main forms of accuracy which is often sought relates to the distribution of probable outcomes rather than the actual expected single figure projection.

Finally, there are certain, totally unpredictable factors — wars, economic crises etc. — which can completely destroy any forecast's basis and thus render it totally inaccurate. (It is worth noting, however, that even when crises do not distort the picture, a considerable proportion of the inaccuracy in most traffic forecasts has proved to be a consequence of inaccurate projections of the independent variables, rather than calibration errors or flaws in the model structure *per se.*) The oil crisis of 1974 is the classic example of an unpredictable event; here an unforeseen rise in fuel prices caused a sudden and dramatic change in the demand for travel. Almost by definition it is impossible to allow for such events when forecasting, but the problem may be recognised if forecasting is conducted on two levels. Pearman and Button (1981) suggest that at the lower level forecasting should follow one of the currently established types of model (see below), although offering more information about the robustness of projections in the light of short-lived distortions to normal patterns of behaviour (using, for instance, simulation techniques of the Monte Carlo kind). The second, higher level projections would involve 'scenario' analysis and would provide planners and decision makers with some, not necessarily quantified, guide to the possible impact of sudden, dramatic changes in the environment in which transport operates. This is clearly a move away from the mechanistic approach of offering exact forecasts and, by necessity, use of the predictions would involve a greater degree of subjective application but the final outcome may prove to be more accurate forecasts in the wider sense. It is also an approach which conforms closely to developments which are taking place in the wider investment appraisal methodology.

Theoretical consistency

The 29 June 1974 issue of *Business Week* expressed the view that 'a forecast, essentially, is the statement of a theory with specific values instead of abstractions. When the forecast goes seriously wrong, it suggests that something is wrong with the theory'. Quite obviously one can question the validity of this statement — forecasts may go wrong, for example, because of inappropriate application of a perfectly sound theory or because of defective calibration of essential parameters without, in either case, the underlying theory being defective. Nevertheless the theoretical foundation of a forecasting model is important. What are the desirable properties sought in a forecasting model? Certainly detailed replication of the real world is both impossible and, given the problems of forecasting exogenous variables, usually impractical. John Maynard Keynes argued over forty years ago that 'The objective of a model is to segregate the semi-permanent or relatively constant factors from those which are transitory or fluctuating so as to develop a logical way of thinking about the latter, and of understanding the time sequences to which they give rise in particular cases'. The difficulty then becomes one of deciding, in the forecasting context, what are semi-permanent factors. One, semi-tautological answer is supplied by Friedman (1953, p.41) who argues that 'Complete "realism" is clearly unattainable, and the question whether a theory is realistic "enough" can be settled only by seeing whether it yields predictions that are good enough for the purpose in hand or that are better than predictions from alternative theories'.

One school of thought (Tanner, 1978) argues that it is so difficult to construct a long-term forecasting model which simulates in detail the effects of various socio-economic influences on traffic patterns, that simple extrapolative forecasts based upon time trends offer a more useful forecasting tool. The forecasts produced by the Ministry of Transport and its successors throughout the 1960s and 1970s accepted this view. The long-term nature of official requirements (up to forty-five years) favoured the adoption of forecasting techniques which could produce usable results over the period and which gave the appearance of being insensitive to year-to-year changes in the expectations of variables such as real income and fuel prices. The conventional economic models of demand did not meet these criteria at the time. More recently, however, Ben-Akiva (1974) has expressed an alternative view in his advocacy of disaggregate causal models, namely, 'In general, it is impossible to determine the correct specification of a model from data analysis. It should be determined from theory or a priori knowledge based upon experience with, and understanding of, the phenomenon to be modelled'.

One's view of the importance and the desirability of a firm theoretical foundation to underlie traffic forecasts often depends upon what it is that one wishes to obtain from the forecasting exercise. If it is simply numerically accurate forecasts then the theoretical base may prove less important. The design and calibration of elegant and theoretically sound mathematical models of car ownership in this case is transcended by the practical necessity to produce acceptably accurate numerical forecasts for policy purposes. Alternatively, if one accepts Heggie's

(1978) view that traffic models should, in addition to providing predictions, assist in understanding and explaining behaviour and aid in policy formulation, then theoretical considerations increase in importance. Further, if the forecasts are to be treated as neutral, irreversible facts then once again the underlying importance of theory is likely to be over-shadowed by the need for accuracy. Should the forecasts, however, be seen as sensitive to the actions of policy makers, either those directly involved in the transport sector or those concerned with broader macro-economic policy, then an understanding of the workings of the transport market together with a sound theoretical appreciation of the ways in which policy affects this market becomes important.

Flexibility

Flexibility in forecasting may take a variety of forms. Firstly, it is often useful if a forecasting framework may be used in a variety of applications. Throughout the 1960s the majority of UK transport policy initiatives focused on the large-scale expansion of transport infrastructure both at the urban and interurban level (the motorway system, for example, expanded from 153 km in 1960 to 2,483 km in 1979 while nearly 2,000 km of trunk route were made into dual carriageways between 1970 and 1979), but subsequently the emphasis has moved away from comprehensive, investment-intensive transport planning and has been replaced by a rather more *ad hoc* piecemeal approach (Department of Transport, 1977). Consequently, traffic forecasting models need to be adaptable, capable of meeting the needs of those involved in relatively small-scale road improvements, parking schemes, public transport subsidies, car-pooling arrangements, pollution controls, vehicle restriction policies etc.

A forecasting model may also need to be flexible to permit the testing of different policy options, i.e. it is often desirable that it is 'policy sensitive'. This feature of demand forecasting models tended to be less important where an overriding philosophy, e.g. the idea in the 1950s that all demands for road space should be met, dominated official transport policy, but has become rather more desirable in recent years with the acceptance that transport policy should seek to satisfy a diverse range of socio-economic goals rather than simply fulfil stipulated traffic targets. Policy began, from the mid-1970s, to emphasise a need to reverse previous trends, using incentives to persuade the public to break existing habits, especially those relating to urban car use. In the United Kingdom such new policies were pursued in several provincial town centres with some vigour. A 'balanced transport policy' was, for instance, introduced into Oxford by adopting a package including escalating parking charges, extinction of on-street parking, closure of some streets and attempts in general aimed at making public transport more attractive. The 'zone and collar scheme' tried in Nottingham was another example. This overall change in the basis of transport planning can perhaps be traced back to the late 1960s when the transport element of the Greater London Development Plan came under considerable criticism for its excessive reliance on the then conventional road building philosophy. Specifically, '. . . there is ample evidence to support our view that, whether for reasons of administrative difficulty, political reluctance, or inertia, the potentials of management measures, and of restraint by parking controls, have not been adequately used and are far from sufficiently exploited' (Department of the Environment, 1973).

When considering policy sensitivity it is useful to distinguish between two different forms of policy which may influence transport demand — both may prove to be important in the forecasting context. There are broad macro-economic policies affecting income, fuel prices etc. which exert strong influences on traffic patterns as a whole. These types of policy are captured in most forms of traffic forecasting framework quite simply because they determine the long-term, aggregate growth path of travel demand. There are, however, also micro-economic policies affecting traffic management, urban public transport provision etc. upon which local traffic patterns are dependent. Consequently, while forecasters of national and possibly regional travel behaviour require their methodology only to be sensitive to macro policies, those concerned with local predictions are often interested in the sensitivity of their forecasts to micro policies. In the latter case, macro-economic policies are often treated in much less detail since they are exogenous to the appraisal in hand, although some allowance must still be made for them if viable counterfactuals are to be established.

Economy

Traffic forecasting may be expensive and one oft sought quality in a forecasting framework is economy. Economy may result from several features. Data collection is normally a labour-intensive exercise and, consequently, costly. In addition, the marginal increase in information falls off quite sharply with increases in sample size. It therefore makes sense not to spend money on data collection beyond the point where the sample is adequate. The obvious problem is in deciding what is 'adequate' especially in cases when it is not possible to decide upon the exact form of analysis and forecasting until after the data has been collected. Use of census and other easily accessible official statistics offers economies and was, for example, one of the reasons for the development of category analysis forecasting procedures (see below).

Even where aggregate data is imperfect for the actual forecasting exercise at hand, it may prove a helpful input into elementary, preliminary analysis and offer useful insights into the actual type of detailed data which should be sought.

Where sample surveys are employed, the forecaster may either seek a methodology which requires a small data base or one which does not necessitate expensive sampling techniques. The advocates of disaggregate household based forecasting models, requiring only about 600 household surveys, point to the advantages of the method over the 10,000 or so samples required in the zonally aggregated, sequential models employed in the 1960s. The advances in disaggregate modelling are a result of both pressure to devise more cost effective methods of forecasting and developments in the theory of consumer behaviour. (There has been some questioning of this apparent advantage in recent work (for example Bates, 1979) on the grounds that economy in the data base is only obtained by increasing the potential error in the forecasts.) Activity analysis also claims economy in sample size, and much of the work conducted in Oxford during 1976 was based on a household sample of about 60 households.

Economy may also be achieved in the costs of model calibration and prediction. Calibration is less of a problem today than, say, a decade ago. The development of standard computer software and desk top calculators combined with the widespread availability of high-powered computing facilities has relaxed one of the formerly binding constraints which confronted traffic forecasters in the 1960s. Nevertheless in some circumstances, especially in Third World countries, a simple methodology requiring only relatively basic computational aids and technical skills may be a very important quality sought by forecasters.

While the widespread availability of computing facilities does now facilitate the easier and cheaper application of advanced models, this availability is also not without its own dangers. In a paper by Pearman and Button (1973), commenting upon some earlier work by Lesley (1971) concerned with examining the structure of urban public transport, one such danger became apparent. Lesley had made use of a standard statistical regression software package to appraise the importance of a number of 'macro-parameters' on the public transport system of 34 European cities. His empirical results, however, were based upon regression planes *constrained through the origin* which, in effect, invalidated the conclusions he reached given the nature of the statistical 'package' he employed. As the authors said, 'Regression analysis is deceptively simple and in practical terms even more so since the widespread availability of computer software. This leads to a double danger: misinterpretation of the package itself and the general misuse of regression techniques'.

Comprehensibility

It is not simply 'technicians' who consider traffic forecasts and since forecasting can make no pretence to being an exact science, many lay people, usually those affected by the implications of the forecasts, may wish to consider the validity of the forecasting methods employed. The forecasting method must appear consistent with the other elements of the transport planning exercise, and not be simply a self-fulfilling prophecy. (Of course, the opposite may be desired by the policy makers.) There are, however, potential problems. The extrapolative methods of forecasting car ownership employed in the appraisal of inter-urban road investment in the early 1970s, for instance, were relatively straightforward to understand and, in consequence, came under severe public scrutiny (e.g. Adams, 1974; Gershuny, 1978). The criticism were so vocal that in 1975, traffic forecasts were deemed 'matters of policy' and placed outside appraisal at public inquiries. Inspectors at public inquiries were duly told not to permit questioning of any traffic forecasts. Such measures, however, proved extremely unpopular and it is possibly less damaging to indicate explicitly the inherent weaknesses in any forecasting methodology rather than present forecasts as scientific and unquestionable fact. A practical difficulty is still likely to arise, however, as forecasting models become more technical and their output less easily understood (e.g. discrete choice models yield probabilities while interactive models have a relatively high 'quantitative' element – see below). As with many other aspects of transport appraisal there may be important trade-offs which have to be made, in this case between the accuracy or cost of forecasts and the public's willingness to accept their validity.

Form of output

Forecasts are normally thought to yield the future level of per capita car ownership, but in practice different forecasting methods tend to offer different *forms* of prediction. In some cases this is unimportant or simple conversion factors may be applied, but this is far from the normal situation. The early extrapolative models of car ownership produced expected average per capita ownership predictions which at that time ideally suited the needs of those concerned with appraising trunk road investment. Later they provided suitable inputs when COBA, a computerised procedure employed to appraise small-scale road schemes, was introduced (see Department of Transport, 1980). Such forecasts are, however, of much less use at the urban level where an entire local network comes under scrutiny. Here forecasts of non-car, one-car and multi-car owning households are often thought more useful since it is this trichotomy which is important in determining future travel patterns. Attempts to apply conversion factors to the per capita forecasts have been made (for example, see Pailing and Solesbury, 1970), but this complicates the forecasting process and introduces the possibility of a compounding of forecasting errors.

The form of prediction provided by one sub-model in the overall traffic forecasting exercise must dovetail into that which follows it. It must be remembered that the demand for car ownership is derived from the demand for its use which in turn is derived from the demand to reach some final destination. One of the current difficulties in car ownership forecasting is that while there have been considerable efforts made to improve this stage in the overall traffic forecasting exercise, the car use models tend to remain rather basic and do not easily accommodate the probabilistic predictions provided by causal ownership models. At a higher level of abstraction, the underlying assumptions of many existing traffic forecasting methods conflict with recent developments in appraisal techniques. Much of the current philosophy underlying transport analysis is now based not upon the classical assumptions of maximisation, but rather upon notions of satisficing, and methods employing multi-criteria project appraisal techniques are now being assimilated into official transport policy making. For internal consistency within the overall appraisal process, therefore, there is a need for the output produced by the traffic forecasts to be compatible with the implied behavioural assumptions underlying the complete appraisal methodology. The need to revise car ownership forecasting models in this way was highlighted by Pearman and Button (1981) and is implicit in Dix's (1977) advocacy of interactive forecasting models when he argues for 'behavioural realism' and an emphasis on 'understanding the phenomenon'.

Trade-offs in forecasting attributes

What is quite clear when considering the various qualities outlined above which are sought from traffic forecasting models is that many of them are mutually exclusive or, at best, major trade-offs have to be made between the extent to which the different attributes desired may be achieved. This is why in practical terms, it is important to be extremely clear about the exact way forecasts are going to be used and to establish from this the relative importance which should be attached to each of the qualities outlined. It is interesting to note that over time 'fashions' in forecasting have changed and the importance attached to the various attributes of different forecasting methods have fluctuated in the eyes of analysts. In particular, at the local, urban level, as financial constraints have tightened, economy has become a prime consideration and now far more care is taken over the basic data collection exercise than a decade or more ago. Similarly, since many of the parameters formerly thought to be relatively stable over time, or possibly changing in a steady, readily discernible way, can no longer be taken as given, the forecasting exercise also has become part of the learning process with forecasting models serving the dual role of predicting and increasing our understanding of the basic, underlying influences on travel behaviour.

While some of the trade-offs which forecasters have to make are fairly obvious, others are less so. One of the major difficulties at present is the desire to improve the theoretical foundation of forecasting models while at the same time opening the transport planning process to wider debate and discussion (e.g. Department of Transport, 1978). Modern economy theory is complex and while it was relatively easy to explain the early extrapolative methods to the proverbial 'interested lay-man', the theoretical underpinnings of discrete choice models are less easy to communicate. A further problem is that of trading off cost against 'quality' of data employed. Large household surveys have now tended to be replaced by smaller, more detailed ones designed to meet the needs of disaggregate forecasting models. While this offers some financial economy, the types of survey undertaken are, per household, more expensive and, with the gradual acceptance of activity analysis based forecasting, are likely to become even more so in the future. Basically, one must spend more to obtain greater detail of the way in which household decisions are reached. Whether the search for such information is likely to be cost effective in the future will, to a considerable extent, depend upon the advances which are made in the overall transport planning and forecasting process of which car ownership modelling is only one part. There is little point in having an extremely detailed and sophisticated car ownership model if the forecasts produced can only be utilised in simple, unreliable trip generation and modal split models. This is one reason why interest in the various components of traffic forecasting has varied over time as one stage moves ahead of the others and a catching up process follows.

The forms of traffic forecasting model

Since different approaches to traffic forecasting have associated with them their own specific advantages and weaknesses it is helpful in assessing the practical problems of forecasting to consider the main, broad types of methodology individually. Table 9.1 provides a very general guide to the different techniques of car ownership forecasting, listed in

209

Table 9.1
An outline of the main methods of car ownership forecasting

Technique	Features	Example	Refinements	Advantages	Limitations
Extrapolative	(i) Based on product life cycle theory (ii) Time series based (iii) Normally uses official data (iv) Normally highly aggregated (v) Produces deterministic forecasts (vi) Calibrated using a variety of point fitting and regression techniques (vii) Used for long-term forecasting	Tanner (1962) $$C_t = \frac{s}{1+be^{-ast}}$$ C_t : cars per capita at time t s : saturation level of car ownership a : actual rate of per capita car ownership growth at any level of ownership b : position on curve for any value of s t : time	(i) Incorporation of additional socio-economic variables (Tanner, 1974) (ii) Use of more sophisticated growth patterns (Tanner, 1978) (iii) Introduction of lagged effects (Tanner, 1979)	(i) Cheap and easy to calibrate (ii) Output is readily comprehensible	(i) Lacks policy sensitivity in its basic form (ii) Dependent upon past *trends* holding in the future (iii) Empirically has proved a poor predictor in the short term (iv) Highly sensitive to the saturation level employed
Spatial econometric	(i) Uses either official data or sample surveys aggregated spatially (ii) Generally employed at regional or urban level (iii) Based on aggregated, zonal socio-economic variables (iv) Usually calibrated using simple equation regression techniques	Tanner (1963) $$C_r = d_1+d_2A+d_3B+d_4C+d_5D+d_6E$$ C_r : cars per head in area r A : income per taxpayer in area r B : SEG composition in area r C : Population of urban areas in area r D : Population density in area r E : Distance north of area r	(i) Lower levels of spatial aggregation (Button, 1973) (ii) More complex model specification (McCarthy, 1978) (iii) Pooling of time series and cross-section data (Pearman and Button, 1976)	(i) Does not require specialised computer software (ii) May embrace a range of socio-economic variables (iii) Relatively simple to transform variables	(i) Assumes intra-zonal structure will hold in the future (ii) Use for urban land-use studies requires large data base
Discrete choice	(i) Based on utility theory (ii) Usually household based (iii) Uses sample survey data (iv) Economical in use of data	Bates, Roberts and Gunn (1978) $$P_t(1+) = \frac{S(1+)}{1+e^{-a_1(t)}\,Y_t^{-b_1(t)}}$$ $P_t(1+)$: probability of a household owning a car at time t	(i) Introduction of nested models (Train, 1980) (ii) Incorporation of car ownership models with other transport and land use models (Lerman, 1976)	(i) Can be calibrated from small sample survey (ii) Highly policy sensitive	(i) Probabilistic output is sometimes difficult to interpret (ii) Aggregation to the zonal level for wider planning purposes is difficult

Method	Characteristics	Example	Recent developments	Advantages	Disadvantages
	(v) Based exclusively on socio-economic data (vi) Normally employs some form of logit framework (vii) Produces probabilistic forecasts	t : time $S(1+)$: saturation level of one-car households Y_t : household income at time t			(iii) Requires specialised computer software for calibration (iv) Problem of incorporating car price variable
Stock adjustment	(i) Based on neo-classical consumer theory (ii) Usually looks at national car stock (iii) Uses time series, official data (iv) Distinguishes between new and replacement demands	*Stone and Rowe (1957)* $$Q_t = (r-\lambda)\,C_{t-1} + \lambda \sum_i a_i X_{it}$$ Q_t : stock of cars in year t r : replacement demand as fraction of previous stock λ : constant indicating wish to close gap between desired and actual stock X_{it} : socio-economic variable i (e.g. income, car prices etc.) at time t	(i) Introduction of 'state adjustments' to make model dynamic (Houthakker and Taylor, 1966) (ii) Differentiation by car 'type' (Blomqvist and Haessel, 1978)	(i) Offers results which are easily understood (ii) Can be estimated from readily available data	(i) Of limited use at the local level (ii) Makes strong assumptions about perfect markets, continuous demand curves etc. (iii) Assumes the car is used optimally
Interactive	(i) Non-mathematical in form (ii) Relies upon specific, intensive small stratified surveys (iii) Offers both quantitative and qualitative forecasts (iv) Attempts to explain 'causes' of car purchasing decisions	*Jones (1979)* The HATS procedure developed at Oxford confronts households with a map and some blocks representing their location and current activities. In response to questions about changes in household travel patterns and character, the interviewee is invited to plot new travel patterns and illustrate the rearranged activities on the board	(i) The development of more sophisticated interview procedures (Dix, Carpenter and Pollard, 1980)	(i) Highly policy sensitive (ii) Flexible with respect to the types of car ownership forecast which can be produced	(i) Untried for large-scale traffic forecasting exercises (ii) Expensive interview techniques required (iii) Limited to fairly short-term, response forecasting (iv) No statistical significance tests possible
Category analysis	(i) Forecasts ownership for particular classes of household (ii) Uses cross-sectional data (iii) Often used in land use/transport studies	*Mogridge and Eldridge (1970)* Forecasts for London were produced by categorising households by income, residential density and employment. There were 6 income groups, 6 residential groups and 2 employment groups	(i) Development of hybrid models combining categories as dummy variables in regression models (Button, 1976) (ii) Combined with simple data analysis in techniques such as analysis by medians (Button, Fowkes and Pearman, 1980a)	(i) Offers easily understood methodology and results (ii) Minimal computation necessary (iii) Does not specify specific response surface	(i) Difficult to test significance of variables/classes (ii) Treats variables as discrete (iii) Requires a large data base if all cells are to be filled adequately (iv) Offers weak forecasts for many household classes that may grow in future

no special order, outlining their features, their merits and their limitations. Again it is important to emphasise that while the table specifically relates to one particular aspect of traffic forecasting, the comments are of general applicability. Rather than discuss this table in detail — it is, hopefully, self-explanatory — it is possibly more fruitful to take a very broad brush approach and, again drawing upon car ownership for our illustrations, separate traffic forecasting methodology into four basic 'schools' and look at the practical limitations of each in turn.

The extrapolative school

At the simplest level extrapolation is the continuation of an existing time trend into the future. While conceptually straightforward, its application may pose some quite serious practical difficulties. The specification of the exact growth path has presented problems in the forecasting of national car ownership growth in the United Kingdom with earlier assumptions of a symmetric logistic path over time giving way to an asymmetrical power-growth function (Tanner, 1978). The reason for such changes is that extrapolation implicitly assumes that relationships between, in this case, car ownership and the factors influencing car ownership remain the same over time and that their influence is exerted in such a way that it can be reflected in a known cumulative distribution traced out over time. Problems arise not simply in deciding upon the appropriate distribution (Button, Fowkes and Pearman, 1980b, outline some of the difficulties here) but also in deciding the eventual asymptote (the saturation level of car ownership) which is going to be reached. The saturation level of car ownership assumed by the forecaster is of central importance when employing an extrapolative framework. Basically, what is the time path and where is it going? Solutions to these problems involve considerable effort in statistical analysis, but also a degree of subjective assessment and 'feel' for the way that trends are likely to go in the future. Both the choice of growth path and the assumed saturation level are essentially determined subjectively albeit with some statistical information to back up the eventual 'guestimates'. As Tanner (1962, p.264) pointed out in his early paper, 'The algebraic form of the forecast curve is largely open to choice'.

While there are difficulties in providing accurate extrapolative forecasts (table 9.2 gives some indication of the various projections of national vehicle ownership provided at different times by the TRRL extrapolative model compared with actual figures), it is also impossible to make them 'policy sensitive' without considerably modifying the basic approach. Almost by definition, extrapolative models are not

Table 9.2
Comparison of national car ownership projections using TRRL
extrapolative technique with the actual figure for 1975

Year of publication	Base year for calculation	In base year	Cars per person		
			Forecast for 1975	Forecast growth p.a. ÷ Actual growth p.a.	
1962	1960	0.11	0.28	1.14	
1965	1964	0.16	0.32	1.57	
1967	1966	0.18	0.31	1.67	
1969	1968	0.20	0.30	1.84	
1970	1969	0.21	0.28	1.66	
1972	1971	0.22	0.27	1.62	
1974	1972	0.23	0.26	1.48	
			(Actual = 0.25)		

Source: Based on Tanner, 1978, p.20.

policy sensitive since they assume that previous trends will continue
into the future (i.e. that policy will remain constant). In itself this
assumption poses problems and may lead to circularity; with the forecasts becoming almost a self-fulfilling prophecy if they form the basis
of transport policy. Gershuny (1978), for instance, argues that the
extrapolated car ownership forecasts formed the main support for
road building in the 1960s but these new roads in turn encouraged
greater travel and vehicle use which then proceeded to validate the
car ownership forecasts. Similarly, Senior (1975) argued that 'the
forecasts are true only if the road-building programme continues. The
road-building programme will continue only if the forecasts are true.
If one is assumed then the other follows. If either is denied then both
collapse'. Whether such circularities are actually important is an empirical question, but one the forecaster should be aware of and be prepared
to address himself. Of course, if policies do change then the
insensitivity of the extrapolative framework is exposed. In the United
Kingdom some attempts have been made to make national car ownership models policy sensitive by incorporating a limited number of
socio-economic variables, namely, some measure of income (Y) and
motoring costs (PM). The basic model had by 1977, for example,
become:

$$C_t = \frac{S}{1 + (b + at + f \log Y + g \log PM)} - N \qquad (9.1)$$

Compared with the basic logistic extrapolative model (see table 9.1,

213

column 3) this is clearly much more complicated to calibrate and requires substantially greater informational inputs. In particular, it is necessary to have external estimates of the elasticities associated with changes in the socio-economic variables. The complexity also makes it rather more difficult for the non-specialist to understand. Additionally, it is not clear just how policy sensitive it is. While it may be a useful method of assessing the broad impact of, say, a change in vehicle excise duty or in petrol tax, it is unlikely to offer such assistance at a more local level where detailed policies may involve parking restraints, bus subsidies etc. It also means a movement away from one of the main advantages of the extrapolative framework, namely the fact that the independent variable (in the earlier case, simply time) is readily predictable. The introduction of income and motoring cost variates produces the need to forecast these variables to the target date and, although they are to some extent within the control of government policy, this can never be done with certainty.

The planning school

The forecasting procedures which can be generally classified under this broad heading derive from the particular needs of local, usually urban, transport planners. The main feature of these models is that they are not concerned with travel as such, but focus on the physical manifestations of travel decisions, namely traffic patterns. Since policy sensitivity is important to planners, the extrapolative framework has severe defects but at the same time, and particularly in the early years of land-use/transportation planning, there was really no necessity to understand the workings of the transport market, providing reasonably accurate long-term forecasts were produced. The spatial econometric and stock-adjustment models of car ownership outlined in table 9.1 are approaches which fall within this school. Although the stock adjustment model has some foundation in economic theory, it is nevertheless similar to other approaches of this school in that the main objective is to forecast *levels* of vehicle ownership rather than gain an understanding of how individuals or households decide to become car owning.

Since planning school models tend to be relatively highly aggregated, they are inefficient in their use of data, concealing important intrazonal or intra-vehicle type variations. The spatial econometric approaches to car ownership modelling are well designed to meet the needs of traffic forecasting, employing the traditional, four-stage sequential method of forecasting (i.e. zonal trip generation, trip distribution, modal split and traffic assignment). The output is usually at the level of the zone and, being deterministic in form, fits particularly well into conventional aggregate trip-end and modal choice models. Practical problems may arise, however, if the proposed investments under review are likely to affect the internal structure of a traffic zone or alter the different, relative degrees of accessibility enjoyed by individual households within it.

Stock-adjustment models pose serious problems when used to separate influences of different vehicles, household and macro-economic characteristics on the structure of vehicle demand (see Hensher and Manefield, 1981). The underlying assumptions of the stock-adjustment model, especially that of a perfect car market and the optimal utilisation of vehicles by owners, also pose questions as to its practical usefulness to transport modellers.

Although forecasting models from the planning school can be adapted to take disaggregated household data they are really aggregate models and attempts to modify them tend to increase both the problems of calibration and the complexity of forecasting. In their cross-sectional forms they also require a substantial input of data to ensure that the dispersions around the aggregate means are reduced to a statistically acceptable level. Thus, the emphasis on the zone as the basic unit of study is useful in terms of technical design of transport facilities but considerably reduces the efficiency of forecasting models.

The causal modelling school

This approach is highly disaggregated and uses specific sample survey data to model the causes of household travel demand patterns. Such models then permit, by introducing predicted values of the causal variables, future travel behaviour and, *ipso facto*, traffic patterns to be forecast. Category analysis only just falls into this school; it could almost come within the planning school but its emphasis on the household rather than the zone or vehicle market justifies it being deemed causal. Causal types of model have the virtue of being policy sensitive and are extremely flexible in their application. With the exception of category analysis, which lacks statistical sophistication, such forecasting models are normally calibrated on relatively small, and hence cheap to collect, data bases (although the sampling techniques required to ensure suitable stratifications may offset this apparent economy to some extent).

The difficulties with causal models, which in the context of car ownership forecasting are typified by the regional highway traffic model (Bates, Gunn and Roberts, 1978) at the national level and, from the United States, the General Motors' automobile model (Burns, Golob and Nicolaidis, 1976), are the complexity of calibration and the form of the forecasts produced. (This complexity does not apply to category analysis, although in many ways this may be seen as a crude form of causal model.) The main problem is that the households are either car owning or not, whereas most economic models of consumer behaviour have traditionally assumed households select amongst *continuous levels* of quality or bundles of goods. To cope with this logit, or similar, techniques are employed and calibration is usually by maximum likelihood procedures. In some cases it is necessary to introduce an exogenously determined saturation level of household car ownership, but this may be circumvented by the adoption of appropriate computer software (e.g. the employment of maximum likelihood techniques, rather than simple regression routines, permits saturation to be estimated simultaneously with other parameters — see Bates, Gunn and Roberts, 1978). Even when a saturation level of car ownership is determined independently of the main model, the fact that the basic data contains observations representing almost the entire range of possibilities, including very poor and very rich households, means that no external information need be employed, unlike the extrapolative models.

The usual approach is to treat zero-car, one-car and multi-car owning households separately, giving the possibility of making different assumptions about the growth path of each — the RHTM car ownership forecasting approach is to treat one-car ownership as a log-logistic function of household characteristics but multi-car ownership as a simple logistic relationship, i.e.:

$$P_t = \frac{S\ (1+)}{1 + e^{-a_1\ (t)}\ Y_t^{-b_1\ (t)}} \tag{9.2}$$

$$P_t(2+|\ 1+) = \frac{S\ (2+|\ 1+)}{1 + e^{-a_2\ (t)\ -\ b_2\ (t)\ Y_t}} \tag{9.3}$$

While there are advantages in using household data, one problem with these models is that they are normally based upon cross-sectional survey data. This snapshot view permits the extraction of long-run elasticities but, in doing so, clearly assumes that household demand responses remain invariant with respect to time. While the team working on the RHTM attempted to assess the stability of their various parameters by making a succession of cross-sectional estimations this has not altogether been proven a success in retrospect. At the national level, the availability of a regular series of large sample surveys makes

216

this possible, but at the local level one cannot normally conduct such a series of tests, although a limited number of follow-up studies are now gradually being conducted to appraise the performance of earlier methods. Reliance, at the urban level, must be placed exclusively on the 'snapshot view'. In a sense, therefore, this approach is also extrapolative because the models used, although not assuming a constant relationship between traffic and time, do extrapolate past relationships between traffic and a set of specified socio-economic variables into the future.

An interesting suggestion for circumventing some of the practical problems of cross-sectional forecasting, although financially costly, is to base traffic forecasts on panel samples rather than cross-sectional stratified samples (Hensher and Manefield, 1981). The idea is to move away from the single cross-section and embrace dynamic considerations by taking a panel of households and by repeated, possibly annual, surveys of this sample examine how parameters in a structured logit model change over time. This is obviously more complex, as well as more expensive, than the conventional causal approach but it does directly confront the problem of cross-sectional bias.

The activity analysis school

The activity analysis or interactive approach towards traffic forecasting represents an attempt to move away from the mathematical biases of the other schools where mathematical convenience has often been given priority over a thorough appreciation of why particular traffic patterns are likely to emerge. The aim is to produce a forecasting framework which gets close to the essential decision process underlying household travel behaviour. Rather than, for instance, just incorporating a variable such as household status within a mathematical format because it is statistically significant (or data is available!), interactive modelling seeks to explain *why* status affects travel behaviour and to make use of this understanding in the forecasting of travel behaviour. To date the approach has only been applied in small-scale studies (e.g. Jones, 1978, used it in his study of local school bus operations in the United Kingdom, while Phifer, Neven and Hartgen, 1980, employed it in their appraisal of energy constraints in the United States), mainly because of the specialised data collecting techniques required.

Ideally, it is argued, an interactive forecasting model should exhibit six main properties (Heggie, 1978):

1   It should involve entire households and allow for interactions between their members.

2   It should make existing constraints on household behaviour explicit.

3   It should start from the households' existing pattern of behaviour.

4   It should work by confronting households with realistic changes in their travel environment and allow them to respond realistically.

5   It should allow for the influence of long-term adaptation of household behaviour.

6   It should be able to tell the investigator something fundamental that he did not know before.

Some of the practical difficulties in meeting these requirements are highlighted in the work of the Oxford University Transport Studies Unit and the 'household activities travel simulator' (HATS) which it developed (see also table 9.1). This forecasting procedure presents a small sample of households (usually stratified to reflect the socio-economic composition of the local population) with a board showing a map of the surrounding area combined with a 24-hour 'trip representation of coloured pieces' reflecting how current activities of each household are spread over space and throughout the day. The various transport policies or investment options (including the do-nothing state) are postulated and the effect on the different households' activities throughout the day and over space are simulated by adjustments to the strip representation. In this way, changes brought about in the transport system after investment may be seen to influence the entire 24-hour life pattern of each household and unsuspected changes in 'remote' trip-making behaviour can be traced back to the investment. The emphasis, by being focused on the micro-unit, should permit much clearer insights into the overall, long-term effects on travel patterns of transport investments.

The difficulties, besides the costs, are that while the approach embraces interactions *within* households it is less certain that it predicts the consequences of interactions *between* households. Each household will almost inevitably assume that those it interacts with, e.g. in terms of social meetings, co-ordinating school trips etc., will retain their existing travel patterns or make guesses about how they will adapt to the investment. In the long term, of course, the various changes in the travel behaviour of individual households will, due to experience, adapt to those of their neighbours. The adoption of Delphi-type procedures may offer a method of coping with this problem but only at the cost of more interviewing and greater complexity. The problems of developing a viable, large-scale interactive framework for use in transport planning for the large conurbations, however, seem to be acute.

Possible future developments

Much of the effort in the past has been directed at improving the mathematical and statistical sophistication of traffic forecasting models. This emphasis seems to be changing, in part, one suspects, because traffic forecasts have not always been as reliable as one might have hoped, nor the techniques quite as flexible and practicable as have been claimed. Certainly one of the areas where greater emphasis is currently being placed is the collection of better and more relevant data. Here, for example, the recognition that there are important interactive effects between several of the standard variables employed in local level car ownership forecasting has called forth attempts to collect, rather more systematically, longitudinal data, so that the stability of such inter-dependences may be assessed. Dynamic effects may, as we have noted in the previous section, be incorporated in traffic forecasting by the wider use of panel surveys, although, almost by definition, this must be a long-term process. Goodwin and Mogridge (1980) have also attempted to develop a more general theoretical framework to take into account the dynamic consequences of changes in factors influencing car owner-ship both in an equilibrium and disequilibrium context. More work on operational models of this kind is, however, still needed. Activity-based forecasting frameworks now offer the scope for improving our under-standing of how interactive effects influence long-term trends in travel behaviour, but their usefulness in other than small-scale local appraisals seems likely to continue to be limited by the specialised data collection procedures which they require.

Equally important is the recognition that the series of different decisions regarding various aspects of travel choice, e.g. whether to make a trip, where to make it, which mode to use etc., are simul-taneously determined rather than discrete, sequential decisions. The movements away from the sequential approach to so-called 'explicit demand modelling' (Button, 1976b) represent the recognition of this need amongst members of the planning school of forecasters and the development of disaggregate causal models also permits greater cognisance to be taken of this simultaneity. Train (1980), for example, looks jointly at household decisions regarding car ownership and mode choice while Lerman (1976) considers location, housing, vehicle owner-ship and mode to work within a single framework. The car ownership forecasting sub-model is still normally treated as independent of other travel decisions and ownership forecasts used fed into the main traffic models as an exogenous influence. Perhaps the single most pressing problem at present, therefore, is the integration of the car ownership forecasting model into the overall transport forecasting exercise. The improvement, in terms of forecasts, obtained from this type of approach is likely to be considerably greater than those likely to result from further, minor refinements to the calibration procedure or the specification of existing single equation models.

One of the practical reasons why forecasters may have avoided using simultaneous models of transport demand (including car ownership) in the past is that such models are more difficult to handle on computers and are more expensive to run. This objection is much weaker with the advent of the new generation of machines. At the theoretical level, however, the incorporation of household logit models of car ownership (which are now, possibly, the most generally accepted models among forecasters) into a system of equations is extremely difficult to carry out. Further, at present, knowledge of the exact specifications of the equation system is limited due to the dearth of relevant empirical data. In the short term it may be possible to improve causal modelling by making use of aggregate parameters, e.g. elasticities, in certain of a set of household-based equations. Some knowledge of specific parameters has already been obtained in zonal level studies, where the problem of a discrete dependent car ownership variable does not arise. Clearly, aggregation bias will exist in such studies but this could well be small relative to the simultaneous equation bias which certainly accompanies the single equation forecasting models of car ownership.

In summary, we have attempted in this chapter to look at the practical problems of producing car ownership forecasts. It should be quite apparent that these are often at least as important as the purely abstract and theoretical debates on forecasting methodology which are more often found in the transport literature. The actual needs of those seeking car ownership forecasts and, indeed, traffic forecasts more generally change over time and there is an inevitable lag between the new demands placed on forecasters and their eventual response. One of the main difficulties is that those using the forecasts seldom make it clear to those developing the models and making the predictions what exactly their requirements are. In the past, developments in statistical analysis have often been made independently of the needs of practitioners and have been discovered almost by accident – the result has been that the techniques have not always perfectly met the practitioners' needs. Greater co-ordination and better communication between those undertaking the forecasting and those using the projections would seem one way of moving forward in the future. To some extent the establishment of the Standing Advisory Committee on Trunk Road Assessment in the United Kingdom represents a movement in this direction.

References

Adams, J., 'Saturation planning' in *Town and Country Planning*, 1974, vol.42, pp. 550—4.

Bates, J.J., 'Sample size and grouping in the estimation of disaggregate models — a simple case' in *Transportation*, 1979, vol.8, pp. 347—69.

Bates, J.J., Gunn, H.F. and Roberts, M., *A Disaggregate Model of Household Car Ownership*, Departments of the Environment and Transport, Research Report 20, HMSO, London, 1978.

Ben-Akiva, M.E., 'Structure of alternative travel behaviour structures' in *Transportation Research Record*, 1974, no.526, pp. 26—42.

Blomqvist, A.G. and Haessel, W., 'Small cars, large cars and the price of gasoline' in *Canadian Journal of Economics*, 1979, vol.11, pp. 470—89.

Burns, L.D., Golob, T.F. and Nicolaidis, G.C., 'A theory of urban households' automobile ownership decisions' in *Transportation Research Record*, 1976, no.569, pp. 56—74.

Button, K.J., 'Motor car ownership in the West Riding of Yorkshire: some findings' in *Traffic Engineering and Control*, 1973, vol.15, pp. 76—8.

Button, K.J., 'Category analysis and household multiple regression models of trip generation; a possible reconciliation' in *International Journal of Transport Economics*, 1976a, vol.3, pp. 19—27.

Button, K.J., 'The use of economics in urban travel demand modelling; a survey' in *Socio-Economic Planning Sciences*, 1976b, vol.10, pp. 57—66.

Button, K.J., Fowkes, A.S. and Pearman, A.D., 'Car ownership in West Yorkshire: the influence of public transport accessibility' in *Urban Studies*, 1980a, vol.17, pp. 211—5.

Button, K.J., Fowkes, A.S. and Pearman, A.D., 'Disaggregate and aggregate car ownership forecasting in Great Britain' in *Transportation Research* (A), 1980b, vol.14, pp. 263—73.

Button, K.J., Pearman, A.D. and Fowkes, A.S., *Car Ownership Modelling and Forecasting*, Gower, Aldershot, 1981.

Department of the Environment, *Report of the Panel of Inquiry into the Greater London Development Plan*, HMSO, London, 1973.

Department of Transport, *Transport Policy*, Cmnd 6836, HMSO, London, 1977.

Department of Transport, *Report of the Advisory Committee on Trunk Road Assessment*, HMSO, London, 1978.

Department of Transport, *COBA—8*, London, 1980.

Dix, M.C., 'Report on investigations of household travel decision-making behaviour' in E.J. Visser (ed.) *Transport Decisions in an Age of Uncertainty*, Martinus Nijhoff, The Hague, 1977.

Dix, M.C., Carpenter, S.M. and Pollard, H.R.T., 'The second car; owner-ship and usage decisions', *Transport Studies Unit WP 130*, Oxford University, 1980.

Friedman, M., *Essays in Positive Economics*, University of Chicago Press, Chicago, 1953.

Gershuny, J., 'Transport forecasting: fixing the future' in *Policy and Politics*, 1978, vol.6, pp. 373–402.

Goodwin, P.B. and Mogridge, M.J.H., 'Hypotheses for a fully dynamic model of car ownership' in *Transport Economics*, Proceedings of the 1980 PTRC Summer Annual Meeting, Seminar L, PTRC, London, 1980.

Heggie, I.G., 'Putting behaviour into behavioural models of travel choice' in *Journal of the Operational Research Society*, 1978, vol.29, pp. 541–60.

Hensher, D.A. and Manefield, T., 'A structural logit model of automo-bile acquisition and type choice: some preliminary evidence' Mimeo, 1981.

Houthakker, H.S. and Taylor, L.D., *Consumer Demand in the United States 1929–1970*, Harvard University Press, Cambridge, Mass., 1966.

Jones, P., 'School hour revisions in West Oxfordshire: an exploratory study using HATS', *Transport Studies Unit, Technical Report 1*, Oxford University, 1978.

Jones, P., 'HATS: a technique for investigating household decisions' in *Environment and Planning* (A), 1979, vol.11, pp. 59–70.

Lerman, S.R., 'Location, housing, automobile ownership and mode to work: a joint choice model' in *Transportation Research Record*, 1976, no.610, pp. 6–11.

Lesley, L.J.S., 'A parametric analysis of European urban public trans-port' in *Traffic Engineering and Control*, 1971, vol.12, pp. 584–7.

McCarthy, C., 'The determinants of regional variations in private car ownership: some evidence from Irish data' in *Annals of Regional Science*, 1978, vol.12, pp. 14–23.

Mogridge, M.J.H. and Eldridge, D., 'Car ownership in London', *GLC Intelligence Unit Research Report No.10*, 1970.

Pailing, K.B. and Solesbury, W.B., 'The future proportion of non-car and multi-car owning households' in *Traffic Engineering and Control*, 1970, vol.12, pp. 244–7.

Pearman, A.D. and Button, K.J., 'The analysis of urban public trans-port: some comments and suggestions' in *Traffic Engineering and Control*, 1973, vol.15, pp. 132–4.

Pearman, A.D. and Button, K.J., 'Car ownership – a social and econo-mic perspective' in J.S. Yerrel (ed.) *Transport Research for Social and Economic Progress*, Gower, Aldershot, 1981.

Phifer, S.P., Neven, A.J. and Hartgen, D.T., 'Family reactions to energy constraints' in *Transportation Research Record*, 1980, no.765, pp. 12–16.

Senior, M., 'Driving into the future' in *Ecologist*, 1975, vol.5, pp. 341–3.

Simon, H.A., 'Rational decision-making in business organisations' *Nobel Memorial Lecture*, 1977.

Stone, J.R. and Rowe, D.A., 'The market demand for durable goods' in *Econometrica*, 1957, vol.25, pp. 423–43.

Tanner, J.C., 'Forecasts of future numbers of vehicles in Great Britain' in *Roads and Road Construction*, 1962, vol.40, pp. 263–74.

Tanner, J.C., 'Car and motorcycle ownership in the counties of Great Britain in 1960' in *Journal of the Royal Statistical Society* (Series A), 1963, vol.126, pp. 276–84.

Tanner, J.C. 'Forecasts of vehicles and traffic in Great Britain', *Transport and Road Research Laboratory Report*, LR 650, 1974.

Tanner, J.C., 'Long-term forecasting of vehicle ownership and road traffic' in *Journal of the Royal Statistical Society* (Series A), 1978, vol.141, pp. 14–63.

Tanner, J.C., 'Choice of model structure for car ownership forecasting', *Transport and Road Research Laboratory Supplementary Report*, SR 523, 1979.

Train, K., 'A structured logit model of auto ownership and mode choice' in *Review of Economic Studies*, 1980, vol.47, pp. 357–70.

10 Port investment appraisal in developing countries
J. A. Holt

Introduction

The performance and potential of alternative general cargo shipping technologies and their port requirements are outlined in the first part of the chapter. The merits of various objective functions which developing countries may employ to evaluate port improvements and how queuing models may be used to obtain information pertinent to the appraisal procedure are discussed and illustrated later.

Shipping technology and port requirements

Containerisation now dominates the general cargo trades between developed countries and many ports in developing countries are facing an increase in the use of this mode, especially for imported goods. It is worthwhile considering the likely direction and impact of technological change in general cargo shipping, with regard to developing countries.

The main characteristics of general cargo are its heterogeneity of nature and diversity of shape. Traditional break-bulk cargo handling produces two major drawbacks. Firstly, ships spend too much time in port because of the limited speed of cargo handling. Gilman (1977) estimated that for a cargo flow comprising mixed industrial goods handling rates between 200–500 tons per day are common, though the use of a variety of unit load methods including a limited number of containers, may allow liners to achieve up to 1,000 tons per day. Thus, Meek (1975) noted that though the 'Priam' class of ship operating on the Europe—Far East service in 1974 had achieved a 10 per cent increase in the proportion of time spent at sea, compared with 1966, due mainly to the greater use of unitised cargo, such vessels were still spending 40 per cent of their time in port. In such circumstances, investments in vessel size without corresponding improvements in port performance simply increase the costs of vessel time in port and reduce the productive revenue earning time of the vessel at sea. Therefore, since port time tends to vary directly with the volume of cargo carried, shipowners are unable to gain any potential economies of scale from increasing vessel size where conventional cargo-handling methods are employed.

Secondly, break-bulk general cargo shipping is particularly labour intensive both in terms of the costs of manual cargo handling and stowage and in terms of crew costs per ton of cargo carried where potential economies of vessel size cannot be realised (crew costs vary little with vessel size). The replacement of manual cargo handling requires the conversion of such cargo into standard units of suitable size and weight for rapid mechanised handling. Such unitisation may reduce the mainly labour-related cargo-handling costs and improve vessel productivity in port, allowing the realisation of scale economies in the marine sector.

There are several alternative forms of cargo unitisation available to ship operators, including containers, trailers, barges and pallets. In addition, developments in recent years have produced a wide range of options in ships and their operating configurations. Whilst cellular containership systems represent a specialist form at one end of the spectrum, intermediate alternatives with full or part container configurations include large modern liners, roll-on roll-off ships and barge-carrying vessels.

Gilman (1977) explored the relationship between route conditions and the choice of handling technology for routes to developing countries for the ship types in table 10.1. Comparisons of the efficiency with which different types of ship provide transport capacity on a route are problematic, given that ships vary widely in size and speed, and in their relationship between weight and space-carrying capacity. In general cargo shipping, therefore, it is normal to examine comparative ship costs per ton of cargo carried on a given route, allowing for differences in the potential for cargo handling which in turn may depend on the route structure operated, the balance of cargo flow, cargo type and port operational efficiency. In consequence, there is no unique set of relationships between ship costs for various types of general cargo vessel since each will have different sensitivities to these

Table 10.1
Comparisons of marine and port sector costs of general cargo ships

	Cargo DWT	Bale capacity cubic metres	Speed knots	Daily costs at sea $	Index of cost/ton mile DWT	Index of cost/ton mile space	Daily costs in port $	Index of daily cost in port	Cargo-handling capability tons/day
Conventional									
Standard liner	14,600	19,430	14	7,353	100	100	5,729	100	150–500
Modern liner	12,000	16,860	18	9,230	119	113	6,650	116	300–800
Large modern liner									
Break-bulk configuration	23,000	30,860	16	12,645	95	95	9,685	169	400–1200
Break-bulk + 170 TEUs on deck	23,000	35,940	16	12,645	95	84	9,685	169	1000–3000
Containerships									
560 TEU	12,000	16,800	19	12,568	153	146	9,593	167	1500–5000
1,200 TEU	23,000	36,000	22	22,957	126	107	15,007	262	3000–8500
Roll on Roll off									
Breakbulk + 200 TEUs on deck	21,000	57,140	22	24,852	156	73	18,084	316	1500–4000
Trailer type operation	21,000	51,430	22	24,852	156	163	18,084	316	8000–10000

Source: In part, Gilman (1977).

TEU represents a 20-feet equivalent unit.

constraints (including route length). Gilman, as shown in table 10.1, considered three strongly competing systems: cellular container, conventional including part container capability, and roll-on roll-off, and identified the factors controlling their comparative performance.

Containers provide the main form of unitisation and fully-cellular containership systems were first established on deep-sea routes between major industrialised regions with high-volume balanced trades; high port costs; and high proportions of full container load (FCL) traffics served by well developed inland transport infrastructure. However, in the context of developing countries the specialised container system incurs certain disadvantages. For example, it is often necessary for reasons of marketing or geography to maintain complex route itineraries requiring considerable vessel diversion, whereas the system performs best where port time and the number of ports served can be minimised. In addition, routes to developing countries are often characterised by low cargo volumes which may be subject to directional or seasonal imbalance with the need to reposition empty boxes thereby increasing the costs of the container system. Fully cellular container systems may also shut out lucrative heavy lift cargoes, awkward loads and bulk commodities in liner parcels which may be unitised in a better way.

Container systems achieve their maximum potential where the proportion of door-to-door FCL movements is high. In developing countries, where the average general cargo consignment is small this is unlikely to apply, and there will be a high proportion of less than container load (LCL) movements which require stuffing/stripping at consolidation depots within or close to the port. Finally, many developing countries may be described as capital and foreign exchange scarce and often suffer from chronic unemployment, thus affecting the perceived benefits of container investments with expensive capital outlays on ships, containers, cranes and port facilities thereby displacing labour. Counter to this argument is the view that conventional break-bulk berths though labour intensive will not achieve the same speed of ship turnround as a container berth, and can create higher overall capital requirements.

From Gilman (1977) it would appear that the cellular container system tends to be rather inflexible for the needs and operating circumstances of many Third World trades and unit costs appear particularly sensitive to vessel diversion; cargo imbalance; and variability in port turnround performance. This does not necessarily mean such routes should support labour-intensive conventional break-bulk systems since these must be matched in the ports and hinterlands of trading partners where labour costs per ton handled may be up to ten times higher. In practice, container systems to LDCs which involve predominantly LCL traffic may retain a high labour component and simply transfer the labour cost from the port to the cargo consolidation depot.

Roll-on roll-off (Roro) ships and modern cargo liners can operate in full or part container configuration and achieve many of the advantages of fast low cost cargo handling while retaining considerable flexibility in the use of space and the choice of packaging and handling methods. In particular, Roro permits the rapid handling of wheeled cargo into large garage decks and thus combines most of the flexibility of a cargo liner with the quick turnround of a cellular containership. A well managed large Roro may discharge up to 8–10,000 tons per day (depending on mode of operation and slave trailer–fork lift mix) and can regularly handle that wide band of high freight cargo that does not lend itself to containerisation including aircraft parts, long loads, agricultural and construction machinery.

Although specialist port facilities will normally be required to maximise the potential on regular Roro trades (to allow for bow, stern or side-door access) with an angled stern ramp a Roro can load/discharge at any berth that can take the ship, without any special cranes, docks or shore-based handling facilities. This is often claimed to be a major advantage when viewing the prospects for non-containerised routes. Whilst the capital outlay on cargo handling for a Roro system is probably less than for a cellular container system the main disadvantage is that the capital and operating costs of the ship are probably higher than for other ship types with the same cargo capacity, because Roros are physically bigger given their high cubic/cargo weight ratio.

A distinction can also be made between pure Roro and those vessels where Roro capability is a subsidiary one, which adds flexibility to the cargo-handling operation and space utilisation on board the ship.

Roros perform particularly well in response to short-run port congesion by increasing effective port capacity. Savings in ship waiting time costs outweigh the low density of cargo stowage and resultant space loss especially where road trailers are employed. In the long run, when port investment is undertaken fully cellular containerships may regain comparative advantage over the Roro particularly on longer routes.

The design of conventional cargo liners has evolved to meet the changing cargo and service requirements as owners have attempted to take advantage of modern cargo-handling methods. Ways in which ships themselves have been adapted include larger hatch openings (or twin hatches) which reduce the need for horizontal movement in the hold; flush hatch covers which make it possible to store containers and heavy lifts on deck; and improved lifting gear which may be used in preference to quay cranes. These investments in turnround performance have occurred in the search for a flexible multipurpose ship which can operate in a range of general cargo and small bulk trades. As shown in table 10.1, these tend to be very large liners which obtain economies of increased size in the marine sector with good cargo-handling capabilities and can also utilise a high proportion of capacity in carrying containers in non-cellular operation.

Although these ships can achieve the best results when a simple route structure is operated they can more easily accommodate multi-port itineraries and are less sensitive to cargo imbalance than containerships. The primary reason for this relates to the lower daily costs of such vessels which therefore do not generate the same diseconomies of unproductive time either in port or at sea. The system is labour intensive and is sensitive to cargo type, performing best when cargo is homogeneous.

A further sea transport system that might yet replace the traditional cargo liner is the barge-carrying vessel (bcv) but the system has not yet proliferated. This system is highly flexible from the cargo point of view accommodating both break-bulk and unitised cargoes. It is ideally suited for raw or semi-processed or finished materials of value sufficiently high to present inventory problems but not high enough to stand high freights, especially parcels of between 250 and 8,000 tons, at regular intervals. However, a preponderance of bulk goods with a relatively low value may not create high enough revenue for such an expensive system. The system can carry barges for reefer and dry cargo, and liner parcels of bulk liquids, and it can serve ports with adequate potential cargo volumes but with inadequate infrastructure. In theory, cargo handling is divorced from ship turnround and thereby vessel time in port is minimised. However, if the bcv has to enter conventional port facilities the advantages of this very expensive ship are diminished. This through-transport system allows door-to-door or door-to-pier service between any two sites having 9 feet of water alongside and in consequence the number of cargo-handling stages is minimised. Further, cargo-handling costs into and out of barges may be lower than for conventional ships due mainly to shorter crane cycles and open hatch access. However, the bcv system is particularly sensitive to delay, given the high cost of ship waiting time and in practice it has proved difficult to obtain the necessary cargo volumes and balance to avoid operating them as rather expensive containerships.

Whilst it is very difficult, in the context of LDCs, to compare the capital and operating costs of various types of port facility a number of observations may be made. In most ports, terminal construction rather than dredging represents the major investment required to accommodate fully cellular container services. There is considerable variation in size and layout depending on the ship type and method of container handling employed. Typically, an increase in ship length leads to a more than proportionate increase in carrying capacity so that the

229

number of containers a berth may handle, and hence the required storage area, increase sharply with berth length. The amount of space needed will also depend on the length of time containers remain at the terminal prior to shipment and the handling/stacking system employed.

Ship-to-shore transfer in a container berth is generally done by shore-based gantry cranes normally with a lifting capacity of 30–40 tonnes and an average cycle time of 2–3 minutes. Maximum throughputs are rarely sustainable in practice due to low berth occupancy; low ratio of ship working time to total ship time at the berth; and poor box stowage, especially for smaller ships on multi-port itineraries. The transfer of containers between quayside and storage area and inland transport may be undertaken by one of three basic methods in common use: trailer systems, straddle carriers and container yard gantry cranes. Trailer systems, where each container is placed on a trailer and towed between the quay and storage area by tractor, are easier to organise and offer high accessibility. The system is rather expensive in the use of space and requires a large investment in trailers, though these may be used for non-containerised general cargo handling.

Straddle carriers are highly manoeuvrable and can be used to stack boxes thereby allowing a more intensive use of land although a higher standard of surfacing is required. The employment of yard or even the berth gantry for landside operation is more expensive but with intensive use may prove economic, especially in restricted areas. Given the high fixed costs involved unit costs are sensitive to the volume of through-put. In the early stages of container build-up, ports in LDCs may use conventional berths and cranage for limited numbers of units and, at higher traffic levels construct multipurpose terminals with shared equipment and facilities. In particular, trailers, sideloaders and front-lift trucks are more versatile than straddle carriers in so far as they may be used to handle non-containerised cargoes in slack periods.

Whilst modern conventional shipping may sometimes require less port investment than specialised systems, this does not necessarily mean that no new investment is needed. Existing break-bulk facilities are often operating at full capacity and are characterised by narrow aprons, quay obstructions and inadequate transit sheds which may prevent improvements in vessel turnround time. Even where there is spare capacity, depth restrictions, turning circle or dock gate dimensions may prevent the berthing of the larger, modern multipurpose ship. UNCTAD (1976) put forward the concept of a terminal able to accommodate a variety of vessel types and handle a range of break-bulk and unitised cargoes. Such multipurpose facilities are envisaged as a means of coping with the transitional period during which unitised traffic gradually builds up, but before it reaches the volume at which specialised berths become justified. Table 10.2 reproduces the basic details of such a

Table 10.2
Main characteristics of multipurpose terminal

Terminal throughput (tons per annum)	650,000
Length of quay (metres)	360
Covered area (square metres)	20,000
Basic open storage area (square metres)	21,000
Pre-stacking and marshalling area (square metres)	18,000
Delivery, receiving zones (square metres)	14,400
Parking area (square metres)	7,200
Other operational areas (square metres)	19,400
Total terminal area (square metres)	100,000
Roro	1
Gantry crane	1 (35 tons)
Heavy lift crane	1 (30 tons)
Mobile cranes (quay)	2 (15 tons)
	2 (6 tons)
Mobile cranes (yard)	1 (20 tons)
	2 (5 tons)
Tractors or tugmasters	6
Chassis or Mafi trailers	18
Forklift trucks	15 (3 tons)
	5 (10 tons)
Straddle carriers	3

Source: UNCTAD (1976).

multipurpose terminal. The increased flexibility and sophistication of such facilities can only be achieved at the expense of a trebling of capital cost. It is argued however, that although attainable throughput is obviously dependent on cargo mix it may easily be five times as high as a conventional berth.

It is clear that modern shipping technologies may reduce the scale of capital requirements in the port and shipping sectors and may offer savings in long-run unit costs. Overall, therefore, technologies which combine fast low-cost cargo handling with flexibility in the use of carrying capacity and are able to cope with complex route itineraries may have a comparative advantage in the context of developing countries. Even where capital is scarce and labour abundant the choice between shipping technologies cannot be formulated as a simple trade-off between the increased capital intensity of unitised ship and port systems and savings in labour-dominated cargo-handling costs. Investment appraisal procedures which measure the real impact of alternative developments in marine transport and their corresponding port requirements need consideration.

Port investment appraisal — alternative decision criteria

Goss (1979) argues that few ports have formulated explicit financial or economic objectives and often implicitly aim to maximise cargo throughput subject to a financial constraint. Without guidance on what is to be maximised or minimised it becomes difficult to judge port investment acceptability. Nevertheless, three main objective functions may be proposed for port investment appraisal.

Financial tests

Account may be taken of estimated money costs and revenues accruing to the port through its pricing and expenditure systems and profit maximisation may be pursued. The main problem with such financial tests arises where prices do not reflect the opportunity costs of resources involved in providing port services. Goss (1967) identified that the commonest form of charging for ships was a fixed scale per gross or net registered ton covering a stated (and quite often lengthy) stay in port. The dues on cargo usually take the form of charges per ton weight, but are sometimes quoted per standard barrel, case or bale and occasionally *ad valorem*. The conclusion drawn is that the prices of individual port services are not based on cost, whether these be total, average, marginal, short-run or long-run. In addition, Heggie (1974) argues that publicly owned ports rarely keep comprehensive cost accounts and do not price port services on a commercial basis. Thus, given that the main financial objective of a port is to equate total cost with total revenue (inclusive or exclusive of subsidy), prices are often adjusted to attain this objective by some averaging procedure. The consequences of such policies that are a port's resources in the short run may be misallocated since neither the use of excess capacity is encouraged nor is excess demand curtailed; cross-subsidisation is common with financial losses on individual port services being covered from profits accruing elsewhere in a port; and importantly, no criterion is provided by which a port can identify where investment or disinvestment, which will benefit both the port and port user, should take place. Indeed, if the investment encourages the use of fewer, larger vessels or permits faster turnround, it is quite possible that, on the original scale of charges, the port authority's revenues may in fact fall. Any attempt to raise port charges significantly may divert vessels to competing ports.

Some observers suggest that the correct approach is to use discounted cash flows on an appropriate pricing system. However, this raises difficulties, for example, in the calculation of marginal social opportunity costs which are similar to those encountered when undertaking social cost—benefit analyses. Further, if port demand is inelastic with respect to port charges, then the real benefit of port improvements remains unchanged, whatever pricing policy is adopted. For example, the real benefit of a reduction in ship waiting time which comes from the construction of a new berth is not affected by increased port charges to finance the berth nor is the financial gain. In such circumstances, the port charges simply reallocate or transfer the benefit.

Economic tests

Since port investment decisions in developing countries often have to be made where there are no adequate prices for major inputs and outputs, then the maximisation of world real income is often proposed as an objective function. This has led to a wide application of cost—benefit analysis to evaluate the social profitability of projects.

Normally social benefits are compared with the opportunity costs involved in the project. The real benefits to the ship operator arising from a port improvement, such as a new berth or more efficient cargo handling, will be reflected in increased ship productivity which may take the form of either a reduction in ship turnround time in port or saving in the marine transport costs because the port can accommodate larger and more productive ships. It is possible to evaluate such benefits. Goss (1974) developed an annuity-based technique for estimating the long-run opportunity cost of ships' time, and Heaver (1972), and Gilman (1977) amongst others have evaluated the economies of scale available in the bulk and general cargo trades respectively.

The main problems with this approach relate to the evaluation of real benefits and real resource costs where money values are the product of market distortions. When constructing economic tests for port investment proposals it is often possible to commence with the commercial accounting data used in financial analysis and then to adjust these to economic or shadow values. The main adjustments include the deduction from the cost stream of the project of all direct and indirect taxes and other transfer payments which do not constitute direct claims on real resources; the deduction from the benefit stream of all capital, operating and other subsidies which are not payments linked to the output of port services (taxes, however, should be retained on the benefit side, since they reflect in part consumer surplus and hence value); the use of shadow prices to value labour, capital and foreign exchange, when appropriate (see below); and the inclusion of secondary benefits which may arise when a port improvement stimulates the employment of resources, outside the project, that would otherwise remain unemployed. Secondary benefits are usually difficult to justify. Though such cost—benefit calculations are necessarily complex one solution lies in the context of linear programming where the many inputs and outputs of the economy are viewed as a linearised system. The shadow prices of these inputs and outputs are obtained by maximising a social welfare function subject to the constraints of resource availability. However, assuming direct evaluation of market distortions permits the derivation of shadow prices then port investment decisions can be taken on the basis of the net present value criterion.

The NPV may be derived by discounting the net benefit each year at the social opportunity cost of capital, where the net gain B in year j from the project is given by:

$$B_j = \sum_{i=1}^{n} a_{ij} P_i - \sum_{k=1}^{m} f_{kj} V_k \qquad (10.1)$$

where a_{ij} ($i = 1 \ldots n$) and f_{kj} ($k = 1 \ldots m$) give the output and input coefficient respectively; and P_i and V_k are the shadow prices.

Goss 1967 identified the need to optimise the combined costs of ports and ships, therefore the economic test for port improvements becomes one of comparing ship queuing costs with the costs of expanding port capacity (through additional berth or crane provision, or channel deepening and widening), valued at the relevant shadow prices. To illustrate this approach, the question of what capacity a port should have in terms of its approach channels may be considered. Holt (1978) argued that, given that the rate of ship arrivals changes over time, there is an optimal amount of channel capacity which will maximise total net benefits to both shipowners and the port authority.

At one extreme, the port could maximise utilisation of its channel capacity and minimise the costs per ship handled to the port; this, however would involve the largest delays to shipowners. At the other extreme the port could provide wide enough channels to eliminate all queuing time for shipowners, but the port would incur high capital dredging costs in constructing such capacity.

The problem of reconciling capacity with variations in demand over time is one of trading off extra capacity costs against delay costs to shipowners. In relatively simple cases queuing theory can be used to produce a solution. However, where a port approach channel is used by many types of vessel with different transit-time capabilities due to vessel size or due to the nature of the ship's cargo, and where vessels leave and enter that channel at different points for general or specialised berths, queuing theory is too simplistic to be useful. Simulation models can be developed to provide the information necessary to optimise capacity utilisation and capacity size.

For different amounts of capacity provision, it is necessary to know:

(a) total waiting time associated with a given amount of capacity (in terms of channel widths, depths, and port control regulations), for a predicted number of ship arrivals;

(b) the value of the ships' waiting time;

(c) the discounted cost of providing a particular level of capacity; and

(d) predicted future arrival rates.

(a) and (b) provide supply information, whilst (d) provides demand information; (c) is self-explanatory.

If for a given predicted demand the reduction in ship queuing costs exceeds the costs of expansion, appropriately valued and discounted, the investment is worthwhile. Where demand is perfectly inelastic, with respect to waiting time, this becomes analogous to determining the minimum cost solution for different levels of predicted demand for port capacity, in each future year. De Weille and Ray (1974) extended this methodology by assuming rather than deriving a particular demand curve. Their pragmatic approach to estimating future demand functions involved firstly predicting the demand in each future year (on the basis of some assumed growth rate), given a specified ship waiting-time cost level. This provided a single point on each annual demand curve, the shape of which was then determined by assuming a certain elasticity between ship waiting-time costs and the volume of ship arrivals. The gross benefit of the port investment is then measured by adding to the reduction in queuing costs the consumer surplus accruing to traffic generated by this reduction.

Figure 10.1 illustrates two demand forecasts 1985, and 1990, and also two levels of capacity provision. For example, capacity level 1 might be with channel width x and level 2 with $2x$. Alternatively, capacity level 1 may be where vessels transit the channel on a first-come-first-served basis and capacity level 2 may involve traffic regulations or scheduling by vessel size and type. Nevertheless both capacity levels involve the port in different cost outlays and have different relationships between ship arrivals per unit of time and average waiting time costs per vessel. It should be emphasised only average costs are represented in the supply curves and not marginal social costs; this assumes that the port authority does not concern itself with congestion in its pricing policies.

In figure 10.1, little problem is envisaged in 1985 with capacity level 1; investment in capacity level 2 would generate benefit $CBAE$ to existing port users through reduced average waiting time. Further,

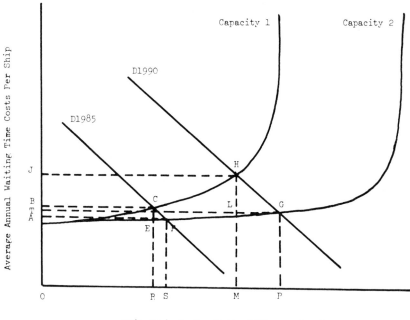

Figure 10.1   Two levels of demand forecast and capacity provision

lower waiting times would generate some new traffic in 1985 as depicted by the movement along the demand curve. *RS* would be the generated traffic, i.e. at traffic level *S* new traffic only just regards it as beneficial to use the port with new investment, whereas at traffic level *R* the new traffic needed little inducement in terms of improved performance, to switch to the port. Consequently the benefit to this generated traffic can be represented by the consumer surplus triangle *CEF*. The total consumer surplus resulting from investment in capacity level 2 in 1985 would be *CBAE + CEF = CBAF*. This would have to be set against the cost of expanding physical capacity and the extra operating costs at this new level. This is not the end of the story because possible benefits from an investment will be spread over many years. The exercise described above can be repeated for future years. For example figure 10.1 also shows the demand curve for 1990, where with capacity level 1 average delay costs per ship have risen substantially. Consequently the gains from investment in extra capacity are greater. The area *HJTL* represents the benefit to users in 1990 who would use the port anyway, without new investment, and the triangle *HLG* is the extra benefit to generated traffic attracted by the lower delay costs resulting from the investment. The total benefit in 1990 would be area *HJTG*, and this would have to be discounted, at an appropriate discount rate, either to the present or to some common time period when all costs and benefits could be compared on the same basis. This exercise could be repeated for all years and the discounted benefits could be compared with discounted costs, and if benefits exceed costs then the extra capacity provision is justifiable. For sound investment several alternative levels of investment provision with their different costs and different abilities to generate congestion relief and benefit should be assessed simultaneously. Further, assuming that they are mutually exclusive in nature and involve different outlays, the project with highest net present value to capital cost ratio should be chosen. Once the most rewarding scheme has been identified it only remains to decide on the optimal starting date for the new investment. This involves deferment testing, which simply requires a check to be made that the benefits accruing during the first year of the project are at least equal to the potential savings which could be realised by postponing the investment by one year.

The optimum amount of capacity for a specific point in time is provided when:

(a) the marginal amount of capacity provision has a positive net present value when discounted at the appropriate discount rate, and

(b) the benefits of that extra capacity during that particular year exceed the cost saving possible from postponing the investment by one year.

This analysis is general and can accommodate changes in capacity provision and utilisation not only generated by new investment in channel deepening or widening, or extra berth provision, or by the introduction of traffic scheduling and regulation, but also can accommodate changes in capacity provided by the introduction of new pricing policies designed to make better use of existing capacity. This can be illustrated in a diagram similar to figure 10.1.

Figure 10.2 again shows the relationship between average waiting costs and arrival rates for two levels of capacity provision. It also shows the associated marginal social cost curves which depict the extra waiting costs imposed on all other traffics from the addition of a small increment of traffic at different levels of traffic flow (arrival rate). Although an investment in new capacity may be an alternative path

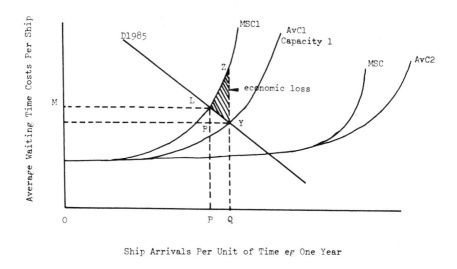

Figure 10.2   Effect of the introduction of marginal social cost pricing

open to the port in 1985, a switch to marginal social cost pricing, which will also produce an optimal allocation of resources, may generate an acceptable net present value. Figure 10.2 assumes that the port charges at average cost and generates a traffic flow of OQ in the first instance. Now QY equals the marginal social benefit accruing to traffic OQ, but QZ is the marginal social cost of accommodating this traffic $(QZ > QY)$. This means the port is being over used in the short term. If optimal pricing is introduced such that traffic up to the point where marginal social benefit equals marginal social cost is accepted, then OP traffic would be forthcoming at an average waiting time of LP. Therefore with efficient pricing triangle LZY is the area of 'economic loss' avoided (and is therefore a gain) by moving from OQ to OP traffic flow. The economic worth of this move could be assessed in exactly the same way as an investment, as it too represents a change of economic capacity provision.

A modification to the above calculations, may be necessary if we are interested in the maximisation of net benefits (real income) to a specific country rather than the world as a whole. The accrual of benefits will depend upon the incidence of those transport costs that are affected by the port improvement scheme. De Weille and Ray (1974) argued that all benefits will accrue to a national economy if the ship-

238

ping industry is operating under fully competitive conditions which force it to pass on port cost reductions in the form of freight rate reductions. Laing (1977) also contends that since shipping lines tend not to make excess profits they must pass on the benefits of port improvements. However, even if benefits from port investment are passed on to shippers in the form of lower freight rates, it is not necessarily the importers and exporters of the developing country that benefit most. The distribution of benefits between the LDC shippers or consignees and their counterparts at the other end of the trade depends on the elasticities of demand and supply for the commodities traded. It can be shown that for LDC exports where the elasticity of supply is less than the elasticity of demand, the majority of the benefit from a lower freight rate will be retained within the LDC, and the greater the difference the higher the proportion that will be retained. Similarly, for LDC imports, where the elasticity of supply is greater than the elasticity of demand, the majority of the benefits will be retained within the LDC and the greater the difference, the higher the proportion that will be retained. It is difficult to generalise about the elasticities facing developing countries, since much depends on the commodities traded, the strength of competition, and the constraints on free trade. Port investments generally have fairly long lives and so it is long-run elasticities which are most relevant. These tend to be higher than short-run elasticities as producers and consumers have more time to react to changes in price. This infers a greater increase in trade and thus a greater overall benefit from a freight rate reduction than with low elasticities, but offers little guidance to how this benefit will be shared between LDC and foreign importers and exporters. In practice, with worldwide inflation, the benefits of port investment may merely be a less rapid increase in freight rates than would otherwise have occurred. The principles outlined above regarding the distribution of benefits remain valid, however. In such circumstances, it becomes necessary to modify the NPV calculation to include only that proportion of consumers' surplus assumed to remain within the investing country and that proportion of the capital costs which is borne by the investing country.

Finally, if a port improvement project is being undertaken by an international aid agency then financial and economic tests may be regarded as complementary, not alternatives. For example, the World Bank will not normally finance port projects unless it can be demonstrated that the project represents a desirable use of national resources and will also be able to sustain itself financially either with or without assistance from the government.

One problem of applying the NPV criterion to port projects (which may be regarded in part as export, and import, substitution projects) in developing countries is that foreign exchange is normally the most distorted factor. Typically, the exchange rate will be undervalued giving rise to a chronic balance-of-payments deficit position and the use of the official exchange rate will wrongly value the imported inputs and the exports of output.

It is sometimes suggested that failure to improve port facilities may lead to ship operators bypassing national ports which would then become only feeder ports. Port investment may then represent some import saving on port charges and trans-shipment together with export earnings from expenditure by foreign shipowners in the national port.

The economic tests described above compute the return to the primary factor capital; therefore as an alternative, the implied return of the primary factor exchange rate may be compared with its shadow price. This method determines the cost of foreign exchanges in terms of the domestic resource costs, when capital is assigned its shadow price. Cohen and Shneerson (1976) suggest that an advantage of applying this method is that the results are consistent with the comparative advantage of the country. Thus a developing country will have a comparative advantage in the port sector if the domestic-resource cost of foreign exchange earned or saved is lower than the accounting exchange rate.

Thus, reconsidering equation (10.1) above, the net foreign-exchange coefficient will equal the difference between the marginal dollar revenue obtained by adding port services (x_j) and the marginal dollar outlay on imported inputs (m_j). If the shadow price of domestic currency per dollar is given by eo, the net gain B in the year j of the project can be expressed as:

$$B_j = (x_j - m_j)eo + \sum_{k=2}^{m} f_{kj} V_k + \sum_{i=1}^{n} a_{ij} P_i \tag{10.2}$$

Therefore, the domestic resource costs (DRC) per dollar of the port project is:

$$d_j = \frac{\sum_{k=2}^{m} f_{kj} V_k + \sum_{i=1}^{n} a_{ij} P_i}{x_j - m_j} \tag{10.3}$$

The terms in the numerator express the direct value added of domestic factors valued at opportunity costs and the opportunity costs of non-traded domestic goods that are used in producing port services respectively. Net foreign exchange earned is measured by the denominator. The domestic resource costs can be defined as the net expenses in domestic currency divided by the net revenue in dollars. Thus, DRC reflects the opportunity costs of value added of domestic resources (including the net value of non-traded goods) as a fraction of the net change in the balance of payments (including alternative income foregone within the net value of domestic traded goods). The decision criterion is that acceptable projects should have domestic resource costs which exceed the shadow price. The DRC earned on port projects can then be compared with that in other sectors, for example, shipping.

Whilst such a criterion may be of interest to those LDCs with particularly chronic international payments problems it should be pointed out that, firstly, a positive cost–benefit NPV will normally be consistent with a balance-of-payments improvement and, secondly, that all industries are import saving or export earning at the margin and it may be difficult to justify industry-specific action (to support port investment) as a means of pursuing a macro-economic target on external balance.

The analysis of ship and port systems

When a port is faced with the problem of congestion in any one phase of its operations, various options may be available by which port capacity may be increased. Particular reference will now be made to the case of berth expansion where the criterion chosen for optimising port investment is that of minimising total ship and port system costs. The methodology employed can be applied equally well to other port improvements such as cargo-handling facilities or channel deepening which may reduce congestion and shipping costs per unit of cargo if the use of the port by larger vessels is permitted. Wanhill (1974) in a study of port planning at Mina Zayed in Abu Dhabi expressed as berth costs (BC) plus port time cost (PTC). Berth costs are taken as the total number of berths multiplied by the average cost per berth (ac_b). However, the number of berths required for a given total cargo tonnage may be regarded as a function of the cargo-handling rate (r), such that $BC = f(r)$. Port time costs are comprised mainly of waiting time and service time, multiplied by the average vessel cost per unit of time (ac_v). Waiting time is taken as a non-linear function of cargo-handling rate, the average number of vessels present in the port per unit of time ($\bar{v}$), and the number of berths which is in turn a function of the cargo-

241

handling rate. Therefore, total port usage cost may be expressed as

$$TC = f(r)ac_b + [\ g(r, f(r), \bar{v}) + \frac{Q}{r}\ ]\ ac_v \qquad (10.4)$$

Given the total cargo tonnage, the cargo-handling rate, and the probability density function governing the chance of having v vessels present in the port per unit of time, then it is possible to minimise equation (10.4) in terms of port time and number of berths. Therefore, it is necessary to obtain information about the operating characteristics of port systems for different levels of berth and cargo-handling provision in order to determine the differences in ship waiting time.

If ships arrived at ports with complete regularity, and if the time taken to discharge and load such ships was constant, it would be a relatively simple matter to determine the ship waiting time involved for various levels of berth and cargo-handling capacity. In practice however, neither the timing of ship arrivals nor the service times for individual ships are known. Using the techniques of queuing theory it is possible to derive the distribution of the number of ships present and hence to estimate waiting time, for a wide range of arrival and service distributions. Typically, a Poisson arrival process is assumed such that the time between successive arrivals is a random variable with a negative exponential distribution, though an Erlangian or negative exponential distribution may be considered more realistic.

Yamada (1981) considered the question of optimum berth provision at Yamashita Pier, Yokohama as part of a wider analysis of port and ship systems. Generally, ship arrivals at the port are random and a Poisson distribution was indicated, as follows:

$$f(x) = \frac{(\lambda t)^x\ e^{-\lambda t}}{x!} \qquad (10.5)$$

where x = number of ship arrivals in time t
       λ = mean ship arrivals in unit time.

The berthing period was indicated by an Erlangian distribution, as follows:

$$f(t) = \frac{(k\mu)^k}{(k-1)!}\ t^{k-1}\ e^{-k\mu t},\ (x \geqslant 0) \qquad (10.6)$$

where t = berth time of the ship
       k = phase of Erlangian distribution
       μ = mean number of ships served in unit time.

The distributions of ship arrivals and berth times are given in figures 10.3 and 10.4 respectively. The mean value of ship waiting time (t_w) for berthing was derived for the $m/E_k/S$ model by using the formula:

$$t_w = W_q (1 + c^2)/2 \qquad (10.7)$$

where W_q = the mean value of ship waiting time in the $M/M/S$ model
   c = the coefficient of variation

and

$$W_q = \frac{\mu a^S}{(s-1)! \, (s\mu - \lambda)^2} \sum_{n=0}^{s-1} \left[\frac{a^n}{n!} + \frac{a^S}{(s-1)! \, (s-a)} \right]^{-1} \qquad (10.8)$$

where s = number of berths
   a = λ / μ.

Given cargo-handling rates of 2,400 and 3,600 tons per day for each vessel and that the cargo lift per ship visit was 4,000 tons of general cargo, total port and ship costs were calculated for a range of annual cargo throughputs and for 1−16 berths. Whilst total costs were defined in a manner similar to equation (10.4), the cost of warehousing and interest charges on the cargo value were also included. Figures 10.5 and 10.6 reproduce the results from Yamada (1981) and show the relationship between total system costs, the number of berths and annual cargo volume.

Whilst such models provide important information on the potential performance of investment alternatives it is important to recognise the particular assumptions made with regard to the time interval between arrivals. In the above case inter-arrival times are regularised, other models assume that the arrival time of one ship does not affect the time when any other ship arrives and that the service times of different ships are independent. However, the actual arrival times of scheduled general cargo and container services may vary significantly with the state of the service; the terminal and tidal conditions; and equipment and cargo availability which influence ship working rates. In consequence, waiting time may be concealed by slow steaming and schedule variation. Edmond and Maggs (1978) identified factors which may affect the application of queuing models to container services in particular. They investigated a number of single and multi-server models with a range of assumptions with regard to ship arrival and service rates. The main conclusions were that although simple queuing models may give a reasonable approximation to some aspects of container operations, a

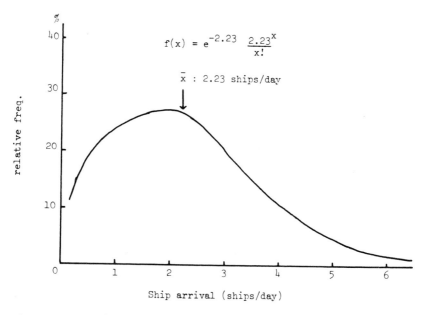

Figure 10.3   Distribution of ship arrival at Yamashita Pier

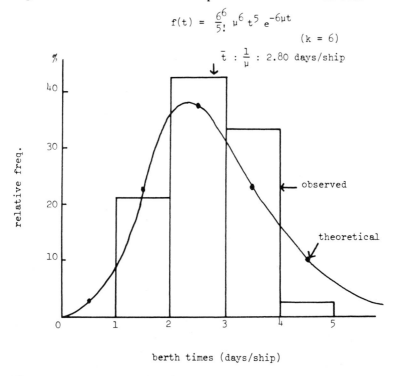

berth times (days/ship)

Figure 10.4   Distribution of berth times at Yamashita Pier

244

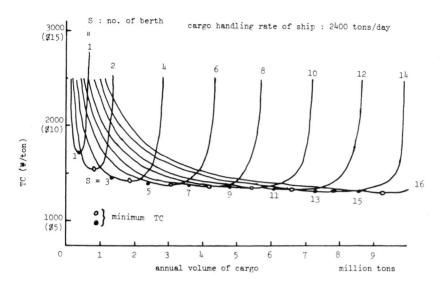

Figure 10.5 Relation between TC, number of berths and annual volume of cargo — 2400 tons per day

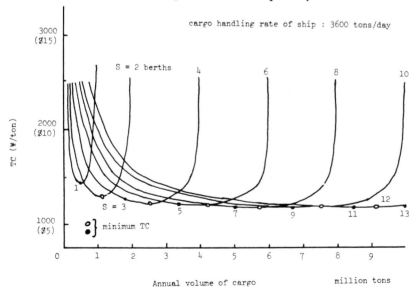

Figure 10.6 Relation between TC, number of berths and annual volume of cargo — 3600 tons per day

245

group of such models may be more useful for investment planning provided the choice of model and parameters, and the evaluation are carefully undertaken. Queuing models with arrival rates and ship working rates dependent on the state of the terminal and the service appeared particularly useful. It would appear that queuing models offer a quick and inexpensive way of obtaining the basic data necessary for the economic evaluation of port investment alternatives. Simulation models may prove to be too time consuming given the complexities and interactions involved in representing all of the relevant port and ship operations.

Conclusions

The choice of appropriate cargo-handling systems for ports in LDCs is a critical one. Modern multipurpose ships offer relatively inexpensive and flexible capacity on trades with limited volumes of containerisable cargo. However, where the high capital costs of containerships and container terminals can be spread over appreciable cargo volumes, fully cellular systems may provide the cheapest overall solution. Put simply, the objective of the port investment decision should be to minimise the sum of the costs of ships' time in port and the costs of the port facilities and their operation. Costs should be valued in terms of their real impact on the economy particularly with regard to the shadow prices of foreign exchange and port labour. The costs of ships' port time is directly proportional to the average time spent in port and queuing models may be used to calculate these times for alternative ship and port systems. There is little incentive for LDCs to invest in expensive terminals and equipment unless an adequate share of the overall benefits is passed on to them. Whether a developing country will achieve this depends on the effectiveness of port pricing, the extent to which freight rates reflect cost savings, and the elasticities of demand and supply for the commodities traded.

References

Cohen, D. and Shneerson, D., 'The Domestic Resource Costs of Establishing/Expanding a "National Fleet"' in *Maritime Policy and Management*, 1976, vol.3, pp.221–36.

De Weille, J. and Ray, A., 'The Optimum Port Capacity' in *Journal of Transport Economics and Policy*, 1974, vol.8, pp. 244–59.

Edmond, E.D. and Maggs, R.P., 'How Useful are Queue Models in Port Investment Decisions for Container Berths' in *Journal of the Operational Research Society*, 1978, vol.29, pp. 741–50.

Gilman, S., 'Shipping Technologies for Developing Countries' in *Journal of Transport Economics and Policy*, 1977, vol.10, pp. 24—44.

Gilman, S., Maggs, R.P. and Ryder, S.C., *Containers on the North Atlantic*, Marine Transport Centre, University of Liverpool, 1977.

Goss, R.O., 'Towards an Economic Appraisal of Port Investments' in *Journal of Transport Economics and Policy*, 1967, vol.1, pp. 249—72.

Goss, R.O., *A Comparative Study of Seaport Management and Administration*, vol.1, HMSO, London, 1979.

Heaver, T.D. and Studer, K., 'Ship Size and Turnaround Time' in *Journal of Transport Economics and Policy*, 1972, vol.6, pp. 32—50.

Heggie, I.G., 'Charging for Port Facilities' in *Journal of Transport Economics and Policy*, 1974, vol.8, pp. 3—25.

Holt, J.A., 'Port Traffic Management Systems: Alternatives and Optimisation' in *Proceedings of the Third International Symposium on Marine Traffic Systems*, 1978, pp. 131—54.

Laing, E.T., 'The Distribution of Benefits from Port Investment' in *Maritime Policy and Management*, 1977, vol.4, pp.141—54.

Meek, M., 'Operating Experience of Large Containerships', 1975.

UNCTAD, 'Technological Change in Shipping and its Effect on Ports', 1976.

Wanhill, S.R.C., 'A Study in Port Planning: Mina Zayed' in *Maritime Studies and Management*, 1974, vol.2, pp. 48—55.

Yamada, T., *Analyses of Seaport and Ship Systems*, unpublished paper, Massachusetts Institute of Technology, 1981.

Subject index

Civil Aviation Authority 20–2, 23, 30, 32, 35, 39
COBA 8, 11, 159, 160–1, 163, 165, 167, 171, 172–3, 176, 192–3, 207: *COBA-9 Manual* 159, 167
Commission of Inquiry (Kyeemagh-Chullora Road) 108–32 *passim*
Complete ignorance rules 173
Computational costs 157, 197, 199, 206, 209, 210
Consumer surplus 193, 195, 233, 235, 236, 239
Containerisation 99–100, 102, 225, 227, 228, 230, 231: disadvantages for developing countries 227, 229
Contingency allowances 163–4
Cost–benefit analysis (*see also* Planning Balance Sheet): development of 4–14, 140, 159; existence of alternative approaches 4, 12–14, 50, 68–80 *passim*, 128, 142–8; limitations of 7–8, 10–12, 16, 140–2; of airports 11, 13, 14, 19–39, 68–70, 123–4; of Channel tunnel 15, 88–106 *passim*, 182; of ports 17, 224–46 *passim*; of roads 8, 11, 108–32, 142, 156–77 *passim*, 182–94 *passim*, 198–220 *passim*
Cost-effectiveness 50, 71, 140
Cross-import method 175

Decision making under risk 71, 165
Decision making under uncertainty 164 (*see also* Uncertainty)
Decision making with incomplete knowledge 165

Delphi procedures 172, 218
Demand modelling (*see* Traffic forecasts)
Developing countries 206, 224–46 *passim*
Development benefits (of airport) 20–1, 34
Disaggregate models 139, 206
Discount rate and discounting 8, 9, 141–2, 160, 201, 237
Discrete choice models 209, 210
Distributional effects 3, 6, 9–11, 34–5, 52, 101, 142, 143, 183, 184–5, 188, 194, 238–40: spatial 98–9, 186
Distributional weights 9–11, 185, 238–9
Do-minimum alternative 160
Do-nothing alternative 121, 218
Double counting 4, 13

Ecological effects 123
Energy costs 109, 121, 149, 150, 162, 185, 190, 202
Environmental effects (*see also* Pollution *and* Noise) 7, 12, 117, 125–6, 148–9, 156: of airports 20, 23; of Channel tunnel 89, 92, 97–8, 104
European Economic Community (EEC) 90, 91, 92, 95, 96, 98–9, 100
Explicit demand models 219
Externalities 3, 20, 23, 92, 97–8, 145
Extrapolative models 121, 200–1, 207, 209, 210, 212–14, 217

Factor profiles 144–5
Financial appraisal 2–3, 4, 71, 148, 151: of Channel tunnel 90–1, 101; of Leeds/Bradford Airport 19, 24, 27–8, 32–4, 37, 38; of ports 232–3, 239

Flood Control Act 1936 (USA) 7
Forecasting error (see Traffic forecasts)
French Engineering School 4—6
Fuel prices (see Energy costs)

Generalised costs 138
Goal achievement matrix 14, 143—4
Goods vehicles (see also Traffic congestion): speeds 181, 190—1, 195; value of time savings for 181—2, 186, 190—2, 200—1
Greater London Development Plan 11, 59, 68, 159, 205: Inquiry 60
Greater London Plan 59

HATS model 211, 218
Hicks-Kaldor criterion 10
House of Commons Transport Committee 90—1, 93, 94, 95, 96, 102, 105
Hurwicz criterion 165

Incomplete knowledge 165
Incremental analysis 160
Industrial Revolution 4
Intangibles 63, 109, 151—2
Interactive models 208, 211
Internal rate of return: Channel tunnel 92, 103; Kyeemagh-Chullora Road 111; Leeds/Bradford Airport 19, 24—5, 27
Inter-urban roads (see also motorways) 7, 8, 11, 20, 77, 98, 108—32 passim, 156—7 passim, 200—1
Investment criteria (see Cost—benefit analysis and Transport Investment Appraisal)

Land-use planning (see also Transport planning and Town planning): administrative dimension 50—2, 54; ideology of 48, 53—4; politics of 52—3, 54, 57—68 passim; practitioners 44—8, 81; rational—central-rule approach 60; urban structure 46, 150, 210
Land-use transportation studies 65, 67 (see also Land use planning)
Leitch Committee (Advisory Committee on Trunk Road Assessment) 13, 109, 158, 159, 161, 171, 176, 187, 188, 189, 191, 192, 194
Logit models 216—7, 220

Marginal social cost 232
Maximax 165, 166
Maximin 165, 166, 167
Measurement error 162
Minimax regret 167
Modal choice 45, 79, 138, 157, 197, 209, 214, 215, 219
Monte Carlo simulation 172, 202
Motorways 7, 142, 147, 201, 204
Multiple criteria decision methods 12—14, 71, 146, 161, 176
Mutually exclusive projects 164

Need 3
Net present value: Channel tunnel 93; Kyeemagh-Chullora Road 111; Leeds/Bradford Airport 19, 26—7, 32; Ports 234, 238—9, 240—1
Net present value—cost ratio 93—4, 192, 237
Noise: abatement 13; aircraft 20, 97; costs of 137, 141; road 97, 115, 137, 148

Name index

Aaronovitch, S. 81, 86
Abelson, P. 108
Ackoff, R.L. 144, 153
Adams, J. 207, 221
Agunwamba, C.C. 170, 178
Albers, G. 43, 52, 72, 75, 76, 82
Aldcroft, D.H. 81, 82
Alford, R.R. 85
Allais, M. 169, 178
Altshuler, A.A. 61, 82
Anderson, E. 32, 39
Apgar, M. 68, 82
Arctander, P. 43, 82
Arrow, K.J. 176, 178
Ashford, N.J. 16, 133, 148, 153
Ashley, D.J. 172

Bachrach, P. 47, 82
Banfield, E.C. 61
Banister, D.J. 77, 80, 82
Baratz, M.S. 47, 82
Barback, R.H. 17
Barber, G. 179

Barrell, D.W. 7–8, 17
Bates, J.J. 67, 82, 206, 210, 215, 216, 221
Baumol, W.J. 144
Beesley, M.E. 108ff
Beggs, J.J. 61, 62, 83
Bellomo, S.J. 87
Ben-Akiva, M.E. 203, 221
Bishop, B. 134
Black, J. 43, 63, 65, 66–8, 77, 82
Blomqvist, A.G. 211, 221
Blonk, W.A.G. 82, 86
Bouchier, D. 81, 82
Boyce, D.E. 42, 82
Brand, D. 153
Brecht, B.E.F. 42
Brussee, C.R. 153
Bruzelius, N. 183, 195
Burns, L.D. 215, 221
Button, K.J. 16, 58–60, 62, 75, 82, 196ff, 198, 202, 206, 208, 210, 211, 212, 219, 221, 222

253